Teaching and Learning History

Teaching and Learning History

Geoff Timmins, Keith Vernon
and Christine Kinealy

SAGE Publications
London • Thousand Oaks • New Delhi

First published 2005

 SAGE Publications Ltd
1 Oliver's Yard
55 City Road
London EC1Y 1SP

SAGE Publications Inc
2455 Teller Road
Thousand Oaks, California 91320

SAGE Publications India Pvt Ltd
B-42, Panchsheel Enclave
Post Box 4109
New Delhi 100 017

Library of Congress Control Number: 2004116090

A catalogue record for this book is available from the British
Library

ISBN 0-7619-4772-8
ISBN 0-7619-4773-6 (pbk)

Production by Deer Park Productions, Tavistock, Devon
Typeset by TW Typesetting, Plymouth, Devon
Printed in Great Britain by Athenaeum Press, Gateshead

Contents

Acknowledgements   vii
Note on abbreviations   ix
Teaching and Learning the Humanities in Higher Education   xi
Foreword   xiii

Introduction   1

1 The state of the discipline   9
   Introduction   9
   Internal divisions   11
   The history front of the 'Culture Wars'   21
   External pressures   28
   History today   34

2 Progression and differentiation   39
   Introduction   39
   Progression and differentiation implementation issues   40
   Progression and differentiation survey   42
   The content dimension   45
   The skills and primary source dimension   52
   The teaching and learning and assessment dimensions   57
   Conclusion   63

3 Content matters   67
   Introduction   67
   Benchmarking and content   69
   Time depth and geographical perspectives   71
   Diversity of specialisms   79
   Reflexivity   87
   Dissertations and content   91
   Conclusion   94

4 The historian's skills and qualities of mind   96
   Introduction   96
   Benchmarking, skills and the historian's qualities of mind   98
   The role of skills in undergraduate history   102
   Teaching discipline-specific skills to history students   108
   Teaching generic skills to history students   119
   Conclusion   130

5 Learning and teaching   132
   Introduction   132
   Benchmarking and history learning and teaching   133
   The role of the history tutor in learning and teaching   134
   Lectures   138
   Seminars and group work   146
   Using ICT in undergraduate history teaching   153
   Conclusion   167

6 Assessment issues   170
   Introduction   170
   Assessment criteria   171
   Statements of attainment   179
   Developing assessment criteria: a small-scale case study   185
   Assessment by coursework and examinations: general
      considerations   192
   Assessment in practice   197
   Conclusion   206

   Conclusion   211

   Appendices
   1 Sampling approaches   216
   2 Websites for learning and teaching in higher education
         history   218

   Bibliography   221
   Index   241

Acknowledgements

We are greatly indebted to many of our fellow historians for the help they have given in writing this book. Our colleagues at the University of Central Lancashire have provided guidance on many of the matters we discuss, both John Walton and Dave Russell helping particularly by reading and commenting on early drafts. Susan Bailey also provided invaluable research assistance. Historians from other higher education institutions in Britain readily responded to our requests for information and those who answered our survey questions are acknowledged in Appendix 1. Alan Booth and Paul Hyland have greatly inspired and encouraged our work, both through their own writings and through the highly instructive learning and teaching events they have organised in recent years as part of the *History 2000* and the *History, Classics and Archaeology Subject Centre* programmes. We would also like to thank those of our colleagues who have contributed in various other ways to our book, especially in relation to their own practices. They are John Davis, Elizabeth Foyster, Wil Griffith, Ann-Marie Kilday and Harvey Woolf.

We are also indebted to higher education historians in the United States and Australasia, both for providing details about their learning and teaching approaches and for discussing issues with us. In particular, we would like to thank Robert Blackey, Gary Cross, Peter Frederick, David Goodman, Jeanine Graham, Diana Long and Andrew Markus.

Ellie Chambers, our series editor, has provided constant support and advice as the book has progressed, alerting us to various ways in which the text could be improved both in terms of content and presentation. We are particularly grateful for her efforts on our behalf. Her colleague Jan Parker has also offered valuable advice and encouragement.

All too often, books can take longer to complete than optimistic authors anticipate. We had hoped to finish ours by the summer of 2003, in time to mark the retirement of Joe Pope from his position as Head of the Department of Historical and Critical Studies at the University of Central Lancashire. Despite missing this occasion, we hope Joe will nevertheless be pleased that we dedicate our book to him in recognition of the long-standing support he has given to developing progressive approaches in degree-level history teaching.

Note on abbreviations

Abbreviated book, booklet and article titles are given conventionally in textual references using author's surname, date of publication and, where appropriate, page numbers. However, abbreviated title references to university websites are given by institution and document title, since author and date of publication are seldom stated. The same approach is adopted in citing the websites of other educational organisations. Dates noted in parentheses after website entries for universities and other organisations give the last date on which the authors visited the sites. On-line essays are noted by author and date where given, but by author and abbreviated title where date of publication is not stated.

Teaching and Learning the Humanities in Higher Education

SERIES EDITORS: Ellie Chambers and Jan Parker, The Open University

This series for beginning and experienced lecturers deals with all aspects of teaching individual arts and humanities subjects in higher education. Experienced teachers offer authoritative suggestions to enable beginning and experienced lecturers to become critically reflective about discipline-specific practices.

Each book includes an overview of the main currents of thought in a subject; major theoretical trends; appropriate teaching and learning modes and current best practice, new methods of course delivery and assessment; electronic teaching methods and sources.

Features include :

- discussion of key areas of pedagogy: curriculum development, assessment, teaching styles, professional development, appropriate use of C&IT
- case study illustration of teaching certain problematic topics
- the findings of educational research and sample material of all kinds drawn from a range of countries and traditions
- suggestions throughout for critical decisions, and alternative strategies and follow-up activities, so that all teachers are encouraged to reflect critically on their assumptions and practices.

The series sets out effective approaches to a wide range of teaching and teaching-related tasks.

The books are intended as core texts for lecturers working towards Membership of the Institute for Learning and Teaching, for adoption by training course providers and as professional reference resources.

The books are also suitable for PGCE, and Further and Higher Education courses. In countries with less formal plans for lecturer training but a longer tradition of serious attention to pedagogy within the higher education culture, the series will contribute to the scholarship of teaching and learning and professional and organisational development.

Series titles:
Teaching and Learning Modern Languages, Literatures and Cultures
Alison Phipps and Mike Gonzales

Teaching and Learning History
Geoff Timmins, Keith Vernon and Christine Kinealy

Teaching and Learning English Literature (Publication Sept 2006)
Ellie Chambers and Marshall Gregory

Ellie Chambers is Professor of Humanities Higher Education in the Institute of Educational Technology, The UK Open University. Since 1974 she has worked as a pedagogic adviser, evaluator and researcher with colleagues in the university's Faculty of Arts. In 1992 she founded the interdisciplinary Humanities Higher Education Research Group and in 1994, with colleagues, the national Humanities and Arts higher education Network. She regularly addresses conferences internationally and has published widely in the fields of distance education and Arts and Humanities higher education – including the best-selling book for students, *The Arts Good Study Guide* (1997, with Andrew Northedge). Currently, she is founding Editor-in-Chief of 'Arts and Humanities in Higher Education: An International Journal of Theory, Research and Practice' (Sage) and a Member of Council, the Society for Research into Higher Education.

Dr Jan Parker is a Senior Research Fellow of the Open University's Centre for Research in Education and Educational Technology and chairs the Humanities Higher Education Research Group. Founding editor of the Sage journal *Arts and Humanities in Higher Education: an international journal of theory, research and practice* and Executive Editor of *Teaching in Higher Education* (Taylor and Francis), she still teaches and writes on her disciplinary specialism, Greek Tragedy, and is a Senior Member of the Faculty of Classics, Cambridge. She is currently co-writing the Teaching and Learning Classics and Classical Studies volume of this series.

Foreword

These are exciting times for teachers of History in universities and colleges. Recent developments within the discipline have greatly expanded the scope and vision of the subject as a field of knowledge and research, and posed fresh challenges with regard to what it means to learn and speak about the past. Across the world, there is also a pressing need and opportunity for historians to promote the benefits of history education, as many countries transform their higher-education systems, increasing student populations, and extending the range of course provision and the use of information technology to support the growth and development of their societies. Such changes, both within the discipline and in the ways and contexts in which it can be learned, raise many important questions now about what and how History should be taught.

Of course, good historians and teachers have always asked fundamental questions about the nature of the discipline, what knowledge, skills and values a history education should impart, and how best these can be taught and learned. Many historians, individually and through their national communities, have also engaged in vigorous debates about the goals and social benefits of studying History at university, and how the profession as a whole should respond to the criticisms of politicians and other public figures, who have often sought to steer the study of History towards the promotion of particular views and understandings of the past. Thus, there is a long tradition of developing the discipline in the light of reflection and research, and in accordance with the changing patterns and demands of higher education. However, to meet the many challenges of teaching a growing number and diversity of students, meeting their needs and aspirations, and enhancing their learning opportunities, experiences and achievements, a far greater sharing of ideas and knowledge of good practices and innovations is now needed.

Grounded in a careful examination of current trends and practices, *History* offers a fascinating guide both to the ways in which the discipline is currently configured and delivered, and to the means by which its teaching and learning can be enhanced. Following an introduction to the state of the discipline, there are chapters on how vital decisions – about how to ensure progression and differentiation in degree programmes, what should be offered and required in the curriculum, which skills and abilities need to be developed, what teaching and learning methods should be deployed, and how learning can be best assessed – affect every aspect of a history student's education. Such decisions raise many questions about the challenges that face historians today, and they are seldom easy, even for the most experienced of teachers. In every chapter, however, the authors draw upon a wide range of evidence gathered from departmental websites, survey responses, national statements about standards of provision, and personal experiences of teaching to provide a rich and balanced series of discussions. Moreover, though informed by recent research on student learning, the authors keep their focus firmly fixed on the needs and interests of the history teacher.

In providing such a clear, informative and thoughtful exploration of the current state of History in higher education, and in helping to raise the quality of critical debate about its future, this book contributes greatly to the growing scholarship of teaching and learning in the discipline. It should also become a vital resource for all historians who wish to honour the old dictum that, in teaching as in research, the one duty we owe History is to rewrite it.

Introduction

That higher education is undergoing profound change is widely appreciated. The supposed demands of the knowledge economy are putting increased pressure on universities and related institutions, in terms of both the drive to recruit greater proportions of the population and the corresponding desire of financial and political authorities to ensure that standards are maintained and the needs of society and economy are met. Interrelated with these developments has been the implementation of new directions in methods of learning and teaching, not least those arising from the remarkable innovations in ICT, which have greatly enhanced the potential for the globalisation of higher education. The study of history has, of course, shared in the challenges arising from these developments, but, not unconnectedly, history as an academic discipline has also experienced upheavals of its own. In the last generation, historians have debated with much heat, and a degree of light, the underlying assumptions, the methods and the academic and public purposes of their discipline. Whatever the desirability of the changing circumstances in which higher education has come to operate, or their eventual outcomes, both the general and specific contexts in which history is developing as an academic discipline raise profound questions about its nature and purpose at degree level. What should be taught to history undergraduates, by what means and to what ends?

Historians have been far from reticent in addressing these issues. Indeed, there is a substantial and growing international literature dealing with learning and teaching in history at undergraduate level. Much of it reports and comments on new classroom approaches that have been adopted within traditional face-to-face settings, but there is also a good deal to be found relating to the use of virtual learning environments. In both cases, addressing the skills agenda has gained far greater importance, involving students in the investigation and application of primary evidence to a much greater extent than has traditionally been the case.

AIMS AND APPROACHES

In adding to the literature, our aims are to contribute to the process of curriculum planning in undergraduate history programmes and to the ways in which these programmes are implemented. Our approach is partly to review a selection of the contributions made by higher education historians in relation to these matters, on the principle that much can be learned from considering the thoughts and experiences of those addressing the same sorts of issues as ourselves. In making our selection, we have focused on examples that offer particularly innovative approaches to addressing key issues that arise in developing history curricula and devising appropriate learning and teaching strategies. Additionally, we have tried to undertake our review within the context of the wider educational literature concerning undergraduate teaching. Our purpose here has been partly to broaden discussion by drawing on observations and experiences that transcend disciplinary boundaries, but also, as opportunity arises, to benefit from the approaches adopted by colleagues working in other disciplines than our own. This inevitably raises concerns about how to cope with a vast educational literature and about what sort of balance should be maintained between the general and the particular. However, in a book primarily directed towards the history teaching profession, especially to new members of it, the emphasis has to lie strongly on developments within the discipline itself. Our excursions into the broader literature are primarily to obtain insights, some of them theoretical, which help to inform the rationale for the types of practice historians already adopt or might consider adopting.

As to our primary source material, a good deal of reliance has been placed on history department websites. While these sites vary considerably in the amount of detail they give, and can be exceedingly sparing with regard to the rationale for the provision offered, they collectively provide a massive amount of information about current practices, particularly where detailed student handbooks and course unit descriptions are included. Moreover, they facilitate international comparison, for our purposes between Britain and Ireland, North

America and Australasia. For the most part, we have gathered primary material that can be used in discussing key issues, rather than undertaking surveys as a basis for reliable generalisations about existing practice. And even where we have mounted small-scale surveys in relation to particular issues, they have not been designed to yield representative data. The rationale for adopting this approach is discussed in Appendix 1, but it may be noted here that, despite their limitations, non-representational data provide highly revealing and thought-provoking insights into the range of pedagogical matters with which our book is concerned.

HISTORY BENCHMARKING

In determining the content of our book, we have relied on the key issues raised by the *History Benchmarking Statement* made available for British higher education institutions. Published in 2000 by the Quality Assurance Agency (QAA), a body charged with safeguarding the standards of higher education qualifications, the Statement is one of a series covering a wide range of subject disciplines. These statements seek to

> *provide a means for the academic community to describe the nature and characteristics of programmes in a specific subject. They also represent general expectations about the standards for the award of qualifications at a given level and articulate the attributes and capabilities those possessing such qualifications should be able to demonstrate.*

In the case of history, expectations for honours degree students are expressed in relation to five considerations. These are:

- historian's skills and qualities of mind;
- content criteria;
- progression between stages;
- approaches to teaching and learning;
- assessment.

Recommendations are made under each of these headings, in varying detail, summaries of which are made in the chapters that follow (QAA, *History*, 2000).

To regard the history benchmarking statement as an appropriate document on which to base most of our book might cause consternation, not least because of the high degree of prescription associated with the notion of benchmarking. Thus, in reporting on the announcement by the QAA that subject benchmarking would be introduced, John Clare, education editor of *The Daily Telegraph*, went as far as to remark that a compulsory national curriculum would be imposed on British higher education (Clare, 1998). Even in a more measured and informed response, Anthony Bradney of the Faculty of Law at Leicester University condemned benchmarking as 'part of a long-standing attempt to redirect the work of the university away from its traditional task'. He argued that though content was not being prescribed, benchmarking would still act as a constraint, notably because of the emphasis placed on using outcomes to measure quality in teaching and learning (Bradney, 'Benchmarking'). Such arguments no doubt underpinned the less than wholehearted response with which benchmarking was received by British higher education institutions. Only about a quarter expressed support and while most were neutral or had reservations, a minority were either highly critical or opposed to it in principle (Fletcher, 1999).

Whether opinion was similarly distributed among Britain's higher education historians at the time benchmarking was introduced, and whether their opinions may have changed since, is undetermined. What is plain, however, is that the history benchmarking group, which comprised 16 higher education historians, was opposed to prescription from the outset of their deliberations, their chairperson, Anthony Fletcher, remarking that it

> *never entered into our minds that our task might involve establishing a national curriculum in history, or that we would in any way wish to stifle creativity, diversity and innovation in teaching the subject. We've tried to tread the narrow path between writing an account of the subject that is sufficiently challenging, and being too prescriptive about how colleagues should construct a syllabus, teach or assess their students.*

Not least among the reasons for adopting this stance was the recognition that history is a subject 'where staffing levels, cultures and traditions vary widely' (Fletcher, 1999). And added to the concept of difference was that of change.

We insist that teaching and learning are evolving processes and that it is not our intention to freeze the teaching of History in a particular model. Our benchmarking statement should be seen as a starting point: departments and subject groups will have the chance to demonstrate how benchmarking standards can be built on by the provision of additional or perhaps alternative opportunities.

(QAA, *History*, 2000: 1)

KEY ISSUES

What makes the benchmarking document of particular value for our purposes is that it identifies and raises key concerns about aspects of learning and teaching that have to be addressed by undergraduate history teachers, irrespective of the country or the type of institution in which they work. In this respect, a good deal of fundamental deliberation has already taken place on behalf of higher education historians in general. Moreover, this deliberation has been informed by the wide consultations that the benchmarking group undertook, with written responses having been invited to the draft statement and a national meeting arranged to discuss its content. Held at the Institute of Historical Research in London, this meeting was attended by around sixty historians, probably representing around half the higher education institutions in Britain. That the tenor of both the written and verbal responses to the Statement was generally favourable, and appears to have remained so, adds to our confidence in focusing on the issues it raises. And that detailed prescription is avoided makes the Statement a singularly useful reference point for curriculum planning and teaching purposes, since it encourages wide-ranging thought as to the best ways forward for higher education historians in the particular circumstances in which they find themselves.

Foundations of discussion

In presenting our findings and formulating our line of discussion, six chapters are provided. The first is essentially a 'scene-setting' chapter, its function being to give an overview of the development of higher education history teaching in Britain and abroad, thereby creating a contextual framework for the themes covered in subsequent chapters. A key theme is the changing circumstances in which undergraduate history has been taught during recent decades, especially with regard to the rise of various forms of social and cultural history, and the implications of this for curriculum development and the approaches adopted in learning and teaching. The nature of the discussion in this chapter serves as a reminder that to design and implement an effective undergraduate history syllabus has become a complex and time-consuming matter that is by no means free from controversy, that is subject to ongoing development as circumstances change and that requires a wide range of considerations to be taken into account.

The second chapter deals with the crucial matter of progression. It is concerned with ways of meeting the need to provide more challenging activities for students as they move through their programmes of study. But our discussion also embraces the twin concept of differentiation, which, in the context of our analysis, is concerned with the nature and extent of the differences in the activities students undertake from level to level within these programmes. Discussion is built around an outline survey that we carried out into undergraduate teaching in Britain. The survey is broadly framed, dealing with content selection, skills development, teaching and learning, and assessment, thereby providing a further basis for discussion in subsequent chapters, as well as for making international comparisons. The major issues to emerge concern the differing ways in which progression and differentiation are incorporated into history programmes within and between countries, as well as the varying extent to which these concepts underpin each of the key curriculum dimensions. By no means all the findings presented from the survey and from consideration of overseas examples make for comfortable reading, and they lead us to urge that a good deal more could be done to formulate and articulate how progression and differentiation are being achieved.

Specific curricular dimensions

Subsequent chapters turn to each of the key curricular dimensions, making reference where appropriate to progression and differentiation, but broadening the scope of discussion to include other considerations. A start is made with the chapter on content, a matter that can all too easily stir deep passions, especially in relation to ideas about a corpus of knowledge that history students at whatever level of education should acquire and, presumably, remember. Our discussion mainly concerns the need to achieve a balance between breadth and depth of content coverage and to incorporate different types of history, at both programme and course unit levels. Balancing breadth and depth is linked in our discussion with notions of 'deep' and 'surface' learning, and types of history with the problems arising from trying to absorb emerging areas of historical study into the curriculum, especially those associated with the rise of social and cultural history. Underpinning the discussion is the thorny question of how much compulsion is appropriate in history undergraduate curricula to ensure that students achieve some degree of breadth in content coverage when choosing their programmes of study, while at the same time being given sufficient opportunity to pursue their own enthusiasms.

The following chapter deals with skills, a matter that has excited a great deal of controversy among historians. Although clearly it is false to oppose skills and content, still the suspicion lurks that to highlight skills means to downgrade knowledge of the past. Yet the skills of actually being able to undertake historical study have long provided the essential core and orientation of the subject, and continue to drive the organisation of most history undergraduate programmes. What is new in recent times is the quite proper attempt to consider how best to promote historical skills in an overt and structured fashion. Moreover, there are increasing pressures to incorporate other types of skill in history programmes, not necessarily connected with the study of the past, that are transferable to other contexts, particularly the workplace. Many transferable skills are in fact readily nurtured in ordinary historical study, a matter which again has long been acknowledged by historians and employers; other transferable skills are perhaps more alien but, arguably, admissible components of the curriculum. Drawing on a further sample survey we have undertaken into course units that are specifically orientated to the skills dimension of historical study, this chapter argues for the centrality of skills in undergraduate history programmes and discusses the issues arising in terms of curriculum development.

The fifth chapter concentrates on learning and teaching matters. In part, our concern is with planning and implementing traditional approaches to learning and teaching associated with lectures and seminars, neither of which is a stranger to strong and telling criticism. Our stance is not one of abandoning these approaches, but rather one of adapting them so as to promote more active and deeper forms of learning. A significant part of the adaptation process centres on the ways in which higher education historians can make use of ICT in devising teaching and learning activities. The indications are that, despite the difficulties encountered, undergraduate history students are often able to make considerable and purposeful use of ICT, especially by drawing on various types of web-based facility that are being increasingly provided in-house and that are therefore tailor-made to meet the needs of particular programmes. Yet adaptation within face-to-face lectures and seminars also requires consideration and, as is evident from the published literature, may often provide more meaningful ways forward than virtual forms of learning.

The final chapter deals with assessing work undertaken by history students. A major part of the chapter is devoted to problems surrounding precisely what is to be assessed, surrounding the criteria by which assessment can be made, and the statements that identify the levels students achieve within each of the criteria. Stress is laid on the need to find ways in which students' work can be graded with a reasonable degree of accuracy and consistency and which help them to appreciate what is required in order to reach higher levels of attainment. Different types of assessment are also addressed. Included in the discussion are examples of highly innovative approaches that may diminish reliance on essays, both in examinations and coursework. Of particular concern is the question of how far essay writing provides the most appropriate means of assessing course unit and programme outcomes, bearing in mind the wide range of options that are available.

In concluding, key points are drawn out with regard to how curriculum development and learning and teaching approaches can be advanced in undergraduate history programmes given the markedly changed circumstances in which higher education historians find themselves. The line is taken that much can be achieved by reviewing existing practices in relation to the considerations that arise through analysing benchmarking recommendations, especially in articulating, and making known to both existing and prospective students, the rationale for the approaches adopted.

1

The state of the discipline

INTRODUCTION

In his path-breaking discourse on the structure of scientific revolutions, Thomas Kuhn suggests that resort by practising scientists to philosophical analysis and reflective contemplation is characteristic of a period of acknowledged crisis in their discipline. He argues that long periods of paradigmatic stability are marked by quiescence, shared assumptions and fairly routine endeavours along well-established lines. The onset of revolution, however, brings rival versions of how a discipline should be practised, resulting in intense debate, or even a complete breakdown of communication. In this context, resorting to introspection about the underlying nature of the discipline becomes an attempt to find common ground or, failing that, to reconfigure the very nature of the paradigm (Kuhn, 1962). Though Kuhn's discussion is directed towards science, his comments have considerable relevance for the study of other academic disciplines. Why should practitioners turn to theoretical speculations, far removed from their everyday professional work, if all is well with their world?

In the past generation, there has been a deluge of reflexive analysis within the historical profession. Countless books, articles and conferences have pondered the philosophical underpinnings of history, its assumptions, claims and relevance. Methods, sources and theories have been scrutinised and dissected. This prospect of historians, long associated with theoretical naivety and empirical imperatives, wrestling with questions of epistemology and methodology, has provoked bemusement, even consternation, among some observers (Swain, 1997). Not unexpectedly, the phenomenon has been accompanied by a measure of acrimony and has brought with it the nagging worry of whether, or how, to communicate this discord to students.

What, though, has generated this reflexivity and controversy? Is it reasonable to suppose, following Kuhn, that history is in a state of crisis? While it ought to be acknowledged that a froth of public debate does not necessarily indicate deep or pervasive problems, still the issues raised, which must have been considered in the corridors and coffee bars of all institutions where historians ply their craft, have profound implications for the discipline and the way it is taught.

This chapter reviews the state of the discipline of history at the beginning of the twenty-first century in the light of key debates that have characterised it in recent years. Three broad and interrelated fronts on which the study of history has been challenged are considered. They are:

1. The way that the discipline has been convulsed by internal divisions over its scope, content and purpose. Should history be oriented to the great and momentous events of the past or should it deal also with the lives and experiences of ordinary people? More fundamentally, the central epistemological assumptions of the subject have been questioned. What can historians claim to know of the past? What are historians really producing when they write historical accounts? What, indeed, is history for?
2. The controversy surrounding the wider ramifications of, and audiences for, history. Arguably, to a greater degree than most academic disciplines, history has a public face. It is a central component of civic and national identity and so has responsibilities, and is answerable, to a popular audience. In schools, museums and other arenas of public history, the study of the past has been subjected to close external scrutiny, which has had the effect of overtly politicising and censuring developments within the discipline.
3. How academic history has shared in the wider fate of higher education. At issue here is a relative decline in resources together with increasing external intervention, perhaps nowhere more so than in the United Kingdom where the nature of the sector has been radically transformed during the last ten years.

These developments raise serious questions about the nature and aims of history and consequently about what should be passed on to future generations of historians and their wider constituencies. The internal divisions require us to think carefully about what is taught to undergraduates and how they should approach and understand their subject. Public accountability places an even greater emphasis on the need to understand and to communicate what the academic discipline is about, its relevance and significance. Institutional pressures have considerable implications for how we teach an increasingly diverse student body and encourage meaningful learning. External scrutiny demands greater accountability by academics to their paymasters, who comprise both those in the outside world wanting a definable and useful outcome for their investment, and the students themselves, who similarly want something identifiably worthwhile at the end of their studies. In the face of the commodification of higher education, however, what still remains of the liberal and humane project of appreciating the human past? In many respects, the changes and challenges to history have unveiled long-standing tensions and contradictions, which have hitherto been all too readily swept under a carpet of implicit assumptions. If they force historians to address the issues more clearly, they may well have served a valuable purpose.

INTERNAL DIVISIONS

History as an academic discipline

To speak of an academic discipline suggests regulation and boundaries, of what is, or is not, permissible within its parameters (Bourdieu, 1988; Becher and Trowler, 2001; Jordanova, 2000). In academia, such limitations cannot be legislated for but rest on shared assumptions derived from overt or implicit rules, inculcated during training in the field. Inevitably, there will be internal debate over what should or should not be allowed, but most disputes can be accommodated through negotiation or the erection of loose, sub-disciplinary fences. Where there is profound disagreement, however, and protagonists cannot find common ground, a volatile mix of intellectual, professional and personal identities can come into conflict.

In history, significant internal debate has emerged over the foundations and orientation of the subject. At first, the point of contention was whether any particular approach or subject matter should be deemed more central than any other. Out of this debate, characterised as being between the Old History and the New, another even more divisive and consequential problem emerged. It concerns the post-modernist challenge of whether history really can achieve what it has always claimed to do, namely provide a truthful account relating directly to a real and knowable past. The complex and amorphous controversy surrounding postmodernism in history has threatened the whole basis of historical enquiry as traditionally practised although, in many respects, it has simply exposed structural fault lines of long standing. The constitutive tension that has arisen pits the methodology of the discipline against its traditional aims and orientation.

To examine the points at stake here, the development of academic history can be briefly considered.

The creation of the historical canon

Knowledge of the past is not exclusive to academic historians, of course. For perhaps as long as people have been sentient, the past has provided a crucial cultural resource. Myths, legends, sagas and folk-tales combine factual and fictional elements to construct stories about former times that contribute to a sense of identity, community, morality and purpose. More scholarly approaches, which sought reliable evidence for their stories, often retained elements of an instructive ethos in seeking still to transmit messages of virtuous examples to be emulated and misdeeds to be condemned (Plumb, 1969). From Plutarch's 'Lives' to Carlyle's 'Heroes', the study of great men offered examples worthy of emulation. Well into the nineteenth century, Macauley's popular Whig history of England charted the progress of the nation to its justified Victorian pre-eminence.

Conventionally, history as a modern academic discipline locates its origins in the scientised approach of Niebuhr and Von Ranke at the new University of Berlin in the early nineteenth century (Appleby et al., 1995: 72–6). In the physical sciences, vast new realms of knowledge were then being established through processes of inductive empirical investigation. An accumulation of detailed results, derived from repeated experiment or observation, appeared to provide a secure basis for objective knowledge about the natural world. Adopting these methods in the study of the human past through rigorous and detached empirical study of original documents might similarly allow the scientifically-minded historian to show things as they really were, unencumbered by literary or moralising overtones. As professional history became institutionalised in expanding university systems, more or less modelled on the German pattern, the scientific perspective provided a valuable intellectual bedrock (Novick, 1988: ch. 1). Besides the considerable cultural prestige enjoyed by science in the second half of the century, the aim of objective analysis helped to distance professionalising academic history from the romanticised literature of independent authors, now designated amateurs.

Although professional historians subscribed to the principle of objective analysis of sources, many of the traditional purposes of studying the past remained tacitly in place. The modern university was born out of the Prussian cultural revival and the development of history, universities and nationalism were inextricably entwined. Universities were national cultural institutions, repositories and defenders of national identity, with responsibilities to nurture the next generation of national leaders. History still had a key role in illuminating the nation's past and helping to promote national values (Soffer, 1994). At Cambridge University, Seeley found it useful to put forward the idea that the principal purpose of his school of history was to provide a training for future civic leaders (Slee, 1986: 58–65). It was hardly surprising that progressive and positive stories of the noble men and great events of the nation's past should be to the fore within the curriculum, or that historians, almost to a man, white, middle-class establishment figures, should emphasise the role and rise of their kind in national elites and political institutions. Moreover, the most readily accessible documents were state and political records stored in national archives.

The social institutionalisation of the discipline, therefore, channelled its development along certain lines. Of chief concern was the history of the nation as a political entity, with its emphasis on defining battles, diplomacy, leaders and political machinations. While it was important that events and people were properly analysed through scrutiny of extant sources, the social and cultural parameters of the discipline ensured that the objective findings seemed to be overwhelmingly positive. Certainly, it was important that youths be presented with wholesome versions of the nation's past. Yet from the perspective of established historians, it could appear that the story really was progressive, with England's extraordinary rise to global power occurring while extending political freedom and justice, the United States throwing off the shackles of colonialism and conquering a vast wilderness, and everywhere new nations being carved out of despotic empires and civilised values being brought to barbarian peoples.

Professional academic history, then, while seeking reliable evidence for the actuality of the past, nevertheless wove the events thus revealed into national histories that could be a source of pride and instruction for the present. Thus a canon emerged of progressive, national political history, providing a unifying and integrating acculturation for the next generation of civic leaders.

Opposition to such self-congratulatory stories certainly existed in the work of the Progressive historians in the US and labour historians in the UK, both offering somewhat less cosy views of the past and extending the range of topics studied beyond the great and the good (Novick, 1988: ch. 4; Wilson, 1993). Noticeably, however, these historians often operated on the margins of established academia and their overt political associations only served to distance them further from the professionally objective academic history. Meanwhile, the social profile of historians remained overwhelmingly white, male and middle-class. Although they may well have disagreed over aspects of interpretation, gentlemanly and scholarly differences did not seriously detract from the continuing concentration on narratives of political, diplomatic and intellectual evolution, which remained the staple diet in higher education. Not until the post-Second World War period, especially from the 1960s, did serious and sustained challenges to the canonical approach really emerge.

Old and new history

The vast social and cultural upheavals of the 1960s inevitably affected the way the discipline developed, bringing much greater emphasis on history from below – on people and topics hitherto ignored or regarded as unimportant in the historical canon (Burke, 1991). Most western countries enjoyed significant expansion of higher education at this time (although to a noticeably lesser extent in the United Kingdom) and larger numbers of students also brought a measure of social diversification; a much higher proportion of women entered and there was greater participation by members of the working classes and minority ethnic groups. Unsurprisingly, postgraduates drawn from this wider social mix broadened the scope of historical topics studied. At the same time, the civil rights and women's movements, and the general anti-establishment counter-culture, in all of which universities and students were prominent, put a premium on understanding historical forces acting from below. Whole new fields of social history, women's history and black history sought to recapture the experiences and agencies of ordinary people. With the paucity of official documentary sources, different kinds of evidence, especially that obtained from diaries, autobiography and oral testimony, were mobilised to try to recapture everyday life. Theories from the Social Sciences were also adopted to try to gain insights into the overarching social structures of class, race and gender.

So long as higher education was expanding and the new perspectives remained marginal, there was room for all. Initially, the new topics offered variety to the regimen of the established curriculum; traditional views still dominated and the canon remained substantially intact (Stearns, 1993). As new kinds of history and novel subject matter multiplied, however, the canon came to be indirectly, then overtly, challenged. There is only so much time and space available in an undergraduate's timetable. If new material is constantly being incorporated, the curriculum becomes unmanageable; if there is a division into compulsory elements and options, there is the question of what shall be the core and what peripheral. On a more social professional level, constant diversification ultimately results in a sense of fragmentation and loss of identity. A canon provides a sense of unity and cohesion, something identifiably central to a discipline. If everyone has their own version of what is important, the centre breaks down and the very nature of the discipline becomes open to negotiation.

Such problems, recognisable in theory, became more acutely relevant when higher education entered a recessionary phase from the mid-1970s (Novick, 1988: ch. 16). When job security might rest on the issue, the question of what was, or was not, to be admitted to the curriculum became a lot more barbed and when history became overtly politicised in the 'Culture Wars' of the 1980s and 1990s, the debates acquired an entirely new level of acrimony. This volatile cocktail of intellectual, political and social factors underlay the debates of the 1980s, characterised as being between the New History of social movements, forces and structures on the one hand, and the Old History of grand political narratives on the other (Himmelfarb, 1987; 'AHR forum', 1989).

Setting out the positions in polarised terms, to defenders of the established canon it seemed that history from below trivialised the study of the past, including insignificant people and mundane or distasteful topics, which, all too often, did not really have enough evidence to sustain them. Furthermore, the theories incorporated from the Social Sciences were seen as problematical on two counts. Firstly, they seemed to commit the historian, *a priori*, to a certain mode of analysis and they often had clear political overtones, considerations that seemed to undermine the independent objectivity of history. Secondly, theories about class or gender were also designed to account for a particular time (the present) and, although they might be useful to understand a slice of time past, they were too static and could not deal adequately with change over time. New History disintegrated the grand narrative sequences of the received canon.

To new historians, on the other hand, the Old History was narrow, elitist and insincere. In consigning ordinary people to oblivion it trivialised the lives of the vast majority of people who had ever lived. To be sure, it was often the case that new historians were committed in their choice of subject and approach. However, objecting to the political implications of New History and its political perspective from the bottom up hypocritically ignored the equally clear political implications of Old History, which took its political stance, effectively, from the top down. More positively, New History sought to be inclusive and offered a richer view of the past in addressing a wider range of topics and a broader spectrum of voices. Its theoretical approaches could help to reveal the structures of lives and ideas that might otherwise be irrecoverable, and explicit recourse to theory was better than the implicit theoretical perspectives of conventional history.

Inevitably, many historians straddled the divide in their actual studies and, paradoxically, both New and Old History claimed inclusivity: New History through unearthing and celebrating diversity, Old History by providing a unifying narrative to which all could belong. New historians sought to recover the voices of the majority and to include them in a pluralist historical account which more truly captured the actuality of the past. Old historians feared that the fragmentation of historical study and undermining of the canon might lead to factionalism and the loss of a sense of shared heritage that bound communities together.

The new kinds of sources, perspectives and priorities adopted in history from below disturbed many of the social conventions delimiting the discipline, the implications of which are still current. Key among them is what should be taught to students. It is clearly impossible to cover everything, so how do we deal with the overwhelming plenitude of topic and approach? What must be taught, what may be and what is optional, and on what grounds? Since there is no canon of knowledge that every student of history must know, what does comprise the irreducible core of the discipline that binds historians together as historians and that can be transmitted to students? Similarly, just what is history for, why should it be studied and what kind of messages should it seek to communicate? And can history remain a vehicle for citizenship training and a source of communal cohesion if it does not provide a unifying narrative of the national past? If this dimension is not the underlying value of history, what is?

At a yet deeper level, aspects of New History also pose a fundamental challenge to the aim of objectivity, enshrined in the academic discipline from its inception. At the heart of historical practice is a basic epistemological problem that is widely acknowledged but, until recently, rarely fully addressed. The problem is easily stated: historians do not have direct access to the past, so their knowledge of the past is at best second-hand, derived from the relics persisting in the present. From this fragmentary and randomly-surviving evidence, historians attempt to infer the nature and course of past events and then extrapolate from their inferences to try to assess the meaning and significance of those events, addressing issues of cause and effect and continuity and change. With so many disjunctures between past and present, epistemological certainty is impossible and historical understanding is largely a matter of driving posts into the sand until some kind of explanatory structure can be supported. These problems have long been appreciated, but have only really exercised the rare breed of scholar that indulged in the philosophy of history (Collingwood, 1970; McCullagh, 1998). Most historians are not concerned with philosophical problems and the discipline has devised empirical, iterative processes that have generated a vast corpus of practically stable knowledge, rendering the shifting sands of uncertainty largely invisible. Still, the basic problem remains, especially when historians are unguarded in statements about the objectivity of historical accounts and a level of philosophical insecurity persists.

Until the late twentieth century, philosophical concerns did not feature prominently in historical discourse. In the consensus of canonical history, most historians regarded themselves as engaged in a common pursuit of truthful accounts of the past. Liberal, fair-minded scholars were above mean and narrow partisanship and were guided simply by the evidence of the sources. While it could be acknowledged in principle that historians brought something of themselves to their studies, variations of interpretation were expressions of honest, individual differences of emphasis arising from the evidence and could be contained within reasonably genteel debate. New History, though, undermined this consensus by offering explicitly oppositional perspectives. Celebrations of democratic and liberal polities looked somewhat hollow when seen from the perspective of the English urban working classes, slaves in the American south or women just about everywhere. Historical understanding was relative to the position of the historical actor and of the historian who attempted to recover it. Moreover, new historians were frequently wedded to overt, and often politicised, theoretical positions. Although its supposed political neutrality was a myth, received history claimed the high ground of being above political activism and stood in contrast to the consciously committed Marxist or feminist-inspired history that appeared so sectional.

The challenge of postmodernism

Opposition between Old and New History was evident only in certain respects; at other points of contact there remained much in common. Most new historians maintained, with traditional history, that they were addressing episodes of a real and knowable past, accessible through analysis of evidence and susceptible of rational interpretation. From the late 1980s, however, other elements began to be introduced into New History, which, while logically extending its analyses, ultimately threatened to expose the persisting philosophical frailties underlying both Old and New History. New historical study had introduced a range of theories from the Social Sciences, primarily Marxist or feminist-inspired, to help in interpreting social categories of class, race and gender. From the late 1980s, attention began to shift away from these monolithic, modernist social structures towards finer-grained communal and cultural phenomena. A different suite of theories incorporated from anthropology and literary criticism was entertained, which brought poststructuralist analyses to bear. These theories threatened to take historical relativism to its logical conclusion, ultimately rendering history, as hitherto understood, redundant. 'Postmodernism' has come to stand as an umbrella term for this spectrum of approaches and perspectives (Munslow, 1997: 1–6), but two aspects of the advent of poststructuralist theoretical interventions into history illustrate the nature of the challenge. Both arose in new cultural history, itself an offshoot of social history.

Cultural history was given a fillip by E.P. Thompson's classic, Marxist-inspired study of the English working class, through his discussion of the notion of class-consciousness: the view that class was, in part, a cultural construct, not simply an expression of material realities and relationships (Thompson, 1963; Hunt, 1989: 1–22). How people perceived and expressed their consciousness put particular emphasis on the analysis of texts and language, community and ritual. Historians had long studied high culture, religion and ideas, but these usually had substantial textual and documentary sources to sustain them. To access the new realms of popular culture, mass consciousness and belief systems, however, new perspectives were required in which theories derived from cultural anthropology were obviously useful. Anthropology evidently requires alternative belief systems to be taken seriously, that they be understood on their own terms. Similarly, cultural studies indicate that there are no culturally-free means of discriminating between different world-views, and so language and ritual are as much symbolic and representational as reflecting realities in the world. Pursuing this line, however, does take the historian of movements from below some distance from the material disparities of poverty and direct oppression that were the initial concerns of social history.

Cultural history's study of language and texts as representations of a mental world eventually broached the realm of literary theory. Close analysis of texts, of course, is the stock-in-trade of historians. Philosophers of history had long been aware of the hermeneutic problem of alternative readings of texts, and competing interpretations in traditional history rested, in large measure, on different readings of written evidence (Collingwood, 1970). Equally, historians wrestled routinely with the difficulty of rendering the complexities of past events into a single linear narrative, using the devices and tropes of literary narratives. Historians, however, generally depended on a basically realist epistemology that texts did, albeit in complex ways, reflect the views of an author operating in an independently existing world. Some moves towards a linguistic analysis of historical texts had been made by Foucault who, although operating on the margins of history, had been highly influential in several historical genres (O'Brien, 1989). Foucault's studies of how power was mediated through language and knowledge of mental and corporeal processes revolved around the analysis of texts. He sought for cultural discontinuities expressed in the disjunctures between the texts produced under different cultural regimes. There was little attempt to account for how these discontinuities had come about, but rather to define their differences. Historians of medicine, for example, had drawn on the insights provided by Foucault, but had generally historicised them in standard contextual fashion (Foucault, 1973; Ackerknecht, 1967).

If, however, one took seriously the suggestion that all historical evidence can be regarded as a kind of text and, furthermore, that historical accounts themselves are texts, then it was not unreasonable to apply formal techniques of textual analysis used in literary theory (Kramer, 1989). Some of the contributions by leading French theorists, such as Derrida, took the difficulties of analysing texts to extreme conclusions. Since our access to the world is only ever acquired from, or expressed in, some form of text, all we can really deal with are texts. There are no criteria by which we can legitimately infer the existence of a knowable world independent of texts. Similarly, since authorial intent is open to interpretation, we cannot impute singular meanings to texts. Thus it is for readers to draw their own meanings and conclusions from texts, free from the necessity to relate to any kind of external reality. A linear narrative produced by an historian, therefore, is simply one, more or less fictionalised representation of a kalaidescope of occurrences among a theoretically infinite number of possible representations.

One could identify the challenge of postmodernism in history as that of taking to their logical conclusions some of the problems of which historians have long been aware. Few historians would claim to know with epistemological certainty what actually happened in the past, much less what short- or long-term significance or meaning a particular episode may definitively have had. Even while seeking truthful accounts, historians, if pressed, would admit to the contingency of their conclusions. In this way, evidence is a relic, a fragment of representation rather than a direct reflection of reality. Similarly, historical accounts are widely recognised as imposing order on unfathomably complex issues for the sake of clarity and meaning so, to that extent again, there is a fictive quality to historical writing that emanates in part from the historian's own personal preferences, ideals and values. In a replication of New Historians' critique of the Old, postmodernists argue that all historians should cease their philosophical fudges and accept that they are not capturing a knowable reality but, rather, are imposing their own literary reconstructions of essentially unknowable events. Embracing this position would allow historians to reject the pretence of objectivity in speaking to the present, be more honest in stating their underlying purposes, and would give them freedom to construct, openly, accounts that have more pertinence and value to their readers (Jenkins, 1991).

Taken seriously, the extreme relativism of postmodernist positions would make history, as it has been practised for almost two centuries, impossible. If there is no correlation between evidence and reality and everything is open to infinite interpretation, then there is no way of making meaningful statements about the past (or, indeed, the present). If an account calling itself historical has the same epistemological basis as pure fiction, then it is not history in the same sense that the term has had since the emergence of the academic discipline. Given such an elemental assault on the whole foundations and objects of the discipline, together with long-held professional and, one might surmise, personal identities, it is hardly surprising that there was so vehement a debate about the postmodernist stance (Windschuttle, 1997; Marwick, 2001).

In the event, few historians seem actually to have taken postmodernism that seriously and the controversy appears to have died down in recent years (Munslow, 2001: 355–6). The debates, however, have left a very important legacy. In these, perhaps, post-postmodernist times, it is increasingly difficult for historians simply to ignore the tensions inherent in their activity. Intellectual honesty requires them to engage with the issues and to formulate a response. There is nothing inherently wrong with a version of inductive empiricism as an epistemological tool, but if that is what historians do, it needs to be stated clearly and its implications recognised. And what shall historians teach their students? What are they to say about the nature and purpose of their discipline? What can they claim to know? How do they seek valid understanding of the past and how do they relate their findings to the present? Maybe such questions are too unsettling for unformed minds, but can historians simply evade them and hope they go away?

THE HISTORY FRONT OF TH19-E 'CULTURE WARS'

While academic historians debated the nature of their discipline, in a not unconnected development wider political events brought the study of the past under unfriendly outside scrutiny, adding external assault to internal acrimony. During the 1980s and into the 1990s, governments influenced by New Right political thinking achieved a dominant position in several western countries and sought to roll back the liberal developments of the postwar period. With the quite overt politicisation of social studies and the drift towards multicultural relativism in the Humanities, higher education was a prime target. The 'Culture Wars' represented a New Right onslaught on whole areas of academia, education and public culture under the guise of defending received values and standards from those who would foment discord and anarchy (Kaye, 1995). Initially, history was seen as a relatively safe, conservative discipline, but the debates over New History and postmodernism revealed that, here too, the barbarians were at the gates, threatening cherished national mythologies. Academic history itself was still fairly insulated from the assault, but history more generally, especially school history and the public history of museums, was subjected to much greater intervention.

The school history debate

In the United States, the debate about history in the school curriculum was part of a wider educational undertaking concerning the establishment of National Standards (Nash et al., 1997; Fox-Genovese and Lasch-Quinn, 1999: Pt. IV). Alarmed by a perceived decline in educational achievements, the Bush Senior administration launched a project to devise national frameworks for a range of subjects. Academic historians themselves shared many of the concerns that arose as schools replaced or incorporated seemingly old-fashioned history with apparently more relevant social studies. These concerns culminated in a familiar scare story about the ignorance of youth, with 17-year-olds failing to locate the American Civil War in the correct decade. Academic bodies, among them the American Historical Association and the Organisation of American Historians, mobilised in defence of their subject and sponsored the formation of a number of campaign bodies, including the History Teaching Alliance, and the establishment of an academic focus, the National Center for History in the Schools (NCHS) at the University of California, Los Angeles. This centre was deputed to supervise a federally-supported project to devise national standards in history.

To make recommendations on what the standards should entail, the NCHS mounted a wide-ranging survey and consultation exercise, involving large numbers of higher education and school history teachers. Inevitably, there were internal disagreements between panel members, which reflected the wider debates taking place in the discipline in the early 1990s (Kaye, 1995; Nash et al., 1997). In the panel on United States history, tensions revolved around the extent to which the school curriculum should present a more diverse, multiculturalist perspective, or an assimilationist, shared-heritage view. A similar problem confronted the World History panel over whether it should retain the familiar, broadly Eurocentric, Western Civilisation approach, or aim for a wider-ranging, properly global history. Participants agreed, however, that teaching in history should encourage intelligent interpretation, analysis and critical judgement and, to help to pin down these skills, a framework of five standards of historical thinking were drawn up, comprising:

- chronological thinking;
- historical comprehension;
- historical analysis and interpretation;
- historical research capabilities;
- historical issues-analysis and decision-making.

A large number of teaching examples were devised to illustrate to teachers how the standards might be put into practice.

Debate among the participants, however, was dwarfed by the political storm and media frenzy which soon gathered around the standards (Nash et al., 1997; Ravitch, 1999). Despite being a principal initial sponsor of the NCHS work on the history standards, Lynne Cheney from the National Endowment for the Humanities launched a vicious attack on the standards, days before they were published. Other voices, primarily Republican, joined in condemning the teaching examples (though not the standards themselves) for apparently institutionalising political correctness, being anti-American and fundamentally unhistorical. In Washington DC, a 'sense of the senate' resolution was engineered to condemn the standards and all for which they supposedly stood. To try to rescue something from the project, a review was established to reconsider the recommendations, particularly to remove the thousands of teaching examples, which had provoked most of the controversy. It has been claimed that one of the leaders of the National Standards project admitted that there may have been an element of redressing a historical imbalance (Ravitch, 1999). By the time a revised version of the standards was produced, media interest had moved on, but many states were reluctant to risk courting local political controversy by implementing the standards too closely.

In the United Kingdom, a substantially similar, if somewhat less vituperative, debate blew up around history teaching in schools during the 1980s, again revolving around the attempt to create a national curriculum under central, political direction (Phillips, 1998). Traditionally, control of the curriculum in British schools had rested with the schools and teachers themselves, guided at secondary level by independent examining boards, with the state very wary of becoming too directly involved. From the late 1980s, however, the New Right Tory government began planning for a curriculum that would set national frameworks of content and attainment levels. A History Working Group was appointed, which proposed a scheme that built on the work of the Schools Council History Project. This project had been launched at secondary level as a means of countering the reputation suffered by school history for the dull inaccessibility of its content-driven 'names and dates' approach. New kinds of syllabi were devised that emphasised more the active and engaging skills involved in actually doing history using primary sources, as well as the uncertainty of historical evidence and the need to consider varying viewpoints. A national history curriculum that emphasised critical and analytical approaches, and the existence of alternative interpretations, however, was not what the Thatcher government required.

There was noticeable political intervention in the deliberations surrounding the national history curriculum, with even the Prime Minister intervening. Pressure was applied to incorporate more attention to positive and progressive stories of British history and to the assessment of factual recall. Exemplifying the issues was a remarkable controversy over empathy, which was used as a device for encouraging mainly younger children to put themselves in someone else's shoes and imagine what life was like for individuals in the past and why these individuals may have acted in certain ways. This approach was demonised as engaging in mere fantasy and trivialising history; instead, history should be regarded as a serious business of memorising information about great events and important people (Phillips, 1998: 20–1 and 35). Ultimately, the proposals that emerged reflected a compromise with the political pressure, resulting in a huge burden of requirement on school children. A substantial part of the work was instantly undermined when it was suddenly announced that history would not be a compulsory subject beyond the age of 14.

To a much more significant extent than in undergraduate history, where students have a greater degree of maturity and can exercise choice, debate about history in schools is sharpened by the question of what children should be taught about the past. Is it important that the next generation learns unifying and integrating stories that help to weave a strong social fabric, perhaps at the expense of simplification or even an element of falsification? Or are civic values best cultivated by nurturing awareness of diversity and of critical and reflective thinking? These underlying issues were played out in slightly different ways in the United States and the United Kingdom. In the United States, multiculturalism was a key factor: would too much emphasis on difference and diversity foster factionalism, sectarianism and social discord, of which there was already so much? For the United Kingdom, the debate was couched in terms of skills versus content. Traditionalists saw history as the record of the past and wanted children to learn stories about Britain's greatness and exceptionality, not as an uncertain and contested pursuit in which there could be alternative or oppositional interpretations that children could begin to assess for themselves.

The problem of public history

A second historical front of the Culture Wars concerned the political contestation of public history, particularly in museums and heritage sites, both of which form crucial aspects of popular historical education. Public history boomed during the 1980s in historical reconstruction societies, nostalgic gift companies and, especially in Britain, the heritage industry, which flourished in inverse proportion to the destroyed manufacturing base it often celebrated (Hewitson, 1987; Lowenthal, 1985). Heritage became a focal point in a debate about political appropriation and economic commodification of the past and of Britain's place in the world. Throughout the 1980s and early 1990s, Tory politicians frequently attempted to encourage a return to a highly-selective suite of supposed Victorian values, emphasising the nuclear family, self-help, thrift and industry, as well as respect for authority, a limited role for the state and patriotic nationalism. At their worst, heritage sites seemed to conform to this sentimentalised view, with sanitised representations of the past offering comforting myths and an uncritical perspective: life and work under Victorian conditions was not so bad after all.

In the United States, an exhibition at the Smithsonian to commemorate the fiftieth anniversary of the dropping of atomic bombs on Japan provides a particularly acute example of the difficulties in marking an event of profound sensitivity (Nash et al., 1997). The centrepiece was a section of the Enola Gay, the aircraft that dropped the first atomic bomb. The intention was to take visitors through an exhibition covering events from the background to the action and through the immediate effects and aftermath, considering both Japanese and American perspectives. Considerable opposition was generated to the proposed interpretive display, which was purported to denigrate American servicemen and question American motives. Furthermore, the display was to be housed in one of the premier repositories of national history. The exhibition did not take place, however, and the piece of aircraft was displayed largely without further comment. Similar levels of controversy were generated around commemorations of the 500th anniversary of the landing of Columbus.

Such overt conflict over the representation and interpretation of national history was manifested perhaps even more clearly in the events surrounding the Australian Bicentennial in 1988, when the very meaning of the date was problematical (Jonson and Macintyre, 1988). The sesquicentenary of 1938 had been a fairly uncomplicated celebration of the British origins of westernised Australia. Changing political and cultural sensibilities, however, rendered the original landing in 1788 a much more ambiguous affair. As with the Columbian encounter, this symbolic founding of a nation entailed the appropriation of native lands and wholesale extermination of aboriginal peoples who have remained marginalised to the present day. Whether the event was to be a celebration or more reflective commemoration was allied to a desire for some kind of nationally unifying exercise. Inevitably, planners also hoped for a feel-good holiday and opportunity to create tourism revenue. The contradictions were played out in the protracted disputes over organising an appropriate flagship spectacle. Debates during planning between right and left rehearsed the divisions between European ancestry and multicultural present, amid several changes of government. Ultimately an unofficial re-enactment of the first landing, sponsored by a soft drinks company, became one of the highlights. A major educational exhibition, *The Great Australian Jour-*

ney, was tacitly more pluralist, albeit to the recorded bemusement of many outback Australians for whom it was intended.

Marking the Bicentennial was also a central event in Australian academic history. A multi-volume history of the Australian people was devised, together with a five-volume reference series, which occupied a significant proportion of Australian historians for the best part of a decade. Interestingly, the volumes were designed as time-slices rather than as narrative sequences, dealing primarily with particular years at fifty-year intervals – before 1788, 1838, 1888, 1938 and from 1939. This approach provoked debate on all sides as to whether it was a very New History kind of analytical device, or whether the dates chosen were a conservative manoeuvre that managed to avoid critically controversial periods, including both World Wars. Some portions of Australian academia refused to have anything to do with the bicentenary, the journal *Australian Cultural Studies* refusing to acknowledge it at all, while the *Australian Historical Studies'* special issue on the bicentenary opened with a statement of Aboriginal sovereign rights on its first two pages (Jonson and Macintyre, 1988).

Popular understanding of the past comes from a huge variety of sources, probably most importantly in the present day from blockbuster films and television documentaries. Debate about the accuracy and messages contained in the former are beginning to be raised more forcefully, most recently in the British complaint that American films show United States forces as sole victors of the Second World War. Typically, however, corporate film-makers are beyond the reach of both academics and governments. Schools and museums, on the other hand, are central battlegrounds for the control of public education in history. Although the curricula of higher education have remained relatively insulated from political intervention, the controversies over public history exposed the way the discipline had been developing as the new social and cultural history emerged, bringing academic history to political attention. Attacking an orientation towards skills, critical understanding and pluralist interpretations in either schools or heritage implicitly assaulted the way professional historical studies had developed since the 1960s and raised, publicly, questions about what history was for and what academics were doing. At the same time, however, there is a sense in which academic historians had laid themselves open to such criticisms (Nash et al., 1997; Cannadine, 1987). Perhaps more so in the United Kingdom than in the United

States, academics had distanced themselves from public history and done little to communicate to a wider audience the directions history had taken in recent generations.

EXTERNAL PRESSURES

The Culture Wars brought a good deal of largely unwelcome attention to history. Hostile critics found plenty of caricatures to attack, tarring wide swathes of historical practice in their wake, although in higher education traditions of academic autonomy forestalled detailed intervention in syllabi. The changing economic and political climate, however, allowed increasing restrictions to be placed on higher education generally. From the mid-1970s, the expansionary phase came to a sudden end and, during the late twentieth century, higher education in virtually all western countries was adversely affected by waves of economic recession. Reductions in budgets put pressure on practices that consumed resources and brought with them closer scrutiny of what funding was made available.

Although central governments have long been a primary, or even the principal, provider of higher education funds, in recent years they have been more prepared to exercise the rights that paymasters usually enjoy of dictating what shall happen with their funds. At the same time, higher education has been recognised as a prime generator of the new knowledge economy, which implies even more detailed supervision to ensure that knowledge and economy are geared together. Much of this section deals with the situation in higher education generally, especially in the United Kingdom, but it also provides the context for developments that lie specifically within history.

With the waves of economic recession from the mid-1970s, the great expansion of higher education that had occurred during the previous decade could not be sustained. Since the Culture Wars revealed that some of the academic developments paid for by that expansion were anathema to the emerging New Right governments, humanities subjects especially became more vulnerable to the charge that they were irrelevant to the economy and apparently failing to fulfil their duties with regard to public culture (Beck, 1996: 252–5). During the 1980s and 1990s, governments increasingly sought to gear higher education more closely to economic concerns, both through funding regulations and requiring greater accountability to external agencies. Areas with more apparent economic relevance received higher priority, while all disciplines had to pay more attention to preparing students for the world of work. Somewhat paradoxically, while the critical skills of questioning the past were downplayed in schools, in British higher education skills assumed increasing importance, albeit primarily skills that were transferable to the workplace. These external pressures have been common to university systems but have, perhaps, been felt more keenly in the United Kingdom than elsewhere, since the rapid transformation from an elite to a mass system has entailed enormous adjustment in teaching methods, accountability and, potentially, the whole nature of higher education.

The expansion of higher education

Until the mid-1980s, the United Kingdom retained an elite system of higher education, which carried with it a particular approach to teaching and learning and certain assumptions about the nature of the student body ('Trends in higher education', 2000). Barely 15 per cent of school leavers entered the sector, the vast majority of whom studied full-time over three years for an honours degree. Tuition fees were paid by the state and maintenance grants helped ensure that students could devote their whole attention to education without the need to work, other than during vacations perhaps. Only small proportions of students were not school leavers or were studying part-time. Such a highly selective system meant that high standards of basic literacy and competency could be assumed. The basic unit of resource allowed for generous staff–student ratios, which permitted small-group teaching alongside lectures in an educational process predicated on the ideal of a meeting of individual minds. Most students studied for degrees in a named subject which occupied the overwhelming majority of their time. Syllabi could therefore be devised to take a known cohort of students through a planned and progressive programme. Assessment was predominantly, if not exclusively, by summative examination, often occurring only at the end of the course of study.

During the late 1980s and early 1990s, higher education in the United Kingdom was transformed into a mass operation, which equally radically altered its nature and assumptions ('Trends in higher education', 2000). Over 30 per cent of school leavers now entered higher education, together with increasing numbers of non-traditional students who had returned to education after some time away, whether working or raising families. Numbers of part-time students, who regarded study as only one component of their lives, also increased substantially. At the same time, changes to funding increasingly put the burden of costs onto students themselves (and/or their parents) requiring them to take out loans to pay for maintenance and for contributions to tuition fees, and to seek paid employment as a means of offsetting their debts. Inevitably, average entry qualifications became lower than when there was a very selective system, while more students had basic educational needs and a large number of first-generation entrants to higher education were attracted who showed little awareness of just what was involved in being an undergraduate.

Such substantial and rapid changes in the size and nature of the student body occurring without commensurate increases in staffing or resources have had significant consequences for the organisation and practice of higher education. Furthermore, alongside the expansion of student numbers, other educational developments, most notably modularisation, semesterisation and credit accumulation, have undermined the structure of many traditional degree courses. Although allowing for greater student choice and flexibility, these initiatives have also entailed some loss of staff control over programmes of study. The sheer numbers of students have made it much more difficult to maintain individual tutorials or the small size of seminar groups. At the same time, developments in educational technology have enhanced the potential for distributed forms of learning. Altogether, increasing numbers of anonymous students undermine the educational philosophy of a personal meeting of minds in an inspirational encounter between tutor and taught. In mass higher education, more importance has to be given to educational devices and teaching practices honed in the classroom than in the study.

The growth of regulation

The unprecedented expansion of undergraduate numbers in Britain, combined with concerns about the quality of education as the unit of funding diminished, propelled central government towards greater supervision of higher education (Bennett et al., 2000: 1–3). Traditionally, British governments had maintained a respectful distance from the universities and, with an elite university sector, regulation could be maintained largely through peer review and informal ties, exemplified in the external examiner system. Shared understanding of degree standards could readily be applied to a small student population. However, when student numbers doubled in a quinquennium and the number of universities doubled overnight, there was clearly a very different kind of situation with which to contend. A good degree of suspicion and hostility towards expansion was added to the situation by those who supposed that more must necessarily mean worse. Consequently, state observation of higher education, applied from the 1980s, became increasingly intrusive during the 1990s. External review bodies were established to scrutinise university activity in both teaching and research, ostensibly to ensure parity of standards and efficiency of operation.

Examination of research began in the mid-1980s, with the implementation of the Research Assessment Exercise (RAE) (HERO, *RAE 2001*). In theory, the RAE was designed to provide a more secure basis for apportioning state funds for research by periodically reviewing the quantity and quality of research being published by staff in United Kingdom universities. Initially, the RAE was restricted to the established universities but was extended to include the former polytechnics and other higher education institutions that were granted university status in 1992. As significant funding was decided by the periodic inspections of the RAE, with severe implications for staff posts, the exercise rapidly became competitive and bureaucratic. Inevitably, research in universities became geared towards meeting the RAE criteria, arguably leading to less innovative work that would have a lower risk of being incomplete at the time of the next review or of just not working out. With the failure to fund fully the outcome of the most recent review, held in 2001, it has become widely acknowledged that the process needs reviewing.

Meanwhile, assessment of teaching activity had been a feature of public sector higher education, but not of the old universities, through periodic inspection and the work of a central advisory body for academic awards. Through the early 1990s, however, a more comprehensive regimen for scrutinising the work of all higher education institutions was introduced, which operated on a subject basis. The Quality Assurance Agency (QAA) was created to conduct periodic inspections of all departments or sections that taught academic subjects. The inspections determined a numerical mark that purported to measure the extent to which stated procedures to ensure quality of teaching provision were in fact carried out (QAA, *About QAA*).

In the space of some ten years, then, higher education in the United Kingdom had been transformed from an elite, autonomous sector into a mass system, characterised by a diminution in the unit of funding and the imposition of considerable external supervision. To prevent the change becoming a problem for any political party during an election year, a Royal Commission under Sir Ron Dearing was appointed in 1996 to review higher education and to report during the following year, safely after the election. The Dearing Report was a substantial and wide-ranging review, which captured much about the ways in which higher education had changed, even if, in many respects, it was still highly traditional in outlook (*Higher Education in the Learning Society*, 1997). Two of its recommendations that were put into practice carried forward developments of the previous ten years and are particularly relevant here. One was that teaching in higher education should be afforded greater recognition. The other was that, given such rapid expansion, there had to be more explicit consideration of what constituted higher education and of just what was implied by the achievement of a degree. In somewhat inelegant terminology, what did 'graduateness' mean?

In most western university systems, Britain's included, research has been given higher priority than teaching in determining professional status (Brooks et al., 2000: 22–3; Booth, 2004, 249–50). Promotion is based primarily on research and a key reward for aspiring academics is removal of teaching duties. Noticeably, this is true even of long-standing mass systems such as that in the United States, where eminent professors in top-ranking institutions leave mass undergraduate teaching to junior staff or postgraduates. According to received wisdom in the elite United Kingdom university system, there is an intimate relationship between the capacity to do research and the ability to teach through inspirational example; in principle, all academics both researched and taught and no particular skills were required for the latter. The advent of a mass educational system, however, meant that most academics had to cope with increased numbers of students who required new kinds of teaching practices. At the same time, the RAE raised in a particularly divisive fashion the question of whether all academics in fact both taught and researched. Following a Dearing Report recommendation, an Institute for Learning and Teaching in Higher Education was established, which in 2004 became incorporated into the Higher Education Academy. A focus for professional development of learning and teaching in higher education was thereby created, aiming to enhance its recognition and also to promote and disseminate good practice (HEA, *Home*).

The Dearing Report also recommended that quality assurance agencies should pay greater attention to setting out criteria for what constituted higher education. It was suggested that benchmark documents be drawn up for each subject area, which would set out what was required of a student studying the subject at different levels of higher education and try to identify what was meant and implied by graduating with a degree. Framing such benchmarks was deputed to groups of subject specialists whose task was defined by the Quality Assurance Agency as producing 'broad statements which represent general expectations about standards, particularly at the threshold level, for the award of honours degrees in the field' (QAA, *History*, 2000: 1). In history, the benchmark group drew its membership from a range of institutions, representing a spectrum of specialisms and approaches. As a statement of what higher education history is about, and how it seeks to train students in the discipline, the benchmark statement has enjoyed widespread support in the field for being sensible, coherent and non-dictatorial. As noted in our general introduction, the statement and its five components have much value as an account of the fundamentals of the discipline in teaching and learning terms and, as the headings to the chapters of this book, their meaning and significance will be explored in due course.

The developments outlined above have made the system of higher education in the United Kingdom much more like the majority of American or European versions. In many respects, however, the system is still in a transitionary phase. Although in size and structure a mass system, elements of the elite progenitor remain. Most students are ostensibly full time and expect to complete a degree in three years. Most degree programmes attempt to retain aspects of small-group tuition, close supervision and a personalised approach. There is also, however, a tendency to assume that students are better prepared and more aware of what higher education is about than they are. Messages about the cultural capital surrounding higher education could once be transmitted informally through individual tuition, but the situation cannot now sustain that level of support. Similarly, United Kingdom academia may be less well geared to the learning and teaching methods suitable for mass higher education than its United States and Australian counterparts. Higher education in the United Kingdom stills seems to be working through the implications of mass teaching and external supervision.

HISTORY TODAY

Where, then, does this rather dispiriting survey of the problems besetting history over the last ten to twenty years leave us? Is history in crisis, whether through internal division or external intervention? What has become of the various debates? How do the problems relate to the concerns of this book about the teaching and learning of history in higher education? Undoubtedly, any reports of history's demise are highly premature. Although indeed very serious, the disputes of the late 1980s and early 1990s have not materialised into a substantial threat to the essential nature and purpose of history. The discipline seems now to be in a relatively quiescent phase, not in crisis so much but perhaps somewhat punch-drunk and in need of a period of more healthy introspection. For it remains the case that the issues raised in the preceding review, although now subdued, have not really been resolved, and have important implications for how, what and why we teach history at higher education level.

As noted above, the furore over postmodernism abated around the mid-1990s. To a historian of academic disciplines, the course of events has a very familiar ring. A standard scenario in the development of disciplines is that a group of practitioners, often working in peripheral areas, adopt and adapt theories or methodologies from a neighbouring discipline, which they can apply to their particular interests. This displacement of concepts can then become the basis for career development by carving out a specialist niche. If conflict can be provoked, by challenging traditional norms or polarising positions, then so much the better. Ultimately, controversy tends to die down as careers are established and as existing practitioners realise that, in most cases, the challenge can safely be ignored or incorporated into mainstream practice. To a large extent, this seems to have happened with postmodernism in history. Prominent subscribers to the approach have certainly made substantial reputations out of it and established a specialist niche. As far as mainstream historical practice is concerned, however, it is difficult to assess whether postmodernism has been sidelined or assimilated and, if the latter, whether this represents success or not. Undoubtedly, many historians have simply ignored it.

The majority, however, have probably incorporated some of the more perceptive insights it offers into their own work, particularly an enhanced sense of reflexivity, a yet more careful reading of sources and a greater openness to the diversity of historical topics and possible interpretations. Moreover, the current fashionableness of work on cultures, communities and identities certainly draws usefully on postmodernist perspectives. At this juncture, postmodernism does seem to be having greater impact than previous innovations that threatened to overturn history as we know it, such as cliometrics or psychohistory (Evans, 1997).

This interpretation of its social dynamics, however, cannot conceal the serious theoretical challenge postmodernism has posed in exposing the underlying epistemological and methodological tensions pervading mainstream historical practice. Indeed, part of the sometimes hysterical response to postmodernism may be due to the probing of raw philosophical insecurities that it has brought. How we know about the past, how we go about finding out what we can know, and whether what we say we know is irremediably tainted by personal commitments and presuppositions, are questions which have lurked below the surface of history for as long as it tried to distinguish itself from myth-making. All historians have to construct their own answers to these questions, raising in acute form the problem of how we deal with these matters in undergraduate programmes. How are we to communicate to students a full comprehension of the uncertain nature of historical knowledge, while still maintaining that meaningful knowledge and understanding can be had?

One could interpret the advent of postmodernism in history as an attempt to bring some kind of order to the increasing fragmentation of the subject by defining a new centre. Instead of a canon of accepted knowledge, the core would be a corpus of theoretical understanding, as in physical sciences, social sciences and other humanities subjects. A similar effect seems to have been achieved in literary criticism, which was also threatened by explosive disintegration (Graff, 1992). Literary theory offered a way of identifying a unifying corpus of knowledge, which could be applied to the vast array of available literatures. If such was an aim of postmodernists in history, it has thus far failed considerably, but leaves the question of what does bind the discipline of history together? Several recent studies seem to be trying to work towards finding common ground around which historians of all political and cultural persuasions can rally. A quite overt attempt to do so is in the collection of essays self-consciously devoted to 'Reconstructing History' (Fox-Genovese and Lasch-Quinn, 1999). In this volume, an avowedly diverse group of historians seeks to promote calm and rational debate and the unifying theme that is set at the heart of the discipline is the craft of historical study. In a series of statements, the honest toil of the historian with his or her sources is posited as the real foundation of the discipline.

Historians remain a long way from agreeing on any kind of essential core. Practice may well have a better chance than theory in a notoriously empiricist discipline, although the debate about the place of skills in the history curriculum remains convoluted, and confused about just what kind of skills should be featured and how. In the meantime, the issue first raised by the rise of New History persists. There is so much historical knowledge, of such bewildering and ever-increasing range and variety, that the task of deciding what portions of it should constitute an undergraduate curriculum only gets bigger. The issue, however, may already be beyond our reach. To decide on what shall be compulsory and what optional presupposes that teachers can control the choices students make. In the free choice and flexibility of modularisation and credit accumulation, what is to prevent students from putting together arbitrary and incoherent programmes of study? Unconstrained choice may undermine learning by exposing students to material for which they have inadequate preparation. Some kind of balance needs to be achieved between giving scope to students' preferences and strengths, while ensuring rational and coherent progression of knowledge and understanding through a programme of study.

While relative calm that did not entirely denote accord broke out within the discipline, a similar quiescence fell over the external controversies surrounding history. Politicised public disputes over history in schools and cultural institutions abated. National standards were not implemented on a large scale in the United States, although, in the United Kingdom, a national curriculum was imposed, with which schools have had to learn to live. Constant innovation has been a wearying feature of recent education policy, leaving debate ineffectual. The return of left-centrist governments in both the United States and United Kingdom helped to take some of the heat out of the acrimony led by the New Right over public heritage, while renewed economic buoyancy has also contributed to overcoming morbid nostalgia for the past. In the former country, however, academia has once again come under attack with the return of a right-wing government, bringing the accusation that any attempt to understand an issue that implies questioning the role, actions and motivations of the United States amounts to 'blaming America first' (Fine, 2001). Otherwise, higher education has remained more oriented to economic priorities, although there has been some recognition that the capacities best generated in the Humanities do have wider relevance. External supervision has also persisted and, most notably in the United Kingdom, increased. Student numbers have expanded further, bringing people into higher education who have less prior preparation and cultural capital, and the requirement for United Kingdom academics to devise new ways of teaching, learning and assessing to cater for a mass university system has only become more insistent. There are difficult compromises to be considered over how to teach large numbers while maintaining a level of personal contact between teacher and student which has for long been a special strength of university education in the United Kingdom.

However unsettling and distasteful the controversies besetting history may have been, they have at least served to expose underlying tensions and contradictions which demand addressing by historians, both for themselves and our students. Greater clarity about what historians teach, how they promote learning and assess it, how they devise degree programmes and what exactly studying history is for, seems long overdue. When an elite student body could be relied upon to succeed, almost in spite of its tutors, there was little pressure to consider such matters. In a more open and exposed system of higher education, and in a discipline more susceptible to fundamental scrutiny, unstated assumptions and a tacit theory of education by osmosis need to be clearly addressed. On a broader scale, the issues surrounding the relationships between history and citizenship training are as powerful as ever and the resurgent questions of multiculturalism, immigration and asylum are set to raise them again in potent form. History, culture and identity remain persistently volatile matters. What, how and why the next generation learns its history could not be more important.

Key references
Evans, R.J. (1997) *In Defence of History*. London: Granta Books.
Fox-Genovese, E. and Lasch-Quinn, E. (eds) (1999) *Reconstructing History: The Emergence of a New Historical Society*. London: Routledge.

Graff, G. (1992) *Beyond the Culture Wars: How Teaching the Conflicts Can Revitalize American Education*. New York: Norton.

Hunt, L. (ed.) (1989) *The New Cultural History*. Berkeley, CA: University of California Press.

Nash, G.B. Crabtree, C. and Dunn, R.E. (1997) *History on Trial: Culture Wars and the Teaching of the Past*. New York: Knopf.

Novick, P. (1988) *That Noble Dream: The 'Objectivity Question' and the American Historical Profession*. Cambridge: Cambridge University Press.

Websites

Higher Education & Research Opportunities in the United Kingdom: *RAE 2001* at http://www.hero.ac.uk/rae/index.htm

The Higher Education Academy (HEA) at htp://www.heacademy.ac.uk/default.asp

The Quality Assurance Agency, *About QAA* at http://www.qaa.ac.uk

2

Progression and differentiation

INTRODUCTION

A short but crucial section of the Quality Assurance Agency's *History Benchmarking Statement* deals with the notion of progression, recommending that British history departments 'should show how their particular programmes are designed to provide students with the means to gain in insight, competence and performance over 3/4 years'. The document is careful to point out that departments are not expected to conform to a single model in achieving progression. However, two possible approaches are suggested. One requires students to engage in the same type of activities from year to year 'with a variety of subject matter but with a growing competence'. The other is to attach 'particular skills and attributes to particular courses and prescribe how students shall move through them'. A clear expectation is expressed that undergraduates should achieve a higher standard at the end of their degree studies than at the beginning, however their programmes are structured (QAA, *History*, 2000: 6–7).

In addressing the issue of progression, it is useful to adduce the linked concept of differentiation. Thus, whereas the former is concerned with how the curriculum and methods of study can be designed so that the activities students undertake become more academically challenging as they proceed through their programmes of study, the latter, for our purposes, deals with the differences in terms of academic challenge that are incorporated from level to level within these programmes. And these differences are articulated both with regard to the type of demands they make on students and the degree of change they bring.

Statements of progression and differentiation are fundamentally important in helping students to appreciate what is expected of them as they proceed through their programmes of study. They should anticipate, of course, that the work they undertake will make increasing demands on them, but it cannot be assumed that they will know the nature and extent of these demands. Moreover, from the teaching perspective, there is a need to determine and articulate how the nature of the work students undertake varies from level to level so that appropriate learning activities can be devised for them. Without such consideration, there may be little or no differentiation between levels and, therefore, over programmes as a whole.

Our discussion of these matters begins with a section rehearsing the main concerns that arise in applying the concepts of progression and differentiation within higher education history programmes. This is followed by a section which reports the results of a small-scale survey we have undertaken into how progression and differentiation is being achieved in these programmes as far as British higher education institutions are concerned. Subsequent sections analyse the results in relation to content, skills-based teaching, assessment methods and approaches to learning and teaching. A brief concluding section draws out key issues arising from the analysis.

PROGRESSION AND DIFFERENTIATION IMPLEMENTATION ISSUES

To argue for the importance of progression and differentiation in curriculum planning is one thing, but to apply the concepts within a particular situation is quite another. Several issues arise which must be briefly addressed (Timmins, 2003).

The context within which the concepts should be formulated

Plainly account must be taken both of the educational levels at which students are likely to be when they commence degree courses and of where they can be expected to be when their courses are completed. In terms of starting levels, the educational attainment and experience of students often varies considerably, as does the confidence they have in their abilities (Booth, 1997; Booth, 2000: 39–40). Accordingly, there is much to be said for a progression rationale that, during the first year of study, seeks to enhance students' confidence and to help them acquire, probably through compulsory course units, the type of experiences and understanding they will need to cope successfully with more advanced work. As regards finishing levels, issues arise about the understanding and skills that should be acquired by those completing their studies on graduating, as well as about providing adequate preparation in terms of historical skills and understanding for those proceeding to postgraduate study. In this respect, *The Framework for Higher Education Qualifications in England, Wales and Northern Ireland*, published by the Quality Assurance Agency in 2001, is helpful. The framework gives brief, generic descriptors that distinguish the knowledge, understanding and skills that are seen to characterise different levels of award, including those made at honours degree level (QAA, *Framework*, 2001).

Restrictions on individual actions and aspirations

That a framework of progression and differentiation can be seen to impose unwelcome curbs on the way in which higher education lecturers wish to operate raises legitimate concerns. To take an over-prescriptive approach is likely to cause more problems than it resolves; one only has to think of the periodic revisions that have had to be made to the National Curriculum in British schools and anticipate those that have yet to come to appreciate this point. Equally, to allow individual members of course teams to operate at will, especially as regards curriculum planning, scarcely helps students to understand the direction in which they are heading and what is required of them as they proceed. And as Peters et al. point out, with the introduction of modular degree courses, where choice of course units is wide and students from different year groups are allowed to take the same units, the notion of structured progression can lose out significantly (Peters et al., 2000: 138). To chart some middle course between unfettered choice and excessive compulsion is obviously necessary, bearing in mind the growing maturity and independence that students should acquire as they progress. Furthermore, it is important to recognise that any framework of progression and differentiation must incorporate a degree of flexibility if the curriculum is to evolve in response to changing ideas, needs and circumstances. The new challenges posed by web-orientated approaches to learning and teaching are likely to be of particular concern in this respect.

The curricular dimensions to address

Probably there would be no disagreement that the concepts of progression and differentiation should underpin content selection.

Various possibilities can be envisaged here, such as that of provision being made for students to enhance their historiographical and theoretical appreciation as they proceed through their programmes of study. The issue becomes one of deciding on the extent to which such elements should feature at each stage of the programme. But our contention is that progression and differentiation should also be applied with regard to the other major dimensions of the history curriculum identified in the *History Benchmarking Statement*, namely skills acquisition, teaching and learning strategies and assessment regimes. Our reasoning is twofold. Firstly, to concentrate on content alone with regard to progression and differentiation is to overlook other possible ways in which undergraduate work can be made more challenging from level to level. For example, with regard to assessment, it might be argued that, *ceteris paribus*, making an oral presentation with the aid of bullet points is a more demanding task than reading out an essay and should therefore be placed in the final year of the programme or become more prevalent at that stage. Secondly, the implementation of progression and differentiation can be greatly facilitated when viewed across the various dimensions of the history curriculum rather than within just one of its components. For instance, an assessment regime that increasingly emphasises coursework at the expense of examinations might be linked with the enhancement of cognitive skills through the use of primary source material in illuminating historiographical concerns. Such a link is commonly made with regard to dissertation work and it might well be extended to other course units located in the final year of study.

PROGRESSION AND DIFFERENTIATION SURVEY

The comments made so far imply that the ways in which progression and differentiation can be achieved in higher education history programmes will vary considerably from institution to institution. There is no set means of going about the task and templates cannot be provided that may be generally applied. Nor is it desirable that they should be. What can be done to advantage, however, is to discuss the kinds of possibilities and problems that arise with regard to existing practice, so as to inform the manner in which appropriate frameworks of progression and differentiation can be developed. In part, existing practice can be discerned from findings that have been publicised in book and article literature. However, these are all too few at higher education level, though useful guidance can be obtained from discussions of the history element of the National Curriculum in British schools (Watts and Grosvenor, 1995: ch. 2; DES, 1990: 119–65 and 199; DES, 1985: ch. 6; Lee and Shemilt, 2003). To provide a more adequate basis for discussion, it has proved necessary to seek additional information by undertaking a sample survey relating to undergraduate history provision in Britain. To compare with the findings from this survey, exemplary material has been drawn from undergraduate programmes offered in North American and Australasian universities.

The survey results were obtained from 31 of the British higher education institutions offering degree courses in history (about a third of the total), information being gathered in standardised form from websites and through personal contact. Details are given in Appendix 1. A rough balance of coverage was obtained between pre- and post-1992 universities and colleges of higher education, and most regions of the UK were also included, Northern Ireland excepted. However, the sample is essentially based on availability and cannot, therefore, be taken as strictly representative. Nonetheless, the findings offer a useful focus for discussion of the key matters arising with regard to progression and differentiation.

The findings are given in Table 2.1. The table subheadings correspond to the main issues covered in the history benchmarking document, with two or three progression components being noted in each case. The findings are considered in the following sections, but several general points regarding their interpretation may be made at this point.

- In order to provide a broad basis for discussion, information on progression and differentiation was sought under each of the four headings derived from the *History Benchmarking Statement*. However, instances of other possibilities emerged as our survey material was gathered, especially from the helpful observations made by colleagues, and comment is made on these as occasion arises.

- The progression elements are, for the most part, expressed across programmes as a whole rather than between particular levels within programmes. The latter approach was tried out during surveying in order to assess whether a more marked differentiation tends to occur between levels 2 and 3 than between levels 1

TABLE 2.1 *Elements of progression and differentiation in British higher education history teaching*

Progression statement	Number of cases	Percentage of cases
A. Progression in content		
1. Move from breadth to depth in level/course unit coverage	27	87
2. Move away from compulsory taught course units	26	84
B. Progression in skills		
1. Greater use generally of primary sources at level 2 than at level 1	19	61
2. More emphasis on using primary sources in final level course units than previously:		
(a) in special subject/study modules	23	77
(b) in dissertation	31	100
(c) more generally	21	70
3. Pre-dissertation course unit prior to final year	14	45
C. Progression in learning and teaching strategy		
1. Change from lecture to seminar emphasis	22	71
2. Increased opportunity for more independent learning (other than by dissertation)	20	65
D. Progression in assessment strategy		
1. Increasing extent of coursework assessment in taught course units	9	29
2. A marked shift towards assessing students on their ability to deploy/analyse primary evidence	25	81

Note: The percentage figures for items 2a and 2c are calculated from a total of 30 responses, since one of the institutions surveyed does not distinguish between level 2 and level 3 course units.

and 2, but it was found to add considerably to the sampling task and, for the most part, was abandoned. The more general perspective is presented, therefore, with comment on level-to-level differences that did emerge from the survey made as appropriate.

- Because the data may not be representative of general practice, the percentage figures recorded in the table should not be taken too literally; they provide indications only. Yet the results do suggest that some elements of progression and differentiation are widely incorporated into undergraduate history courses, at least in Britain.

THE CONTENT DIMENSION

From breadth to depth

At the outset, it was anticipated that the commonest approach with regard to achieving progression and differentiation in content terms would be that of moving from broadly-based to more specialist coverage. In part, this was because such an approach would conform to the 'research training' model, that Hitchcock, Shoemaker and Tosh have identified as being the most commonly occurring in their recent survey of British history departments. The model essentially involves moving from survey units in year 1 to survey and option units in year 2 and to option, special subject and dissertation units in year 3 (Booth and Hyland, 2000: 53–4). Furthermore, the advantages of the approach, which are noted below, are well rehearsed and may be seen as compelling.

- A broadly-based foundation provides the background knowledge and understanding that students must have if they are to move effectively into more specialist study; they need to acquire a contextual framework to which they can relate their subsequent studies.
- By taking broadly-based course units in the early stages of their studies, students may awaken new interests and will be better placed to make informed choices about the type of course units they wish to choose at a later stage.
- Broadly-based course units can have particular value for students who have little or no historical background, including United States students enrolled on liberal arts or pre-professional programmes (Simons and LaPotin, 1992: 51).
- They can provide a common grounding with regard to content, a consideration of some importance given the varied backgrounds of students taking undergraduate history courses (QAA, *Archaeology*, 2000: 10).
- Moving away from an emphasis on breadth can provide opportunity for more challenging types of learning to be introduced. A case in point is course units that deliberately focus on a limited range of subject matter in order to enhance the scope for in-depth investigation of key historiographical issues using primary evidence.

TABLE 2.2   *History content progression at Royal Holloway College*

Year	Course unit type	Examples
One	Gateway	*The Birth of Western Christendom, AD 300–1215*
Two	Group 1 Group 2	*The Flowering of the Middle Ages: Europe, 1300–1500* *London Urban Society, 1400–1600*
Three	Group 3	*Class, Gender and Nation in Edwardian Britain*

Not surprisingly, institutions offering history programmes in which course unit content moves from breadth to depth turned up in our sample with some frequency, occurring in around four cases out of five. The approach adopted at Royal Holloway College, University of London, which is summarised in Table 2.2, provides an example. The 'Gateway' units featured in the first year 'cover broad sweeps of history, and are designed to open vistas into great areas which are defined chronologically, or thematically, or both'. They pave the way for more specialist units in the second year. Those in Group 1 still cover a relatively long chronological period and/or a broad geographical span, but those in Group 2 are more limited in geographical and/or chronological range and normally address a broad theme, which is 'studied relatively intensively from a variety of angles'. In the third year, highly-focused modules are offered, which normally cover short periods of time and are investigated from a particular angle using primary sources (Royal Holloway, *Structure*).

A key feature of the Royal Holloway approach is that the degree of differentiation between second and third years is lessened because students take one of the thematic modules introduced in the second year as part of their third-year programme. Progression of this 'overlap and move on' type is typical of the 'research training' curriculum model and has much to offer in terms of moving students gradually from one stage to the next, taking them forward but also providing them with the security of the familiar. And the choice of course units available is extended at each level. Even so, the question arises as to whether such an approach always presents sufficient challenge for students, perhaps missing opportunities to move them forward in ways and at a pace they are quite capable of dealing with. There are certainly dangers in this respect if the degree of overlap is considerable and if, as the *Classics and Ancient History Benchmarking*

Statement notes, course units dealing with acquiring basic knowledge are offered to final year students (QAA, *Classics*, 2000: 10).

The approach to content progression that moves from broadly-based to in-depth course units may well be commonplace in all of the three countries under consideration, if to a less marked degree in the United States and Australia than in Britain. To make judgement on the matter, however, is by no means straightforward. In part, this is because, in all three countries, detailed explanation in the published literature about the precise nature of the course units offered at different levels in history programmes, and about how they are taught, is often lacking, giving rise to uncertainty about why particular units are included at one level rather than another. But judgement is also clouded because the degree to which students become increasingly specialised with regard to the modules they take is in part a function of the choices they make, or are able to make, as they proceed.

To tease out these considerations, examples of history units offered in the United States and Australia can be cited. In the former country, the ubiquitous Western Civilisation units give an extremely broadly-based foundation to history programmes at an introductory level. Yet students are not obliged to move consistently from breadth to depth thereafter, though they may well be encouraged, if not required, to take a mixture of broadly-based and in-depth course units. These points are well illustrated in Table 2.3, which is taken from a sample programme that history majors at Ohio State University could follow (Ohio, *Majors*, 2002).

As can be seen, there is a clear move from breadth to depth between the first and second years with a focus on European course units. Further specialised course units on European history are taken in subsequent years, two of them narrowing down to England. Yet the move from year 2 to year 3 is in the opposite direction, with a broadly-based course unit on East Asia opening up a new area of study. Furthermore, a fairly broadly-based African history course unit makes its appearance as late as year 4. Such a programme plainly has advantage in extending geographical coverage of historical content at undergraduate level and may be seen as a useful means of achieving content progression. The question arises, however, as to whether meeting breadth requirements at later stages in a programme can unduly hinder students' ability to deepen their understanding of history in ways that would give them a fuller appreciation of the

TABLE 2.3 *Sample history major course at Ohio State University*

Year	Course unit title
Freshman	*Western Civilization: Antiquity to 1800* *Western Civilization: 17th Century to Modern Times*
Sophomore	*Introduction to Historical Thought* *French Revolution and Napoleon* *France in the 20th Century*
Junior	*History of East Asia to 1800* *History of Classical Greece* *Medieval England*
Senior	*Tudor-Stuart England* *History of Modern Africa* *Senior History Colloquium* *History of the Early Church in the West*

nature of historical study and of the varying ways it can be approached. It may be that, in practice, broadly-based course units offered during later stages of programmes are qualitatively more demanding on students than those offered at the outset, but, if so, the challenge arises of articulating exactly how.

With regard to content progression between first and subsequent years in Australian universities, the most broadly-based course units again tend to be offered on first-year programmes but are not confined to them. Comparison of the junior and senior history units offered at the University of Sydney in 2001/2 illustrates the point (Sydney, *Handbook*).

Junior units

These were designed to provide 'introductions to the study of history, with the emphasis on approaches to history, overview and generalisation'. They include *Early Medieval Europe*, covering the period from the fifth to the eleventh centuries.

Senior units

These comprise:

1. *Thematic units*, designed to continue the overview element, but also to embrace the notion of contrast. Thus *Facism and Anti-Facism* involves a study of facism as both 'a European and global phenomenon . . .' examining 'in a comparative way facist movements in Germany, Italy and France . . . during the 20th century'.
2. *Specialist units*, which deal with particular problems, periods and countries. Among them is *The Spanish Civil War*.

Progressions of this type demonstrate a form of 'overlap and move on' approach to curriculum design that give a marked degree of differentiation; they do not involve exactly the same type of unit being studied at both levels, but still have an element of continuity, in this case with the overview dimension.

One other aspect of content progression within Australian and American universities relates to the course units provided for the study of history at honours level. To turn again to the University of Sydney's programme as an illustration, the *general seminars* and *special studies* seminars offered to honours students may be considered.

General seminars

These address a variety of theoretical, methodological and ethical issues in history. That entitled *Revisionism*, for example, 'addresses the phenomenon of historical re-interpretation that arises when attitudes or developments in the contemporary world force new and often controversial revisions to historical thinking'. Students 'explore the various manifestations of revisionism, in both its positive and negative forms, across a range of intellectual debates, historical events and countries'.

Special studies seminars

These are concerned with in-depth study of a particular area. *20th Century China 1900–1949* provides an example.

The essential point here is that theoretical and methodological dimensions can be seen to feature more strongly in the later stages of undergraduate study. To proceed in this way has intuitive appeal in that such dimensions might be regarded as being harder for students to appreciate than, say, historical causation, though the proposition is plainly debatable. Yet if theory and methodology are to have stronger representation in the final stages of undergraduate history programmes, questions arise about the extent to which they should be incorporated into individual course units, how far they should feature at this level in programmes as a whole, and what role, if any, they should occupy in the earlier stages of study. Are they to be seen, indeed, as a defining characteristic of more advanced provision?

In raising these questions, the matter of how far other types of historical perspective might be used to characterise the nature of final year course units also surfaces. What of comparative history, for instance, an element of which is evident in the University of Sydney's honours-level courses? The Hitchcock, Shoemaker and Tosh survey reveals that comparative history is often understressed in British universities, though they point to cases where it is included at third-year level (Booth and Hyland, 2000: 54 and 58). One example is at York University, where compulsory *Comparative Special* course units taught in the final term require students to study one of a number of themes, such as *Peasants*, *The Family* and *The Media*, in differing chronological and geographical contexts (York, *Overview*). Higher-level course units with a comparative focus can also be found in United States and Australian universities, including the State University of Ohio's *History of the Family*, which deals primarily with Europe and the United States and gives attention to cross-cultural comparisons (Ohio, *Courses*). Yet such units are not compulsory and may not be all that common. Moreover, that they are optional leads to concern that programmes of study which include them might be more challenging to students than those that do not. In Britain and abroad, therefore, it may be the case that all too little thought is being given to the ways in which theory and comparison may be meaningfully fitted into content progression so that all history students can gain understanding of them.

From and towards compulsion

The other main aspect of content progression that arises from our survey relates to the inclusion of compulsory study units within higher education history courses. What is of concern here is the number and location of taught units that all students on a particular course are required to take as they proceed through their programmes of study and what the rationale for them is in terms of progression and differentiation. Excluded from this definition are elements of compulsion that still permit substantial choice in subject matter, as with dissertations, or that require students to select one of a particular type of taught course unit, such as a special subject.

Starting with the British experience, it is plain from our survey that compulsory taught modules commonly arise at level 1 and in some instances they comprise a large part of the provision. At the University of Bristol, for example, first-year students take seven course units worth 120 credits, only one of which (valued at 20 credits) is optional. However, the range of compulsory work undertaken is varied, embracing medieval history and modern European history, as well as ICT for historians (Bristol, *Handbook*, 2004).

Making some course units compulsory helps to realise the advantages, noted in the previous section, of offering broadly-based provision at level 1. Yet the question arises as to the degree of compulsion that should be imposed, bearing in mind the attraction to students that choice can have. Maybe a minimalist approach can be adopted in dealing with this matter, confining compulsory provision in content terms to a single course unit. (And a similar approach might be adopted with regard to the skills elements of provision.) Alternatively, the view might be taken that a thorough grounding in content should occupy a large proportion of the available time, particularly if various types of history as well as major historical themes that will be encountered later on are to be introduced.

Beyond level 1, the indications are that content-orientated course units are rarely made compulsory in Britain, though exceptions occur. At Sheffield University, for instance, a compulsory module entitled *Rethinking History* is included in the second semester of the final year, its purpose being to provide opportunity for students to 'rethink the basis of their discipline and to reflect critically on their experience of studying the past' (Sheffield, *Single Honours*). Offering such a module raises a major issue with regard to how far an element of critical reflection should feature in history programmes more generally during the final year, perhaps within individual course units rather than within a dedicated unit. Either way, a major advantage is that elements of the 'spiral curriculum' approach become a feature of course planning, with students revisiting themes and ideas but from different perspectives in order to give them new insights (Light and Cox, 2001: 93–4).

In United States and Australian universities, the move tends to be towards compulsory taught modules as students come to specialise to a greater extent in history. At the University of Tasmania, for example, those opting for a history honours course are required to take *The Practice of History*, which 'deals with the work of historians both by displaying a wide range of concerns, approaches and controversies, and by an introduction to professional employment' (Tasmania, *Honours*). And to cite a United States example, honours history students at the University of Texas must take the *Seminar in Historiography* unit, usually in the spring semester of their junior year. This unit is specifically designed to prepare students for their senior research project, introducing them to a variety of historical methods and approaches and requiring them to write a thesis prospectus (Texas, *Honors*). In both countries, compulsory taught units are relatively few and seem to be very much concerned with effective dissertation preparation. As in Britain, the impression emerges strongly that, unless there is good reason to do so, there is a prevailing view that students should not be compelled to take particular course units – as opposed to particular categories of course unit. It may be of course that, in practice, freedom of choice is somewhat prescribed with regard to more popular course units. Yet the notion appears to prevail that students are likely to be more motivated by taking course units of their choice than by being compelled to take units which teaching teams might think should be taken.

THE SKILLS AND PRIMARY SOURCE DIMENSION

The literature available on undergraduate history courses shows that considerable emphasis is placed on developing key skills. Much is to be gleaned from this literature on the nature and range of these skills and of their perceived importance in vocational terms, matters that are addressed in detail in Chapter 4. Yet precise statements about the manner and means by which key skills are developed as students proceed from level to level are infrequent. And this is so despite the designation of study units as 'introductory' and 'advanced' or as 'junior' and 'senior', with the clear implication that students need to acquire and demonstrate higher degrees of competency, not least with regard to key skills, as they move from one level to the next.

Nonetheless, some insights can be gained into how skills progression is being achieved by considering the ways in which history courses involve students in the appreciation and use of primary source material. In terms of enhancing the types of skill that historians need to deploy, history programmes that increasingly require students to utilise primary material in more sophisticated ways clearly make greater demands on them; in effect, students are being asked to work in the manner of research historians, albeit at a less sophisticated level of competence. To cite one possibility, they may be required to move from a position where, having become highly proficient in evaluating the reliability of various types of historical evidence, they use their knowledge to critically appraise differing historiographical perspectives.

Dissertation and pre-dissertation course units

The aspect of progression in the use of primary material to emerge most clearly from our survey of British provision relates to the honours dissertation in history. A substantial piece of independent work located in the final year of study, the dissertation features in all the programmes surveyed, though it is not always compulsory and it does not necessarily require the use of primary material. To help prepare students for the dissertation (or presumably so, since a rationale is not always provided) a compulsory course unit dealing with research matters is commonly included in history programmes during the penultimate year; this was so in almost half the institutions we sampled.

It is not always clear that such units enable students to gain hands-on experience in using primary material, though they certainly address fundamental considerations about dissertation preparation. That available at the University of Melbourne, for example, which is entitled *Historical Theory and Research*, is based on two main components:

- The exploration of a range of social theories and methodologies that have influenced the writing of history since the Enlightenment, including empiricism, Marxism, cultural history, postcolonialism, feminism and poststructuralism.
- An examination of the task of writing history; the archival and biographical practices on which history writing is based; and the creative act of transforming historical sources into interpretative narratives to communicate to others (Melbourne, *Information*).

Other research method modules designed for undergraduate historians show a stronger commitment to the use of primary sources, however. Those forming the Senior Seminar unit at Utah University provide one example. Several options are available, with *Sport in American Society* requiring class members to prepare research papers that are based mainly on primary sources and that make an original contribution to historical literature (Utah, *Descriptions*). At the University of Birmingham, to take a British example, a second-year offering *Group Research* requires students to investigate a topic with the aid of primary evidence by working in small groups. The students assume responsibility for the organisation of activities they undertake, and assessment for the unit comprises a group presentation and the submission of joint minute books and individual reports (Birmingham, *Programme*).

Greater use of primary material at levels 2 and 3 than at level 1

In about 60 per cent of our survey programmes, greater use is made of primary evidence at level 2 compared with level 1 and there is also a strong tendency to place greater emphasis on using primary sources in final-level course units than earlier, usually with regard to dissertations and special subjects, but sometimes more generally.

Special subject course units tend to be closely-focused, involving students in investigating issues in depth using primary evidence. Commonly they count as the equivalent of two modules, so that when they are taken in conjunction with the dissertation, a very strong element of work based on primary sources emerges during the final year. As with the dissertation, the transition to special subject work can be eased by devoting attention to the use of primary material in preceding years, and 'pre-dissertation' units may be used towards this end. However, the question remains as to whether too pronounced a differentiation arises if, prior to the final year, programmes give only fairly minimal attention to primary source-based activity. Again, freedom of choice can be an issue here, since students may be able and willing to select course units before their final year that give them comparatively little experience of using primary material.

In some cases, a growing emphasis on using primary sources is accompanied by a progression of compulsory skills-based units phased over the full three years of the undergraduate programme, as at Sheffield Hallam University and at the University of Central

TABLE 2.4   *Progression in skills-based provision at Sheffield Hallam University*

Level	Course unit title	Main features
First Year	*Making History 1 and 2*	Covers skills such as essay writing, library use, group work and IT and considers historical sources.
Second Year	*The Historian and Research*	Develops core capabilities to undertake an independent programme of historical research. Both practical and methodological approaches are adopted.
Third Year	*Dissertation*	Provides opportunity to undertake a substantial piece of historical work based on independent research demonstrating skills accumulated at earlier levels.

Lancashire. Table 2.4 outlines this type of provision (Sheffield Hallam, *Content*). The essential consideration is that the second-year unit *The Historian and Research* is designed to build on the *Making History* units that all students take in both semesters of the first year, as well as preparing students for dissertation work in the third year. And a further element is added to the progression by treating the *Making History* units as a 'bridge' into undergraduate study. At the University of Central Lancashire, preparation for the third-level dissertation lies partly with a compulsory second-level course unit entitled *Sources and Methods in History*. Students work on directed, small-scale projects using primary sources. Skills-orientated units are also offered at this level (of which single-honours history students take either one or two) with the same objective in mind. The importance of using primary evidence to inform the secondary literature rather than for its own sake is emphasised. Differentiation between the two levels is seen to arise in that the dissertation constitutes a much larger piece of work than the second-level projects and offers students a much freer choice regarding the themes they study. The second-level skills-based units all build on the first-level *Understanding History* unit, an element of which involves students in considering the value and limitations of primary source material. Not until the second level, however, are they assessed to any appreciable extent on their ability to deploy primary evidence in coursework assignments.

As in other subject areas, the inclusion of project work in history undergraduate courses prior to the final year is seen to form a crucial element in establishing a skills-based progression. Thus Katherine

Cuthbert argues for the incorporation at an early stage in undergraduate programmes of 'intermediate' or 'apprenticeship projects', which would make students aware of the final-year project and give them an opportunity to begin preparations for it (Cuthbert, 2001: 80–2). Taking a similar line, and again arguing in general terms, Light and Cox suggest that there should not be just a single project but also earlier ones

> *aimed at involving students and developing their initial learning as well as introducing the basics of managing projects. Later projects could then be more in-depth and more capable of being integrated with their earlier learning on the course.*
>
> (Light and Cox, 2001: 94)

Adopting such a policy raises several considerations, including: the number of projects that should be undertaken; what their form and scope should be; the degree of direction that students should be given in preparing the projects; and the extent to which group projects might be preferred to individual projects. If adequate skills-based progressions are to be achieved, and if project work is to be kept in perspective, these questions need to be thought through with some care, a point that has particular validity if freedom of choice is accorded high priority in history programmes.

It is quite evident from the examples cited above that higher education historians are often concerned to incorporate elements of progression and differentiation into the skills-based dimension of their undergraduate courses. But questions arise as to whether more should be done. In particular, how far should history programmes be rooted in the frameworks of skills progression that have become commonplace at all levels of educational provision? That operated on an institution-wide basis at the University of Luton provides an example, and in Table 2.5 the progression strands it contains relating to the skills of analysis and evaluation are presented (Fallows and Steven, 2000: 20–4). It may be that the use of such frameworks is seen as being far too restrictive or not ideally suited to mapping onto existing history programmes. And the statements they contain will certainly need clarification for students to appreciate precisely what the terminology actually means. On the other hand, these frameworks do have a high use value both in helping to decide how the tasks undertaken by students become more demanding as they progress from level to level

| TABLE 2.5 | Progression in analytical and evaluative skills |

End of level	Analysis	Evaluation
One	Should be able to analyse with guidance using given classification/ or principles.	Should be able to evaluate the reliability of data using defined techniques and tutor guidance (where appropriate).
Two	Should be able to analyse a range of information with minimum guidance, apply major theories of the discipline and compare alternative methods/techniques for obtaining data.	Should be able to select appropriate techniques of evaluation and evaluate the relevance and significance of the data collected.
Three	Should be able to analyse new and/or abstract data and new situations without guidance, using a wide range of techniques appropriate to the discipline.	Should be able to critically review evidence supporting conclusions/ recommendations, including its reliability, validity and significance, and investigate contradictory information and/or identify reasons for the contradictions.

and in showing students what is expected of them at each stage of their studies. It is the latter that students are often particularly uncertain about so the inclusion of skills framework statements within course and course-unit guides can be of considerable help to them.

THE TEACHING AND LEARNING AND ASSESSMENT DIMENSIONS

That the two remaining dimensions of our survey are considered together reflects the limited amount of information that could be discovered about them without recourse to a more in-depth survey. Possibly the shortcomings of the survey are largely responsible for this state of affairs. Equally, it may be the case that higher education historians have paid less attention to issues of progression and differentiation with regard to assessment and to teaching and learning than they have with regard to content and skills. Certainly the evidence that can be derived on these matters from an instructive survey recently undertaken by Wil Griffith of the Department of History and Welsh History at Bangor University hardly brought stunningly impressive responses with regard to British practice. Thus, of the 37 institutions that reported back to him, no more than 22 (about 60 per cent) stated that they adopt methods of delivery and instruction that differentiate between levels 2 and 3. And they do so in terms of emphasis or intensity, such as giving more or longer seminars or requiring greater research activity. A somewhat more positive finding might be seen to emerge from that section of the survey concerning assessment, with 'more substantial work of some form' appearing to predominate at level 3. The need for students to demonstrate their ability to use primary source material in dissertation and special subjects is no doubt influential here, as quite a number of respondents mention. It may also be noted that a survey undertaken by Ian Dawson and Joanne de Pennington into fieldwork in British higher education history courses, by no means a major activity admittedly, found no evidence of planned progression in the difficulty of tasks required of students in moving from level to level (Booth and Hyland, 2000: 173).

Moving to independent learning

What can the results of our investigations contribute to discussion of these matters? Turning first to teaching and learning, the institutions in our sample make a good deal of reference to the variety of teaching approaches they adopt. Lectures, seminars and tutorials figure strongly, of course, but references are also made to the notion of encouraging independent learning. At the University of Liverpool, for example, students entering the final year of study are informed that

> *the emphasis is increasingly on independent study. This will normally take the form of a dissertation exploring primary sources on a topic of the student's choice, under the supervision of a member of staff.*
>
> (Liverpool, *Programme*)

Given that the final-year dissertation has come to form a normal component of history undergraduate programmes, it is quite evident that a move towards independent learning is a notable feature of them. Moreover, in many instances, if not generally, the move represents a clear progression in approach to learning and teaching between penultimate and final year, as individual tuition assumes a more important role.

In curriculum planning terms, a major issue to arise from these observations concerns the importance that educational theory attaches to the idea of students moving towards independent learning as they proceed through their programmes of study. Thus the QAA *Classics and Ancient History Benchmarking Statement* (2000) observes:

> *The principal specific desideratum for any honours degree programme is that at least in their final year students will have the opportunity to engage independently in learning and research with limited guidance and within a broad structure of courses, using and further developing the skills and abilities fostered in previous years.*

Adding flesh to the skeleton, Moxley et al., suggest that student development is facilitated by focusing on promoting academic maturity, a process they see as moving students through three stages in the type of activities undertaken. They argue:

> *Students develop an increased capacity to manage their own learning experience as they move from academic foundations to purposeful learning and then to autonomous learning.*

The features they distinguish for each stage, which have strong resonance in the type of activities that characterise undergraduate programmes in history, are set out in Table 2.6. Aside from the increasing demands made on students, striking points about the progression are the nature and degree of task differentiation created at each level and the emphasis given to active learning. It may also be noted that Moxley et al., are concerned to stress the importance of moving towards autonomous learning in terms of promoting retention, a matter of no little concern to higher education historians. 'As students evolve', they remark, 'their persistence increases and retention risks decrease' (Moxley et al., 2001: 93).

A further matter is whether history programmes are placing too great a burden on the dissertation as a means of promoting independent learning. In about two-thirds of the programmes included in our survey, increased opportunity for independent learning other than through dissertation preparation is evident, though the extent to which this opportunity arises may not be marked and no doubt varies. Since the development of independent learners must be regarded as a major function of history programmes, these findings at least raise the

TABLE 2.6   *Stage characteristics in progression to independent learning*

Academic foundations	Purposeful learning	Autonomous
Getting organised	Participation and involvement	Creating own academic agenda
Attending	Engaging material	Acting on own agenda
Completing requirements	Using material	Self-directed learning

question of whether enough is being done to ensure that this end is achieved, particularly with regard to final-year work. Thus, while the notions of students creating and acting on their own agenda fit well with the inclusion of the dissertation at this stage, they could be extended to other final-year units. Shorter projects provide one strong possibility here. They might take a variety of forms, including work placement or intern units. There are also opportunities to incorporate self-designed assignments within existing taught modules. But the crucial point is that of deciding how far both unit assignments and whole units designed to promote an increasing move towards independent learning should be located in the final year of study rather than earlier.

Moving away from lecturing

Aside from independence of learning, the other aspect of progression and differentiation in teaching and learning approaches that arises from our survey is the tendency to move away from lecturing. Such a move was reported in about 70 per cent of the programmes surveyed. The probability is that the change occurs more particularly in relation to final-year tuition, and is facilitated not only by dissertation requirements but also by the inclusion of course units that are strongly rooted in the study of primary evidence. In British universities, special subjects fall into this category and a similar pattern arises with classes aimed at honours students in United States and Australian universities. To take the example of the University of New South Wales, several course units are offered at advanced level during the third year for students intending to proceed to the honours course in history. Taught mainly by seminars and workshops, they are concerned 'with the theory and practice of History and/or devising and implementing research in History' (New South Wales, *Descriptions*).

The potential advantages arising from seminar work, especially that of being able to involve students more actively in the learning process than is usually possible with lectures, may well underpin progressions of this type, though our survey yielded little comment on the matter. But plainly there are key issues to consider in relation to the growing emphasis that should be placed on seminar work in undergraduate history programmes, not least with regard to promoting independent learning and the high-level academic challenges with which it is associated. In this context, the features of 'purposeful learning' identified by Moxley et al. (2001) (Table 2.6) can be particularly well developed in a seminar context.

Move to assessing use of primary evidence

As with independent learning, the move towards assessing students on their ability to utilise primary evidence, which was reported in four out of five of our survey programmes, is closely linked with dissertation requirements and, therefore, tends to occur more in the final year than earlier. And this tendency is reinforced by the inclusion of other final-year modules, including special subjects in Britain and research-orientated course units in Australia and the United States, that are particularly concerned with the appreciation and application of primary evidence. Accordingly, the differentiation associated with primary-source-based assessment can be far more marked between the later than the earlier stages of history programmes.

The manner in which this differentiation is achieved varies.

- One model requires students to demonstrate their ability to use primary material as at least part of the assessment in *every* final-level course unit. This approach is adopted at the University of Central Lancashire, for example, the requirement being that the major piece of course work in each final-year course unit is informed by primary evidence.
- In other instances, the approach is to confine assessment components based on the use of primary evidence to a selection of course units, thereby tending to give a less sharp differentiation in assessment approach.

Such differences raise important questions about the extent to which assessment centring on the use of primary evidence should feature more strongly as students progress and about how widely, by the final year, assessment of this type should be applied. But whatever decisions are made on these matters, assessing students on their understanding and use of primary evidence can enable growing and substantially greater demands to be made on them as they proceed through their programmes of study.

Move towards coursework assessment

As to the move towards a greater degree of coursework assessment in undergraduate history programmes, our survey reveals that considerable differences arise, though in fewer than 30 per cent of cases is this approach used as a progression element. The following examples indicate the extent of these differences:

- In some instances, the move away from examinations from level to level is pronounced, with no examination being given in the final year. This is the case at University College Northampton, for instance, where examinations account for 40 per cent of the assessment at level 1 and 25 per cent at level 2 (Northampton, *Prospectus*).
- In other instances, less marked differentiation occurs, as at Bangor University and Bristol University. At Bangor University, year 1 assessment is 70 per cent by examination and 30 per cent by coursework, the coursework percentages being as high as 66 per cent in year 2 and 58 per cent in year 3, depending on the choice of course units taken. At Bristol University, most first-level work is assessed by examination alone and thereafter 25 per cent of the marks for individual units are usually derived from coursework, though this figure rises to 50 per cent in the case of option course units (Bristol, *Handbooks*).

Not all the institutions in our sample favour assessment progressions of this type, however. Thus at Liverpool University, most level 2 and 3 course units offered during semester 1 are assessed by an essay or other type of coursework assignment, counting for 90 per cent of the marks available, and by seminar attendance and performance, counting for the remaining 10 per cent. In semester 2, the units are mostly assessed by examinations counting for 90 per cent of the marks and by seminar work counting for 10 per cent (Liverpool, *Descriptors*).

Explanations of the varying approaches adopted to distributing assessment between coursework and examinations are by no means clearly articulated in our survey literature, either generally or in relation to particular levels. It may be that many higher education history departments have traditionally used examinations as the sole, or by far the major, form of assessment and are reluctant to move too far from that position because of the advantages they perceive examinations to have. But this is a matter that will be addressed in the chapter on assessment. What must be noted here is not only that the overall balance between coursework and examination assessment is important in curriculum planning terms, but that changes in this balance can be used as a means of adding effectively to the challenges that students must meet as they proceed through their programmes of study.

CONCLUSION

The findings discussed in this chapter indicate that, not uncommonly, a considerable amount of attention is being paid to achieving progression and differentiation in undergraduate history teaching. As far as British practice is concerned, our survey reveals that of the eleven items of information included in Table 2.1, in over 80 per cent of cases positive responses were made in six or more instances, while in almost a quarter of cases they were made in at least ten instances. And in the majority of cases – almost 60 per cent – positive responses were made to between seven and nine of the items. How representative these figures are of the more general position in Britain, or in other countries, is unclear. However, the examples considered in this chapter, by no means all of which relate to the institutions sampled, and many of which can be replicated, suggest that progression elements are strongly embedded in degree-level history programmes.

Yet the indications are that much more could be done. In the first place, that attempts are normally being made to maximise the opportunities to achieve schemes of progression and differentiation – a policy urged at the outset of this chapter – seems doubtful. As our survey results suggest, practice varies considerably in this respect from institution to institution. The impression gained is that, as far as content is concerned, elements of progression and differentiation are very commonly being expressed in terms of a move from breadth to depth and from compulsion to choice, and that sound reasons are being adduced in support of these approaches. Even so, there appears to be less agreement in our survey institutions concerning other content dimensions that might be incorporated into progression and differentiation frameworks, especially comparative study and theoretical application. And the same argument might be made as far as the other elements that enter into the discussion are concerned. With regard to achieving skills progression through use of primary sources, for example, it is striking that while all the programmes surveyed offer a dissertation, mainly on a compulsory basis, programme designers are fairly evenly split on whether or not a pre-dissertation course unit is required. Notable splits also arise concerning the value of providing increased opportunity for independent learning, other than by means of the dissertation, and of increasing the extent of coursework assessment that students experience in taught units. Perhaps sound justification can be offered to support these varying positions, but it may equally be the case that rather more thinking about them is required to ensure that students face greater challenges as they progress.

Secondly, the impression gained from our investigations is that while schemes of progression and differentiation may well be stated as being incorporated into undergraduate history programmes, how effectively they are implemented in practice raises some concern. Thus it is not always clear why course units are offered at one level that might possibly be better placed at a different level in terms of the content they cover. Equally, it is not difficult to find instances where course units offered at a particular level vary considerably as to how they are assessed and as to how far the learning approach requires students to use, say, primary source materials or deploy theoretical perspectives. At issue here may well be the desire to avoid curtailing staff freedom and/or the inability to do so. Yet the perspective of the teacher has to be balanced against that of the learner. To allow for substantial differences in approach within a particular level of provision can be all very well, but the danger arises that students will face considerably more difficult challenges in some course units than in others. Moreover, these could well be challenges that at least some students are ill-prepared to meet. It may also be the case that, given the desirable aim of maximising course unit choice, students can avoid more demanding work by selecting those units which offer them little that is unfamiliar, except as regards of content.

The final concern is whether or not frameworks of progression and differentiation are clearly communicated to students. Certainly, as our survey reveals, practice varies in this respect, the tendency in the advertising literature made available to prospective students being to provide brief details at best. There are, however, historians who can be exempted from criticism of this type, amongst them those at the University of Aberdeen. Their general statement of progression, made available in an online handbook and therefore available to prospective and enrolled students alike, is succinct and to the point and is worth quoting in full. It reads:

> At the 1,000 and 2,000 level the Department's courses introduce students to key themes, concepts and knowledge relating to longer periods of time. At 3,000 and, even more so, at 4,000 level, you will find that courses become much more specialised in terms of chronological, thematical or geographical content. Once at 3,000 level, you will also find that our aims and objectives become more taxing and that, although some courses remain lecture based, our methods of teaching generally place greater emphasis on small group teaching. You will find that our methods of assessment become more diverse, with an element of peer and self assessment and criticism introduced on some 3,000 courses and in all 4,000 Special Subjects. In addition, the use of primary (contemporary) documents is an aspect of all historical study. However, its use and importance increases from Level 1 to Level 4 where primary sources form the core of the course work. You will also find that we expect more of you in terms of IT skills: you are encouraged at 1,000 level, expected at 2,000 level and required at 3,000 and 4,000 level to submit your written work in word processed form; and the introduction to historical computing techniques on second-year courses are developed on some 3,000 courses.
>
> (Aberdeen, *Guidelines*)

In itself, the statement raises a number of interesting points to debate, but what is of consequence here is that students are given sufficient information to enable them to appreciate what is in general required of them in progressing from level to level. Without this guidance they will lack understanding of the thinking that underpins the nature of the provision made at the different levels, and of how this thinking is translated into practice. Consequently, they will not be well enough informed about what is expected of them as they progress and of precisely how expectations change in order to provide them with more challenging work. Essentially, the matter is one of transparency, a theme that is further rehearsed in subsequent chapters.

The type of concerns raised in this chapter about defining and implementing frameworks of progression and differentiation give an overall picture, albeit within this specific context, of key matters that arise in designing higher education history programmes. The task from here on is to examine these key matters individually in greater depth. A start is made in the next chapter with the issue of content selection.

Key references

Booth, A. (1997) 'Listening to students: experiences and expectations in the transition to a history degree', *Studies in Higher Education*, 22: 205–20.

Cuthbert, K. (2001) 'Independent study and project work: continuities or discontinuities', *Teaching in Higher Education*, 6: 69–84.

Fallows, S. and Steven, C. (eds) (2000) *Integrating Key Skills in Higher Education: Employability, Transferable Skills and Learning for Life*. London: Kogan Page.

Hitchcock, T., Shoemaker, R.B. and Tosh, J. (2000) 'Skills and the structure of the history curriculum', in A. Booth and P. Hyland (eds), *The Practice of University History Teaching*. Manchester: Manchester University Press, pp. 47–59.

Websites

QAA (2000) *History Benchmark Statement* at http://www.qaa.ac.uk/crntwork/benchmark/history.html

QAA (2001) *Framework for Higher Education Qualifications* at http://www.qaa.ac.uk/crntwork/nqf/nqf.htm

Timmins, G. (2003) *Progression in higher education history programmes: the conceptual dimension*. History, Archaeology and Classics Subject Centre Briefing Paper at http://hca.ltsn.ac.uk/resources/Briefing_Papers/progression.pdf

3

Content matters

INTRODUCTION

We saw in Chapter 1 how the vast social and cultural upheavals of the 1960s brought a much greater emphasis than hitherto on the concept of history from below. Major new fields of social history, women's history and black history opened up, which sought to recapture the historical experiences and contributions of ordinary people who had largely been ignored, or regarded as unimportant, in an historical canon that emphasised grand political narratives. It was noted, too, that as the new kinds of history multiplied, they came to challenge the dominant position of the established canon in the undergraduate history curriculum. The debate between Old and New historians raised in a particularly controversial manner what, at the root, is a very practical problem, but which has profound consequences. With so much history that undergraduates can study, and with only so much space available in their programmes, it is clearly impossible to cover everything. The underlying issues regarding content are about choosing what should be included and what omitted and about what should be compulsory and what optional.

Questions relating to these matters are inevitably raised in the *History Benchmarking Statement* and provide a focus for the discussion in this chapter. In part, they concern the types of history that students should study, both in terms of range and of any emphasis that might be favoured. But they also embrace other fundamental content matters which arise irrespective of the types of history that are incorporated into programmes. These matters are:

- achieving adequate geographical and temporal coverage – that history undergraduates should broaden their knowledge base over both time and distance is scarcely in doubt, but the balance they should achieve between the breadth and depth of study requires careful consideration;

● providing opportunity for students to reflect critically on the nature and significance of history as an academic discipline – or 'reflexivity';

● enabling students to devise and undertake an extended piece of written work – commonly, but not universally, termed a dissertation – which, as a rule, is informed by primary source material.

Some consideration has already been given to these matters in relation to progression and differentiation, but there is more to discuss in content terms, particularly regarding the forms that these types of study might take.

In seeking to meet the range of content desiderata suggested in the *History Benchmarking Statement*, the question arises as to how far compulsion is required, a matter of concern given the narrow focus in content terms that undergraduate history students often seem to prefer. It should be stressed that, as the first section of this chapter makes clear, the question has nothing to do with central government seeking to introduce a common core of content in all history programmes, in effect a national history curriculum at undergraduate level. Rather the issue concerns the extent to which compulsory elements, as decided by individual course teams, might need to be imposed within the programmes for which they are responsible in order to meet content aims. Core course units that all students are required to take and compulsory groups of course units from which students make choices both enter into the account. So, too, does the notion of requiring tutors to ensure that, in each unit they teach, attention is paid to particular content elements, such as gender history.

This chapter is divided into five sections. The first discusses the general observations on content selection that appear in the *History Benchmarking Statement*, noting the importance attached to students acquiring a varied range of historical knowledge. A section dealing with content coverage in temporal and geographical terms follows, picking up the issue of 'deep' and 'surface' learning. The third section deals with covering varying types of history, raising the matter of how far ambitions in this direction can be realised by recourse to specialist units alone, or whether a more generic approach is required. The fourth section discusses content aspects to do with reflexivity, particularly developing the key theme of where reflexivity issues are best placed within history programmes, given the heavy intellectual demands they can make on students. The final section turns to content matters that arise as far as dissertations are concerned, including the varying forms they take and the differing demands they make on students from one institution to another.

BENCHMARKING AND CONTENT

Benchmarking has provided a major forum for debating programme content in British higher education. Yet, as noted in our introduction, the decision to introduce benchmarking appeared pernicious to many academics, historians included, because of its overtones of state intervention and the creation of a national curriculum for higher education. In terms of content, particularly, academics were apprehensive that external intervention would make the subject overly prescriptive and John Randall, chief executive of the Quality Assurance Agency, was forced to deny in public that this would be the case. In June 1998, he announced that benchmarking was concerned with 'examining what skills and attributes a person should have developed when they graduate in a given subject, not laying down the content of what is to be taught' (*Independent*, 04.06.98). Moreover, the central propositions of the group responsible for the *History Benchmarking Statement* are that:

- history differs from many subjects in not recognising 'a specific body of required knowledge nor a core with surrounding options';
- variation is accepted 'in how the vast body of knowledge which constitutes the subject is tackled at undergraduate degree level'

(QAA, *History*, 2000: 1)

In developing this perspective, the *Benchmarking Statement* also remarks on the uniqueness of history, asserting that its

subject matter, distinguishing itself from other humanities and social sciences, consists of the attempts of human beings in the past to organise life materially and conceptually, individually and collectively, while the object of studying these things is to widen students' experience and develop qualities of perception and judgement.

At the same time, the *Statement* recognises the close links that history has with other subject areas, especially the social sciences, pointing out that, in general, 'students of all types of history – cultural and political as well as economic and social – should have an awareness of relevant and appropriate concepts and theories' (QAA, *History*, 2000: 1–2). This point links back to our discussion in Chapter 2 as to where any emphasis on theoretical perspectives, which might well appear at all stages in history programmes, might best be placed.

In rejecting the notion of a standard or 'core' curriculum, the *History Benchmarking Statement* reflects a line of thinking among British higher education historians which has come to have widespread, if not universal, support. Writing in 1984, John Cannon, professor of modern history at the University of Newcastle upon Tyne, suggested that the rationale for a core curriculum in undergraduate history appeared in part to stem from a perceived need to maintain areas of provision, such as medieval history, in the face of threatened staff cutbacks. But he also remarked on a 'deeper feeling that history has become so fragmented that the various branches can no longer communicate with each other and an overall synthesis is almost impossible'. Yet Cannon was not convinced that he believed in the value of a core history curriculum and put forward four telling arguments against the idea. They are as follows:

- The concept of a core curriculum suggests a body of knowledge that all historians ought to know. Yet such an idea is difficult to maintain, since there 'is so much history, it increases at such a pace, it connects up with so many other disciplines that most professional historians would concede that a lifetime of reading and research leaves one nearly as ignorant as when one started'.
- A widely adopted core curriculum will 'produce a rather standard product and weaken student choice'.
- Even those who agree on the need for a core curriculum will be unable to agree as to what the core should comprise. Certainly the core will grow 'as more and more enthusiasts suggested things that historians should know or master'.
- Taking a stance that might be seen as somewhat cynical, the danger arises of 'harassed administrators' being given the opportunity to argue that anything except the core is expendable.

(Cannon, 1984: 24–5)

While history benchmarking does not support the notion of a core curriculum, no doubt for the kinds of reasons articulated by Cannon, it does stress the importance of historical knowledge, remarking that history programmes 'need to impart such knowledge and also to encourage students to acquire more'. It is suggested that this process can be achieved by ensuring students are not passive learners but that they should be expected to 'read, discuss, write, engage, explore and discover'. In such a way, it is argued, the skills and qualities expected of a history graduate can be 'developed through the process of acquiring, evaluating and discussing historical knowledge in the courses and the independent study that history degree programmes demand' (QAA, *History*, 2000: 2).

Despite lack of prescription, history benchmarking does make a number of general content recommendations under six broad headings (QAA, *History*, 2000: 4). These are given in Table 3.1, along with a summary of the accompanying comments. The recommendations are not particularly controversial nor unfamiliar to those developing undergraduate history curricula. It does not seem likely, for example, that many would share the discomfort expressed by Elton in the 1960s about the inclusion of an historiographical dimension on the grounds that it directed learners away from happenings to debates about what happened, from 'discussing historians rather than history' (Elton, 1967: 192). Nonetheless, major concerns arise as to how the recommendations can be implemented in practice and it is to a consideration of these concerns that the remaining sections of this chapter are devoted.

TIME DEPTH AND GEOGRAPHICAL PERSPECTIVES

As noted in Chapter 2, university history programmes commonly adopt a pattern of providing course units that give a general overview in the early years, followed by course units with a narrower focus in the third or fourth years. It is noted, too, that general overview units located at an early stage in programmes bring considerable advantage by providing students with a context for studying shorter periods and historical themes in more depth, as well as giving a content foundation for those new to the subject, a basis for making informed choice about later options and a means of stimulating new interests. There is more to discuss, however, about the nature of overview course units in relation to achieving the time depth and geographical perspectives

TABLE 3.1   *History benchmarking content recommendations*

Content element	Summary of comments
Time depth	Awareness of continuity and change over an extended time period, to promote understanding of historical process and to provide insights arising from juxtaposing past and present.
Geographical range	The convention of studying more than one society or culture, both for the academic value derived from comparative perspectives, and the social advantage associated with promoting understanding between cultures.
Contemporary sources	The need to undertake 'intensive critical work' on primary sources. These sources might be both documentary and non-documentary.
Diversity of specialisms	The importance of introducing students to some of the varieties of approach that historians use, including economic, social, cultural, environmental and gender history.
Reflexivity	Giving opportunity for students to 'reflect critically on the nature of their discipline, its social rationale, its theoretical underpinnings and its intellectual standing'. They might do so in course units dealing with historiography or historical method.
Extended piece of written work	Focusing on depth of study and concerned with students undertaking 'an extended independent piece of written work with appropriate supervision'. The expectation is that the work will be based on primary sources, though it could take the form of an in-depth historiographical study.

raised in benchmarking recommendations, irrespective of where these are located within programmes. Such discussion extends our analysis of the advantages that overview units can bring, but also highlights some associated concerns. It raises, too, the question of how far adequate exposure to time depth and geographical perspectives can be achieved in history programmes without a degree of compulsion.

Possibilities of overview course units

In addressing benchmarking recommendations, overview course units can plainly bring major advantage in facilitating an appreciation of both long-term continuity and change and of the study of more than one society or culture. And they can do so by differing appreciably in terms of temporal and geographical coverage, as the following examples of introductory units demonstrate.

- *World History: The Big Picture* offered in the School of History at the University of New South Wales. At the extreme in terms of breadth of coverage, this unit 'focuses on the basic features and forces which have shaped human history from the origins of civilisation to modern times'. There are sections devoted to major civilisations (e.g. the Roman Empire and Han China), such transnational issues as trade between civilisations, and 'the origins and nature of modernity, to the 19th century' (New South Wales, *Handbook*).
- *The Medieval World* unit, available at the University of Washington, illustrates a general survey with a more restricted time span than the above, but still offering very broad geographical and temporal coverage. Extending from the late Roman period to the mid-seventeenth century, it deals with political, economic, social and intellectual developments, emphasising 'three distinctive features of European civilisation that developed during this period: the gradual emergence of a distinction between religion and politics; the development of a concept of limited government; and the changing positions women occupied in European society' (Washington, *Catalogue*).
- The *History of Modern Britain* unit, offered at Merrimack College, Massachusetts, takes a fairly broad perspective, but focuses on developments within a particular country. The unit starts with the Glorious Revolution and incorporates the Irish Question, the Industrial Revolution, the British Empire, the effect of the World Wars, and the British role concerning European unity (Merrimack, Catalog: 49).

The ways in which overview course units can be used to address the specific aspects of time depth and geographical range expressed in the *History Benchmarking Statement* can be illustrated by provision made in the history department at Ohio State University. Take, for example, the notion of helping students to develop historical insights by juxtaposing past with present. A key point is the importance attached to the link with regard to the department's programme as a whole.

History is not simply a lot of names, dates and battles. At The Ohio State University, history is alive, and it's probably not what most students expect. In today's world where war, revolution, famine, and social upheaval occur with frightening regularity, history is the key to understanding these crises. History is not a recitation of facts and names but involves analysis and understanding. History is the sum total of human experience, and that experience serves as a mirror reflecting today's events.

(Ohio, *Handbook*)

At course unit level, the link is shown for example in the description given for a general survey dealing with African civilisation from 1870 to the present day.

> It examines the economic, political, social and psychological ramifications of colonial rule in the first half of the twentieth century. The movement towards independence and the emergence of new nations by 1960 would lead us into some of the current problems of Africa – economic decline, military rule, drought and desertification, urbanization and gender issues.
>
> (Ohio, *History 122*)

Linking the past with the present might raise the question of whether very recent times are the proper concern of historians and, more practically, the problem that course content will require constant updating. Yet not to take full opportunity to view current issues, especially those of major importance, in the context of the past misses opportunities to engage with the high levels of interest that newsworthy events can engender among students, as well as to enhance the relevance of historical study.

The Ohio State history programme also shows how overview units can be used to develop an understanding of the comparative perspectives mentioned in the geographical range element of benchmarking. The *Asian Civilisations II* unit exemplifies the point.

> This course is designed to accomplish three goals. First, it will present students with basic information about these cultures. Second, it will offer analytic concepts to organize this information. Third, it will explicitly compare the characteristics of these cultures as they have evolved in the modern era. The most successful students will be those who have mastered the factual information and can use it in both analytical and comparative ways.
>
> (Ohio, *History 132*)

Overview course units can be designed to encompass comparative perspectives and the juxtaposing of past and present, as in the case of *East Central Europe from 1815 to the present* offered at Florida State University.

> This course will examine the social, political, economic, and cultural development of the lands traditionally known as Poland, Hungary, Czechoslovakia, and the Baltic States from the Congress of Vienna to the present. Wherever possible, attempts will be made to present issues within a comparative framework.
>
> (Florida, *Descriptions*)

Such units may be seen to be particularly challenging for students, raising the question of the level at which they are most appropriately located.

A final argument to make in favour of overview units is that their long-term nature makes them extremely useful in confronting students with the issue of periodisation in history. As Peter Stearns points out, this requires that students appreciate both changes that amplify existing trends and those that establish new ones (Stearns, 1998: 291). In practice, significant turning points in the past tend to be predetermined for students by the start and finish dates chosen for the course units they are offered. However, that identifying such turning points can be the subject of considerable controversy among historians raises an important issue for students to address. Why such controversy arises, and how historians go about the business of making a case for significant change having occurred, certainly provide opportunities for discussion that offer valuable insights into the nature and complexities of historical study. And it may well be the case that students will need to make their own decisions about periodisation, most probably with regard to dissertation preparation.

Problems with overview course units

While general survey course units have a particular advantage in providing a convenient means of meeting benchmarking content recommendations concerning time depth and geographical range, there are anxieties about them. One is that students are confronted with the need to cover vast amounts of content, which can seem overwhelming. Another is the danger of encouraging 'surface' as opposed to 'deep' learning. Major characteristics of the former are that students tend to concentrate on memorising information, on viewing their learning as externally imposed and on engaging superficially in terms of cognitive processing. In contrast, the latter is characterised by students seeking to understand through their learning activity, to engage in critical evaluation and to organise and structure content into a coherent whole (Nicholls, 2002: 31–2; Gibbs, 1992: 1–11; Booth, 2003: 35–8).

According to Greg Light and Roy Cox, content overload 'is, perhaps, the most significant problem confronting course design in higher education'. They note, too, that surface learning is at the centre of 'transmission' approaches to teaching, which judge teaching 'by content transmitted, quality of teaching by content chosen and challenge to the student by the quantity and volume of content transmitted'. They continue:

> *Courses where student contact (transmission) time is high, and content overload is a pervasive feature, are associated with surface learning outcomes and a propensity for teachers to focus their teaching on knowledge reproduction, basic comprehension and application at the expense of the higher levels of analysis, synthesis and evaluation.*
>
> (Light and Cox, 2001: 90–1)

One way of dealing with these matters is illustrated in the approach adopted by William Simons and Armand LaPotin of the State University of New York at Oneonta. Writing in 1992, they expressed dissatisfaction with survey courses on American history offered mainly to freshmen and sophomore students on the grounds that a broad chronological approach 'eschews in-depth examination of topics'. Their solution was to introduce a case study approach with a 'Great Issues' format, their focus being on the Salem Witch Trials of 1692. Their objectives were to:

- give students the opportunity to utilise primary source materials;
- demonstrate the diversity of historiography;
- participate in the methodology of the historian by assembling, evaluating and synthesising data;
- convey the relevance of issues that touch upon a number of broad themes.

They also had progression in mind – the case study approach being seen as a means of better preparing students for upper-division history courses – as well as encouraging active participation in the learning process (Simons and LaPotin, 1992: 51–2).

The problem of a drift towards surface learning potentially arises with any content-led course unit in history programmes where coverage of factual knowledge is allowed to dominate over understanding and interpretation. This problem may be particularly associated with general survey units, but there is no reason why units of broad temporal or geographical coverage should not be highly intellectually demanding in their own terms. Thus grasping a big picture of change over time can require acute analytical and synthetic skills. Clearly, individual historians will have their own conception of what can be meaningfully covered in a particular course unit. One might cavil at dealing with a century, another be happy with covering half a millennium. Undoubtedly there are real dangers of encouraging surface learning, but they relate more to issues of how teaching and assessment are conducted than to any particular type of course unit.

Time depth and geographical spread in history programmes

The issue of breadth in content coverage extends beyond individual course units to entire history programmes. The literature describing these programmes commonly states that history undergraduates should ideally achieve a balance between the breadth and depth of their studies and restrictions imposed by offering compulsory units, and/or types of compulsory unit, are directed towards this end. Even so, questions arise about the extent of the balance that should be achieved.

Left to themselves, history undergraduates may well prefer to choose course units that relate as closely as possible to their known interests rather than sampling a wider diet. In doing so, they may well be engaging in the kind of in-depth learning that they find both satisfying and rewarding. And, as Elton has noted, there can be advantage in students working from subject matter they know if they are 'to learn how to handle evidence, weigh up conflicting views, and analyse problems . . .' (Elton, 1967: 195). Moreover, they may well be going some way to addressing the concern Alan Booth raises about achieving coherent programmes of study, especially in modular courses (Booth, 2003: 81). Maybe, therefore, too much can be made of the notion of achieving breadth of coverage in history programmes, even in the early stages.

On the other hand, that students studying history at undergraduate level, especially those majoring or specialising in the discipline, should be allowed to specialise too narrowly might also generate anxiety. Legitimate concerns certainly arise about the range of content they should study. For example, should they experience medieval as well as early modern and modern history? And, if so, to what extent and why? Similarly, in studying more than one society, as benchmarking recommends, how broadly should the net be cast and how much of a student's programme should be directed towards this end? That students might be allowed to concentrate on the history of their own country to the virtual exclusion of others, thereby bringing too little exposure to alternative viewpoints on events, is certainly an issue that needs addressing. But the issue has a deeper dimension with regard to the contrasting society or societies that might be studied. In the case of undergraduate historians in Britain, for example, should there be a conscious effort to counter a perceived overemphasis on eurocentric perspectives? Nor should we overlook the contention be overlooked that the introduction of a new and unfamiliar aspect of history can have a highly stimulating effect on students, leading them to develop entirely new interests.

In seeking to provide answers to such questions, much depends on the degree of compulsion that programme designers are willing to impose with regard to the content they feel students should study. The decision is by no means easy. On the one hand, there is a need to guard against the charge that time depth and geographical coverage are not being met other than in a token way, perhaps through providing the occasional lecture and seminar. On the other, there is a reluctance to curtail students' freedom of choice in what they wish to study, especially on the grounds that they are likely to perform better by taking course units in which they know they have a strong interest rather than those to which they feel indifferent. In taking these considerations into account, the minimalist position might be that of including a compulsory general survey unit in the early stages of a programme. How far compulsory coverage of time depth and geo-graphical elements would go beyond this position would in part be a function of other elements of compulsion that might also enter into the account. Of particular importance among them would be the types of history to which it is felt all students should be introduced, and skills-based work probably involving the use of primary material. These are matters to which our discussion will return.

DIVERSITY OF SPECIALISMS

That, in line with benchmarking suggestions, history undergraduates are offered a diversity of approach to their studies is hardly in doubt. Even a cursory glance at the programmes offered by university and college history departments reveals that it is common to find course units dealing with economic, social, political, cultural and women's history, and of others besides, including local and regional history. However, the manner in which students experience different types of history, the extent to which they do so and the advantages and difficulties they encounter raise issues that are fundamental to curriculum design. It is to these matters that discussion now turns.

The recommendation made by the *Benchmark Statement* is that students should be introduced to some varieties of history 'each with its distinctive focus and theoretical orientation', so they can gain 'a critical awareness that there are many principles of selection and modes of enquiry' (QAA, *History*, 2000: 4). With regard to planning the content of history programmes, two key concerns arise from these recommendations: which of the varieties are to be covered, and to what extent? Both matters lead to a consideration of the importance that particular types of history are perceived to have and whether there is a need to introduce them by some form of compulsion.

Political history

In deciding on the contribution that various types of history can make to students' understanding, there is much scope for championing causes (Stearns, 1998: 284–5). Thus the significance claimed for studying political history, and the great events and figures of the past with which it is linked, is hard to deny. Arguments in its favour are as follows.

● Understanding major political events and situations in the present day, especially, perhaps, in relation to international conflict and inequalities in wealth and income distribution, depends upon an appreciation of their historical context.

- The study of other types of history, particularly social and economic history, cannot meaningfully be divorced from an appreciation of political history.
- Certain dimensions of political history are undeniably popular with students, including those dealing with fascist regimes.

Elton's view, expressed in the 1960s, was that politics 'must always constitute a large part of any undergraduate history course . . .' (Elton, 1967: 190). Maybe this view still has widespread support, though it has become harder to sustain given the growth in popularity of other types of history, especially those dealing with the perspectives of ordinary people rather than the great figures of history. Moreover, the notion of 'a large part' is open to differing interpretations, while decisions have to be made about whether the notion should be applied to course unit offerings in history programmes or to the actual history that all students should ideally study.

Women's history and gender history

The rise of interest in women's and gender history has coincided with a move to appreciate previously neglected or invisible groups within history, as well as reflecting the emergence of a strong women's movement. This growing interest has added a new dimension to historical understanding as patriarchy, rather than class or national identity, and has become a prism through which the past can be understood. Inevitably, a more nuanced understanding of the contribution of women to family, economic and political life has also forced a reassessment of the roles that had been assigned to men.

As would be expected, the growing interest in the study of women's and gender history has been accompanied by their enhanced role in undergraduate teaching and learning, giving rise to a rich variety of course unit offerings. Some of these units, including Michigan State University's *Women in the US from 1869*, add a women's perspective to traditional concerns. It examines:

> . . . US history from 1869 to the present from the perspective of women. Topics will include women in the changing economy; women's legal and political status, differences among women based on race, ethnicity, class, region, age, and political perspectives, sex roles and the changing image of womanhood.

Traditional subjects like the western experience, labor, World War II and the 'sixties' will be recast as we include women in the narrative.

(Michigan, *Descriptions*)

Units of this type clearly offer great potential for students to examine historiographical issues critically and to offer revisionist interpretations, especially when they are given the opportunity to inform their analysis with primary evidence.

How far there is advantage in studying women's history as part of general surveys has been questioned by Mary E. Frederickson, who argues that these courses often marginalise the experiences and contribution of women.

Generally survey courses in American history, largely because of their emphasis on political history, rarely provide students the opportunity to relate the historical to the personal, to discover their own past in the context of the national story. Because of American women's exclusion from the political realm, women's history courses cannot simply follow the traditional political format. Freed from the rigid structure that most survey courses reflect, women's history naturally has encompassed more social, economic and cultural history, the very nature of which emphasizes grassroots participation, collective movements, individual contributions, and demographic analysis.

(Frederickson, 1992: 23)

The view expressed by Frederickson clearly has profound implications for the ways in which women-centred history should be covered in undergraduate programmes. To help in meeting her concerns, units dealing specifically with women's perspectives might be incorporated. But there is also the need in syllabus planning to reflect the importance that an appreciation of changing masculine and feminine constructs can bring to historical interpretation (Smith, 1993: 267–72). Such an approach is evident in *Gender and the Labour Movement 1820–1850*, a course unit offered at Leeds University. It is built around several key issues:

How did working men and women respond to the changes and challenges of industrialisation? How did the social and economic changes of the early nineteenth century affect gender relationships in the home and at work? How far can it be argued that industrial society was 'gendered'? Was the making of the working class a gendered experience? Using a range of contemporary documents, this module analyses the way in which gendered class relations both influenced and were affected by the development of working-class associations by focusing on the early feminist and socialist movements. It also explores the importance of the construction of gender identities in protecting working-class interests.

(Leeds, *Modules*, 2003/4)

Another example is *Gender Politics in Early Modern England* available at the University of Essex, which aims to 'introduce a range of ways of thinking about gender in the past and to encourage the re-examination of the early modern period with the history of women and gender in mind'. The focus is on three key areas, namely 'the gendered body; order and disorder in household and community; and gender in the religious and political life of the nation' (Essex, *Modules*).

Inevitably, gender history also enters into units focusing on family history. One example is *The Family and Gender in African History* offered to graduates at the University of Virginia. As can be seen, both the role of women and gender relations feature in the unit, the latter dimension being set within a framework of social science theory.

Family and gender relations have fundamentally shaped Africa's changing societies, economies, and cultures, just as it has been shaped by them. We will begin this course by exploring various ways of understanding familial and gender relations, as both Africans themselves and social scientists have imagined them. We will then focus on how African men, women and families have participated in, influenced, and been transformed by various processes in African history, including slavery, migration, urbanization, colonial rule, legal change and the development of the postcolonial state.

(Virginia, *Courses*)

Aside from the varying approaches that can be taken to studying women's and gender history, a fundamental concern in curriculum planning terms is how widely and strongly they should feature in teaching programmes. Alongside specialist units dealing with particular themes, general survey units still provide opportunity to address some of these issues, as the Michigan State example reveals. But so, too, do other course unit offerings, and not only those rooted in social and cultural history. Accordingly, the issue has to be addressed as to whether, in line with the stance taken by Cathy Lubelska, 'histories of gender should permeate the curriculum, informing all analyses' (Lubelska, 1996: 55–74). It is a matter that impinges not only on lecture and seminar programmes, but also on the nature of the assignment tasks that are set.

Race and ethnic history

The same types of argument arise regarding the inclusion of race and ethnic issues in undergraduate history programmes. Again, varied approaches are evident, with comparative analysis featuring. Thus, at the University of the West of England, the unit *Comparative Themes in Black History, 1700–1980* is offered, which focuses on

> . . . a comparative study of the history of black communities in Britain (and its empire) and the United States during the last three centuries. A number of distinct phases of black history are addressed including: the experience of slavery; free blacks in Britain and America in the 18th and early 19th centuries; emancipation and its aftermath; the black community in the late 19th and early 20th centuries; the black experience since the Second World War.
>
> (West of England, *Modules*)

Other course units of this type take a rather different emphasis. For instance, the *Introduction to Comparative Studies in Race and Ethnicity* at Stanford University, not only, in its comparative dimension, identifies 'important topics and issues central to the study of ethnic and race relations in the US and elsewhere in the world', but also introduces students 'to how various disciplines approach the study of race and ethnicity' (Stanford, *Courses*).

As in the area of women's and gender history, course units on the history of race and ethnic studies deal with matters that are of fundamental importance in helping students to understand the nature and complexities of present-day society, and to offer informed opinion on race and ethnic matters. In both these senses, the introduction of such units into undergraduate programmes can be seen as a further contribution to fulfilling the social role of historical study. At the same time, the difficulties that may be encountered by including race and gender elements in history programmes can be disturbing. Thus Mary

E. Frederickson who, in the 1980s, taught women's history in the University of Alabama in Birmingham (a centre of the civil rights movement) has written about the 'ghosts' who sat in the back row of her class. Many of the students in the class – both black and white – had direct contact with the civil rights movement. Difficulties were encountered because, since they took a great pride in the civil rights movement, black students in Birmingham shared 'a legacy of courage and hope'. White students in the same city, however, shared 'a legacy of fear'. Fredrickson concluded that it was necessary to face, rather than ignore, the ghosts of history – 'to let them sit with us as we struggle to understand the past and plan for the future' (Fredrickson, 1992).

Local and regional history

A key argument in favour of including local and regional study in history programmes is that opportunity arises for students to explore themes of major importance on a case study basis. Such an approach is evident, for example, in the *Chicago* course unit offered in Fall 2002 by the History Department at the University of Illinois at Urbana-Champaign.

The University of Chicago's pioneering sociologists had the idea first in the early years of the twentieth century: The city might become a laboratory in which to observe and study the process of urbanization and related social problems. Nowhere did urbanization and the other broad forces of change that have transformed life in the nineteenth and twentieth centuries – industrialization, social class formation, migration and immigration – occur more rapidly than in Chicago and nowhere did they unfold with more dramatic results. This course employs the history of Chicago as a particularly appropriate case study of key problems in the field of US social history: the theory and process of urbanization; formation of classes and the evolution of class conflict; immigration, mass migration and ethnic diversity; racial formation and conflict.

(Illinois, *Courses*)

A related consideration here is that locally-orientated historical investigation often helps students to devise viable and manageable case studies, tapping into a rich vein of readily accessible source material that is varied in nature. Furthermore, the research they undertake, especially in preparing dissertations, can often have a high degree of originality, not least through comparative study and the application of theoretical perspectives. Thus the history offerings at the University of Northumbria included in 2002 a unit entitled *Culture, Society and the Internet: Malmo and Newcastle,* which used ICT to enable Swedish and British students to collaborate in the comparative study of postwar culture and society in the two cities (Northumbria, *Descriptor*).

Other arguments for including a strong local and regional element in undergraduate history programmes are as follows.

- Students often have a considerable interest in the localities with which they are familiar and in how these localities developed, even if, all too frequently, they can have a tendency towards antiquarianism and parochialism in their approach. The challenge here, especially in the later stages of undergraduate study, is to ensure that they appreciate the need to contextualise local investigations in relation to historiographical issues. Much can be done here by demonstrating in lectures and seminars how local investigations can inform more general historical understanding and demonstrate its complex nature.
- Often, students are keen to undertake research into the history of these localities, as Mary Joan Cook remarks with regard to teaching a freshman research paper at Saint Joseph College. She reports her students researching the 'layers' of a town's history, first using physical evidence and then moving to oral testimony and documentary sources. The course unit terminates in student presentations relating to themes that have emerged as their investigations unfolded (Cook, 1993: 289–94). Of importance here is the opportunity that arises to give students ownership of the learning process by giving them scope to follow up their interests and enthusiasms.
- There is an argument to be made about higher education institutions having a public duty to be actively involved in promoting understanding of the history of the localities in which they are based. Dimensions of this responsibility can be seen to extend beyond research and preservation issues to provide opportunity for students to learn about how these localities have developed.

Environmental history

Including environmental history in the curriculum offers a further means by which students' understanding of the nature and purpose of historical enquiry can be broadened, especially with regard to the importance of appreciating varied and changing perceptions. The point can be illustrated as far as national history is concerned by reference to the *American Environmental and Cultural History* course unit offered at the University of California, Berkeley. The unit deals with the:

History of the American environment and the ways in which different cultural groups have perceived, used, managed, and conserved it from colonial times to the present. Cultures include American Indians and European and African Americans. Natural resources development includes gathering-hunting-fishing; farming, mining, ranching, forestry, and urbanization. Changes in attitudes and behaviors toward nature and past and present conservation and environmental movements are also examined.

(Berkeley, *Descriptions*)

Environmental history can equally well be used to broaden perspectives with regard to international history, as illustrated by the course unit entitled *The Environment in World History* offered at Stony Brook State University of New York.

This course will investigate some of the crucial ways in which environmental factors have affected human history over time, and the resulting ways in which different cultures and societies have come to imagine nature and the environment. Drawing on a series of case studies ranging from the ancient Mediterranean to the era of Columbus, from problems of environmental management in imperial India to the emergence of environmentalism as a global movement today, the course will use these comparative perspectives to explore the changing relationships between people and the natural world.

(Stoney Brook, *Courses*)

As is evident from both these examples, the value of including course units of this type in the history curriculum is enhanced by the relevance of their subject matter to an understanding of present-day concerns that are of major significance worldwide. Accordingly, the question has to be posed as to how far history programmes, alongside those of other disciplines, should accept their share of social responsibility in this sense. As with other types of history, to include, say, a couple of modules that emphasise environmental matters may be seen as mere tokenism. What is needed, perhaps, is the strength of commitment expressed with regard to history provision at the University of Northern British Columbia. Here, as with other programmes offered at the university, studying the past is seen to give 'a particular emphasis in History on northern, Native, women's and environmental history along with the history of international relations' (Northern British Columbia, *Introduction*).

Content and the role of undergraduate history

Perhaps the most significant point in curriculum development terms to arise from these deliberations is that, in deciding how strongly and in what ways varieties of history should be included in undergraduate history programmes, there is a need to address the role that history is seen to have at that level. In so doing, tensions will inevitably arise, not only because students may resist studying some types of history, but also because tutors will have their own preferences about what they feel they should teach, and what they feel they are capable of teaching, given their specialist interests and expertise. The argument put forward by Cannon that historians 'have to resist the hideous argument that a good historian should be able to teach on any period . . .' may well be met with sympathy, at least in the extreme form it is expressed (Cannon, 1984: 24). Yet in meeting the content needs of history programmes, compromises may well need to be struck in this respect, particularly with regard to introductory course units. And meeting content needs might also be furthered, as Michael Goldberg points out, by empowering students to take more responsibility as both learners and teachers, essentially by giving them scope to follow up their own interests and report back their findings to the class as a whole (Goldberg, *US Survey*).

REFLEXIVITY

Given the widespread debate that has emerged among historians about the nature and purposes of their discipline, not least in response to the rise of new types of history and the growing emphasis on skills acquisition, it is not surprising that consideration of reflexivity has become an important part of the undergraduate history curriculum. Such provision is often linked with discussion of the processes of historical investigation, encouraging students to delve into the uses and limitations of primary evidence and to extend their understanding of the problems associated with historical interpretation. At the root of such work is the desire to encourage students to reflect on, and come to grips with, the complexities of their subject, so that, despite the problems they will inevitably encounter, they will be able to progress with insight and confidence.

Yet if students are to benefit fully from reflecting on the nature and purposes of history, the key question of where within history programmes such provision should be located needs careful consideration. The matter is touched on in Chapter 2, but is further addressed here by considering the types of provision made in the introductory and more advanced stages of these programmes.

Introductory provision

Logically, the nature of the discipline might be seen to come first, because it is from the uncertainty of historical knowledge that the importance of such fundamental aspects of history as debate, analysis of evidence and proper referencing arise. It is difficult to see how historical skills or research methods can properly be addressed without considering from where they are derived. Pedagogically, however, it is equally unreasonable to ask students to deal with something for which they may be ill-equipped. Yet Alan Booth reports that an early debate on postmodernist critiques of history was welcomed by first-year students at Nottingham University as intellectually challenging (Booth, 2001: 493 and 498). And there are other instances where reflexivity dimensions form part of first-year history programmes, as in the case of the compulsory unit *Introduction to History* provided at Murdoch University, Western Australia.

Different societies and different groups within a society construct different histories. This unit is designed to introduce students to the study of these histories. Topics: The European witch crazes; British colonisation of New South Wales and Aboriginal experience of invasion; 'Typhoid Marys'; the significance of the 1914–18 War for Australia; Nazism and the 'Final Solution'; histories of Anne

> Frank; the dropping of the atomic bombs on Japan. By analysing these different histories, the unit introduces students to the historian's craft and to the nature of historical knowledge.
>
> (Murdoch, *Units*)

What should also be considered in deciding about including elements of reflexivity at the first-level stage is that the mindset of new students seems to be somewhat different than it was. Ten years ago, first-year students were still somewhat shocked to find that historians might manipulate evidence to suit their own preconceived ideas; as far as they were concerned, history was the disinterested pursuit of the truth. In an age of spin, students seem much more attuned to the notion that evidence is malleable and absolute truth a chimera. The problem seems to be more that of persuading students that historians are in fact influenced by the evidence, and that some interpretations are more valid than others!

These considerations lead inexorably to the question of what to do with postmodernism. As noted above, Booth finds that new undergraduates can rise to the challenge of considering postmodernist approaches. And Jenkins describes a formidable introductory module dealing with the issue, which is of the type he has run, though he does not indicate at what level nor with what enthusiasm it was greeted (Jenkins, 1996: 87–91). There is a difficult course to be steered here. Most historians have not embraced the postmodernist solution to the problems of historical knowledge which, combined with the undoubted complexity of the issues and the consequent time required to deal adequately with them, as well as the generally adverse reactions of students to theory, suggests that, perhaps, this is one area of historiography that is best left to advanced or postgraduate levels. On the other hand, many of the new introductions to historiography address, or are in large part responses to, postmodernism, which means that the problems cannot simply be evaded (Evans, 1997, for example).

Provision beyond introductory level

That the conceptual issues involved in dealing with reflexivity are highly complex and the language associated with them often arcane could strengthen the view that dealing with them at first-year level is inappropriate. Certainly many institutions seem to postpone doing so until the second year or beyond, as the following examples demonstrate.

● At Essex University, students are required to take a core second-year unit entitled *Approaches to History*, the purpose of which is to introduce them to 'a selection of key issues and debates in recent thinking about history as a discipline and process'. The students are encouraged 'to think about how history has been and is defined, about the various uses which can be made of the past, and about the problematic nature of "truth" in history' (Essex, *Modules*).

● At Ohio State University, students in the final year of the honours programme are offered a seminar concerned with the 'nature of historical judgment and interpretation; the roles of evidence, approach, and presuppositions' (Ohio, *Courses*).

● At California State University, Hayward, an upper-division course unit on historiography is provided, which deals with the development of historical writing from antiquity to the present (California, *Catalogue*).

Perhaps, following the example set by these institutions, it is better to ensure that students have some familiarity with actually doing history, and have a knowledge base on which to draw, before addressing directly the problems inherent in what they do. Alternatively, this approach could be seen as incoherent. Is it reasonable to allow students to study for several months, perhaps a year, before suggesting that there are profound problems with what they have been doing?

At whatever stage in the programme discussions of the nature of history appear, they have the benefit of actively promoting reflection on what history is all about and how historians operate. Such reflection might logically come at the end of a degree course as at the beginning, thereby providing a means for students to reflect on what they have learned in the previous years. Yet few institutions appear to develop this kind of terminal experience in an explicit way. One that does is the University of Sheffield, where the *Rethinking History* course unit gives an opportunity for students to

> . . . rethink the basis of their discipline and to reflect critically on their experience of studying the past. It asks them to consider the purpose of the study of History, the kinds of questions that historical enquiry can answer (and those it cannot) and to articulate what distinguishes History from other branches of the humanities and social sciences.
>
> (Sheffield, *Rethinking*)

To leave issues of reflexivity entirely to the final stages of study misses the opportunity to encourage thinking about them at earlier stages. In curriculum planning terms, therefore, the central issue is one of deciding where the emphasis on reflexivity should lie within pro-grammes. And this consideration takes us back to the familiar themes of how far the responsibility of developing aspects of provision should lie with specialist course units and/or should permeate course unit offerings in general.

Overall, course units highlighting reflexivity seem to act as gateways to the serious study of history, offering a rite of passage for students who want to get to grips with the subject in more depth. Opinions plainly differ as to whether units of this type should appear early on in history programmes or be postponed until the later stages, but, whatever approach is adopted, careful consideration is required as to how reflexivity can be encouraged so that students are fascinated by the challenges arising rather than being overwhelmed by the demands being made.

DISSERTATIONS AND CONTENT

In adding to our discussion of dissertations, a number of issues arise with regard to the content matters raised in the *History Benchmarking Statement*. They highlight variations in practice between higher educa-tion institutions and give food for thought about both the nature of the challenges that dissertations offer and how appropriate these chal-lenges might be at undergraduate level.

Using primary evidence

At issue here is the benchmarking expectation that dissertations should be based on primary sources, but, alternatively, that they could take the form of an in-depth historiographical study. Allowing such a distinction to operate in history programmes may be justified on the grounds that both types of activity can undoubtedly be highly academically demanding of undergraduate students. The argument here might hinge on the notion that students are required to formulate and sustain lines of argument throughout a much lengthier study than they are likely to have undertaken previously. But the question remains as to whether a greater challenge arises in achieving historical interpretation by informing reported findings with primary evidence than by reviewing and evaluating reported findings alone. The student using primary material still has to undertake the historiographical analysis, but, additionally, has to obtain relevant primary evidence and incorporate it into the study, with all the attendant difficulties that arise. Moreover, in terms of progression, there is concern that students who are trained to use primary material as they proceed through their programmes of study, but do not do so in preparing their dissertations, will not be given full opportunity to demonstrate the skills and understanding they have acquired.

Free-standing or linked dissertations?

Of further concern is whether dissertations should be free-standing or whether they should arise from, and be linked to, a taught course unit that the student is taking or has already taken. That, as long as they can be adequately supervised, students should be allowed to follow their choice of subject in undertaking a dissertation seems both a reasonable and a desirable proposition. Indeed, the idea that they should be able to formulate and undertake their own area of research can be seen as a progression element – as part of the challenge that is expected of them in the final year of their studies.

Yet if students do not take course units in the general areas of study to which their dissertations relate, they risk foregoing the opportunity to consider contextual material that should inform their understanding; at the very least, there is likely to be gain in enhancing the historiographical dimensions of their dissertations. Furthermore, by not taking a final-level unit taught by the tutor who acts as his or her supervisor, a student may miss out on the regular contact between teacher and taught on which successful dissertations usually depend. That some degree of compulsion should be exercised to avoid these drawbacks may be thought to be going too far, but alerting students to them should nonetheless be regarded as a significant aspect of the guidance given in preparing students for dissertation work.

Dissertation length

It is quite evident from examining website entries that considerable variation exists in the length requirement for undergraduate dissertations, even allowing for the fact that some carry higher proportions of the marks that count towards degree awards. Thus, whereas at Birkbeck College, University of London, the history dissertation length is set at 5,000 words (Birkbeck, *Structure*), at Harvard University, the minimum length of the undergraduate history thesis is 15,000 words and may reach 35,000 words, excluding footnotes, bibliographies, appendices and glossaries (Harvard, *Senior Thesis*). And even in between these extremes the differences can be considerable, with, for example, 8–10,000 words being required at the University of Hertfordshire (Hertfordshire, *Guide*) and 12,000 words at Trinity and All Saints College, Leeds (Trinity and All Saints, *Catalogue*).

Such marked variations in both wordage range and overall wordage raise concern about the differing degree of challenge that dissertation work presents to undergraduate students. Regarding the wordage range, the issues are.

- Some leeway may well be considered appropriate, and argument might be advanced about the undesirability of imposing too strict a limit given the varying nature of dissertations that students write; in some cases, students might be able to improve the quality of their work by making it longer, perhaps to develop a key line of argument in a more nuanced manner.
- On the other hand, argument about the value of being able to undertake pieces of coursework within fairly strict word limits may be seen as more compelling, especially if students cannot easily be disabused of the idea that a strong correlation exists between the length of an assignment and its quality. And to encourage brevity may well work in their best interests in terms of making the task manageable, bearing in mind the other commitments they will need to meet.

As to variations in dissertation length, issues to do with progression and differentiation come to the fore. Viewed from this perspective, the length of dissertation and its nature might be seen to depend upon the type of work done previously. Thus to move from relatively short, secondary-source-based essays to lengthy dissertations strongly rooted in primary evidence is likely to be too great a degree of differentiation. On the other hand, longer dissertations are likely to be a reasonable challenge if students have undertaken small-scale project and/or extended essay work before tackling their dissertation. This is the case, for example, at the University of Nottingham, where students in their second year of study prepare an extended historiographical essay of 5,000 words on a topic of their choice. They are expected to 'plan, research and write a sustained analysis, presenting a well-grounded, independent assessment . . .' (Nottingham, *Information*). How far such considerations explain variation in dissertation length between institutions is unclear, but there is plainly a need to view the matter in incremental learning terms.

CONCLUSION

The content issues raised in the *History Benchmarking Statement* have profound implications for curriculum development. The *Statement* certainly sets a challenging agenda with regard to how, and to what extent, the varied range of content inputs it highlights should be covered.

In considering this agenda, the main points arising may be summarised as:

● Achieving adequate geographical and time depth coverage is an issue in terms of ensuring that students acquire the background understanding they will need for the more specialised study they later encounter. In attaining this end, it may be that students will move from general survey to thematic and/or in-depth course units and that an element of compulsion will be necessary. Yet requiring a broad content coverage in the early stages of programmes can bring problems with regard both to encouraging surface learning and to restricting student choice.

● Our discussion of the diversity of specialisms briefly considered examples of the types of history – political, women's and gender, race and ethnic, environmental and local – that have strong claims to be included in undergraduate programmes. All have value in providing students with insights into varying ways that historical study can be approached. Yet issues arise as to how wide the range of offerings should be; whether all students should be required to study them and, if so, to what extent; and how far they should enter generally into units taught on the programme rather than being confined to specific units. In seeking ways forward on these matters, much depends on the purposes that studying history at undergraduate level is seen to have.

- There is much to consider concerning where reflexivity matters should appear in undergraduate history curricula. The conceptual difficulties involved may appear off-putting to new undergraduates, giving rise to the view that these matters are better left until the later stages of their programmes. Yet there is a case to be made for ensuring that students at least make a start on understanding the nature of history as an academic discipline from the outset of their studies, with opportunities being provided for further reflection as they progress.

- Undergraduate dissertations raise important matters to address in content terms with regard to length, the incorporation of primary evidence and the linkage with course units students are studying or have previously studied.

Key references

Cannon, J. (1984) *Teaching History at University*. London: Historical Association.

Elton, G.R. (1967) *The Practice of History*. London: Fontana.

Lubelska, C. (1996) 'Gender in the curriculum', in A. Booth and P. Hyland (eds), *History in Higher Education: New Directions in Teaching and Learning*. Oxford: Blackwell, pp. 55–74.

Stearns, P.N. (1998) 'Goals in history teaching', in J.F. Voss and M. Carretero (eds), *International Review of History Education Volume 2: Learning and Reasoning in History*. London: Woburn, pp. 281–93.

Website

Quality Assurance Agency for Higher Education (2000), *History Benchmark Statement* at http://www.qaa.ac.uk/crntwork/benchmark/history.html

The historian's skills and qualities of mind

INTRODUCTION

Skills have become an inescapable issue in higher education, generating considerable controversy and confusion. Becoming a graduate is increasingly defined in terms of the capacity to perform high-level tasks pertinent more to the workplace than necessarily connected with a degree subject, and the onus is put on higher education to demonstrate that it is equipping students with those capacities. At the same time, changes in the nature of the student population, and growing engagement by higher education tutors with issues of learning and teaching, are putting more emphasis on communicating to students what is entailed in degree-level learning. The whole area is contentious because it can be regarded as representing the imposition of external criteria on the traditionally autonomous realm of academia. Moreover, for some academics, a dichotomy exists between knowledge (or content) and skills, a degree being seen to deal with the subject matter of a discipline rather than with the mechanics of how the subject matter is generated and certainly not with any extra-academic capacities. Others argue, however, that it is the skills involved in actually doing a subject that are its most important feature. Confusion abounds because the language surrounding skills is very imprecise and it is often unclear just what is being asked for – how to learn, how to work or how to be a better person – and whether such things can in fact be taught or learned (Fallows and Steven, 2000: 3–11).

History has seen its share of the debate. It is not primarily a vocational subject; most students do not study history in order to obtain a particular job and, accordingly, the majority of graduates do not enter history-based occupations. To that extent, history could be seen as a prime example of a self-referential academic discipline and that it is reasonable to maintain that a degree in history should be devoted to knowledge and understanding of the past. Taking this view, any techniques that students require can be absorbed in the process of learning about the past. Time spent on explicitly developing skills is, at best, an unnecessary distraction, at worst, threatening to the principles of higher education. Many historians, however, take the view that it is the process of doing history that constitutes the essential core of the discipline. They emphasise the useful cognitive and practical skills that a training in the subject can provide, a perspective also appreciated by employers. Thus it could equally well be argued that ignoring the skills component and extra-disciplinary ramifications of historical education fails students and misses a large part of the value of a history degree.

Organising a discussion about these issues creates problems. It quickly becomes apparent that the dichotomy just delineated is a chimera, and we would argue strongly that it is artificial to maintain hard and fast distinctions between knowledge and skills. The view that skills development has no place in higher education history is unsustainable, but neither do skills, if unconnected with substantial knowledge of the past, constitute a degree in history. Following from this point, the position taken here is that skills should be conceived of broadly, encompassing and integrating both cognitive and practical capacities. Skills are not necessarily low-level mechanical attributes; they can be as complex and demanding as the task in which they are embedded and can play a valuable role in enhancing reflexive and holistic academic and personal qualities (Assiter, 1995: 11–19; Bridges, 1993: 43–4). Nevertheless, for practical purposes, a rough distinction between content and skills is reimposed here, so that we can focus on those questions that are particularly pertinent to skills development. Attention will be concentrated, therefore, on explicit attempts to promote skills awareness in discrete and dedicated course units rather than on the continual practice and reiteration of those skills through content-led activity.

We start with a section drawing on the *History Benchmark Statement* which, significantly, connects skills development with the nurturing of the historian's qualities of mind. This approach, together with other recent discussions, supports the view that skills should be conceived of in broad educational terms. The section briefly addresses the question of how to classify skills, and a basically binary division is drawn between:

- skills *specific* to the discipline;
- *generic* skills that might be developed more or less incidentally to the study of history.

In the following section further context is set by a brief discussion of the role of skills in higher education history teaching, stressing their centrality to the discipline and the need to address them clearly and directly if we are to fulfil our responsibilities both to students and, indeed, the discipline itself. The two remaining sections review the ways in which subject-specific and generic skills are taught to history undergraduates. They draw on a further sample survey we have undertaken, which relates specifically to skills-orientated course units offered in history degree programmes, as well as a wide range of reported practice. The findings raise a number of key issues to address in terms of curriculum planning and delivery. What skills are being developed and are there others that have been neglected? Where in a degree programme are skills best encountered? What concerns give pause for thought in the drive for skills promotion? What skills of wider applicability could feature in a history degree and how far should historians take responsibility for them? In concluding, we return to the question of the historian's qualities of mind and their place in history degree programmes.

BENCHMARKING, SKILLS AND THE HISTORIAN'S QUALITIES OF MIND

As was noted in the last chapter, the *History Benchmark Statement* places considerable importance on skills but, conspicuously, combines the 'historian's skills and qualities of mind' (QAA, *History*, 2000: 3). Three areas are distinguished: dealing with skills specific to history, wider academic skills pertinent to history, and generic skills developed through the study of history. They are summarised in Table 4.1.

Under the first heading especially, the *Benchmark Statement* insists on the inseparability of disciplinary skills from qualities of mind. The practicalities of being able to do history at degree level entail the development of considerable academic maturity and the acquisition of valuable personal and intellectual qualities. 'History involves', the

TABLE 4.1 *Historian's skills and qualities of mind*

1. Historical skills and qualities of mind
- The ability to understand how people have existed, acted and thought in the always different context of the past
- The ability to read texts and sources critically and empathetically
- The appreciation of the complexity of the past
- The understanding of problems inherent in the historical record itself and a feeling for the limitations of knowledge and the dangers of simplistic explanations
- Basic critical skills: a recognition that statements are not all of equal value, that there are ways of testing them and that historians operate by rules of evidence
- The general skills of the researcher, such as setting tasks, solving problems, formulating questions, bibliographic skills, gathering, sifting, selecting, organising and synthesising large quantities of evidence – and reflexivity should be developed
- Marshalling of argument in written and oral form

2. Wider academic skills
- Skills from cognate disciplines appropriate to specific areas such as economic and social history
- Languages, ICT, numeracy, field work

3. Generic skills
- Self-discipline
- Self-direction
- Independence of mind
- Ability to work with others
- Ability to use information
- Analytical ability
- Written and oral expression
- Intellectual integrity
- Empathy and imaginative insight

---

statement maintains, 'the cultural shock of encountering and sensing the past's otherness and of learning to understand unfamiliar structures, cultures and belief systems'. The appreciation of complexity is seen as 'central to History's character as an anti-reductionist discipline fostering intellectual maturity' (QAA, *History*, 2000: 3). Thus the *Statement* endorses a broad conception of skills, embracing both cognitive and practical attributes which are not reducible to mechanical processes. Some of the implications of the phrase 'skills and qualities of mind' will require further discussion, but it is important to appreciate that skills do not have to be conceived of as routine mechanical tasks but can denote advanced academic ability. The rest of this chapter will adopt, and through the course of the discussion defend, this very wide perception of skills. In a subject-specific context, the term will be used to refer to the processes involved in doing history, that is acquiring and applying the technical and cognitive qualities that historians bring to bear in studying, understanding and interpreting the past, as opposed to simply gathering information about past events. More generally, the term will refer to developing in students the capacities involved in performing adequately in higher education and operating effectively in the world of work.

While the *History Benchmark Statement* indicates a threefold classification of skills, other ways of grouping them have been suggested in the recent literature on undergraduate history teaching. Thus the survey described by Hitchcock, Shoemaker and Tosh provides a very broad review of the ways in which skills feature in the structure of history curricula in English institutions of higher education (Hitchcock et al., 2000: 50–3). They suggest there are eight basic building blocks making up degree programmes, namely:

- introductory methods or skills course units;
- historiography;
- IT;
- broad surveys;
- options;
- document-based studies;
- long essays or dissertations;
- open or general papers.

Such a conception of skills has particular value in pointing out that all kinds of history course unit, including those that are content orientated, can help to develop historical skills, a point that leads back to our discussion in the previous chapter about the inclusion of skills-based elements in general survey course units.

Taking as his context an introductory course unit in history taught at Nottingham University, Alan Booth indicates four types of skills directly relevant to performance in a history degree programme:

- basic study skills;
- high-level intellectual skills;
- communication skills;
- personal skills.

Of especial interest in this classification is that basic study skills are highlighted, among which Booth includes 'researching material, reading strategies, taking notes and, especially, essay writing' (Booth, 2001: 489). This is a curricular dimension that certainly has a claim to high importance in easing the transition of students into higher education and that may well need continued attention as students progress. Taking a more wide-ranging stance, Booth has recently suggested a tripartite division of skills that lie at the heart of developing historical understanding, namely critical analysis, critical reflection and imaginative engagement. Apart from promoting subject mastery, he suggests, acquiring these skills has lifelong significance, enabling students to 'think more deeply and act more purposefully in contexts beyond the university' (Booth, 2003: 24–8).

The scope of our discussion is somewhat different from that in each of the above contributions. We would certainly accept that general historical competence is developed through all types of course unit, but our focus is primarily on *practical* skills and methods developed within dedicated course units. In particular, we wish to consider in some detail the questions of where and how both study skills and skills explicitly for the workplace should feature in history degree programmes. Thus, at the risk of contributing further to terminological instability, though drawing on the wider educational literature (Bennet et al., 2000: 23–4), we adopt another skills classification which enables us to take particular account of these dimensions.

At root, there appear to be two underlying categories of skills:

- those that are specific to a discipline and which need to be grasped in order to operate successfully in a named degree programme;
- those that have wider applicability, often termed generic skills, which can be subdivided into:
  - key or basic study skills;
  - skills of wider applicability, acquired in the course of disciplinary learning;
  - overtly workplace-oriented skills.

Each of these categories will be examined in turn, but it must be stressed that they are not mutually exclusive – skills that are necessary for mastery of a discipline may also be useful for effective occupational practice.

THE ROLE OF SKILLS IN UNDERGRADUATE HISTORY

As noted in the introduction to this chapter, the wider debates that have taken place about skills in higher education have been replicated in the specific context of history. In some respects, the debate between Old and New History, discussed in the opening chapter, encapsulates the tensions. But we have noted, too, a false dichotomy. Of course one cannot acquire or demonstrate the critical skills of the historian divorced from some actual instance. Equally obviously, there is more to a degree in history than merely accumulating factual information. Since our main concern here is with skills promotion, we will focus on the skills side of the equation, a stance which helps to identify skills as being at the very centre of history in higher education.

The craft of history

Historians have long been predisposed to a skills' orientation. That there is an essentially craft basis to history has been acknowledged in such classic introductions to the subject as Bloch's *The Historian's Craft* or Elton's *The Practice of History* (Bloch, 1954: Elton, 1967). Certainly, the language of skills has become pervasive in the programmatic statements of intent provided in university guides, as the following geographically wide selection of examples indicates.

● At the University of Bristol, prospective students are reassured that the skills they develop through studying history will have long-term benefit. They are told:

> Studying history teaches students to conduct independent research, to identify the problems inherent in a question, to assess the arguments and evidence of others, to analyse primary data, and last, but not least, to construct coherent arguments in an accessible and persuasive way.
>
> (Bristol, *Studies*)

● In the United States, a particularly full synoptic statement on skills is made by the History department at Wabash College, Indiana. Five core goals are set, which include the following:

The craft of history: to acquire the habit of the many analytical skills which historians use in recovering, researching and writing about the past; such as, constructing important questions, making inferences from primary sources, putting sources into larger contexts, and making one's own interpretations of the past.

Historical thinking: to develop habits of thinking like an historian: e.g., an appreciation for the complexity of both change and continuity over time and in different ages, cultures and areas of the world; an awareness of historical interpretation and historiographical schools of thought; and an understanding of how events and ideas from the past affect the present.

Self-expression: to become competent, confident and fluent in the oral, written and group skills necessary to speak and write about and explore historical questions.

(Wabash, *Curriculum*)

●   In New Zealand, the University of Auckland's History department notes that:

The study of History teaches skills of value to men and women of the new century. It trains you in acquiring and evaluating information and in conveying a logical argument in a precise and down-to-earth but interesting manner; it helps you to summarise, to analyse, to synthesise, and to communicate.

(Auckland, *History*)

●   As a final example, an unusually frank admission on the importance of teaching skills is contained in the introduction to the history programme at the University of North British Columbia.

The study of the past is also intended to lead to a clearer understanding of the present and thus produce better, more informed citizens. Such objectives are common to any university program in History and, to some extent, teaching these skills is more important than covering vast subject matter.

(Columbia, *Introduction*)

An important factor that may be helping to emphasise the centrality of disciplinary skills arises from the divisive controversies convulsing history over the past ten years or so, out of which many historians feel a need to rediscover common ground. Noticeably, a number of recent books on the current state of history reaffirm the craft basis of the discipline, to which all historians of whatever persuasion can contribute. The books on *History in Practice* and *Studying History* are a part of this trend (Jordanova, 2000; Black and MacRaild, 2000). Moreover, a quite conscious attempt to move beyond debilitating factionalism was founded in the United States-based Historical Society, which was intended to be an inclusive body free from jargon-laden debates and political agendas. Its manifesto, *Reconstructing History*, constantly reiterates the core practices, and thereby values, of serious and open-minded engagement with source material. Members are exhorted to recognise history as 'a demanding and rewarding craft [and to] insist on the importance of respect for common standards in the practice of that craft'. While abjuring a return to Rankean naivety, it is acknowledged that '[d]emonstrably, politics and ideology influence historical scholarship, but they should not trump or supplant the fundamental canons of the historian's craft, which historians of differing perspectives observe' (Fox-Genovese and Lasch-Quinn, 1999: 3 and 299). Skills may yet provide the fundamental core, which theory never has been able to supply for historians.

The craft basis of history also underpins the 'research training' model of degree programmes, which is seen essentially to provide

> an apprenticeship in historical method, acquired by means of a progression through a sequence of units which bears an ever-closer resemblance to the empirical source-based study usually required for research degrees in history.
>
> (Hitchcock et al., 2000: 53–4)

Evidence of the importance of being able to do history in this way is clearly expressed in the pride of place afforded to the final-year special subject or dissertation, the importance of which has been noted in Chapter 2. As the information supplied to students at Cardiff University suggests, student-led dissertations based on original sources represent 'in many ways, the culmination of the experience of "doing history"...' (Cardiff, *History BA*). At Kingston University, London, the dissertation is seen as a key feature of level 3 provision, giving 'the opportunity to undertake an extended piece of historical writing based on primary source materials' (Kingston, *History*). A dissertation is an apprentice's masterpiece; the actual topic is immaterial. What matters is that the finishing student can demonstrate the skills of a practising historian. Special subjects fashionable in British universities are more tutor-led, but similarly involve engagement with historical debates through extensive analysis of primary sources.

Dissertations have an equivalent status in the honours programmes at Australian universities. Typically, honours is a selective programme, taking a further year of full-time study after the ordinary bachelor's degree and requiring a substantial research-based dissertation or thesis. At the University of New South Wales, for instance, a thesis of 15–20,000 words is required (New South Wales, *Honours*). In the same way, a thesis is often required for the selective honours degrees at universities in the United States. In many respects, this approach mirrors the still common practice in most of the United Kingdom of making the dissertation the distinguishing feature between ordinary and honours degrees. Outside Scotland, which has a different tradition and clearer distinctions between ordinary and honours degrees, the standard route in the United Kingdom is to honours, in which the dissertation becomes a crucial element; an ordinary degree is often only awarded when a student has failed his or her dissertation. Since undergraduate programmes in the United States usually only go so far as a major in the discipline, which generally comprises no more than a third of a student's programme of study, the research training model is not so evident. Even the largely undirected majors, however, retain an element of specialisation. Thus the University of Virginia requires major students to complete a seminar or colloquium, which usually builds fairly directly on at least two previous course units. The seminars 'offer the opportunity to undertake historical research in an area of the student's interest, in close consultation with an instructor' (Virginia, *Undergraduate Courses*).

The craft of history and the workplace

Turning to the role of more generally applicable skills, it is remarkable how often history is taken as a prime example of the way in which a humanities subject can fit students for the world of work. The introduction to a decidedly vocational document on skills development takes history as its text:

> *Historians are valued as potential employees for a variety of diverse reasons including the breadth of vision and perspective brought about by*

studying in depth our civilisation and culture, and the 'set' of enabling
skills developed within the rigours of the discipline, including the ability
to analyse problems, sift information, weigh evidence, evaluate solutions
and to communicate effectively. In essence it is believed the possession of
these skills, developed to a high order, by, for example, historians, can be
applied to activities other than history.

(Jessup, 1990)

Few historians could disagree with such sentiments. And it is
noticeable that, with regard to the utility of studying history, the party
political dimensions of the debate over skills in history have not been
clear-cut. While many New Right politicians liked the traditionalism
of old-style history, with its emphasis on knowledge acquisition and
examination, these same characteristics opened the discipline to
charges of irrelevance to modern economic life. New-style approaches
to history, meanwhile, simultaneously defended the critical autonomy
of history to question received wisdom, but were more amenable to
notions of transferable skills.

As in the case of disciplinary skills, current history degree programmes also stress the value of historical training for a career. Typical
is the claim that history graduates at the University of Reading are

> . . . enabled to think clearly and critically, to express themselves with confidence,
> and to work effectively both as individuals and within teams. They are used to
> evaluating and interpreting complex data and, as such, are highly attractive to
> employers.
>
> (Reading, *Prospectus*)

Similarly, the University of California Riverside suggests that

> [b]ecause history stresses change over time and provides the tools for
> comprehending better a rapidly changing world, many of those planning
> graduate work find history an excellent preparation for professional schools such
> as law and business administration.
>
> (California Riverside, *Career Opportunities*)

It might be objected that these blandishments are simply pandering to
the latest buzzwords, and will probably be re-couched when the

jargon changes. Such cynicism is not unfounded but cannot fully explain away the widespread and public commitment of historians to the development of skills, both disciplinary and transferable. In this respect, it is worth emphasising that publicity material also continues to recognise that it is the intrinsic fascination for history and desire for personal development that inspires most undergraduates to study the past (Booth, 1997: 210–12 and 215). A commitment to skills is not an abdication of the intrinsic value of higher education and the study of history; rather, it is precisely those qualities nurtured in the study of history that furnish the personal characteristics desirable both in society at large and in the workplace. Illustrative of this perspective is the highly inclusive statement from the University of Sheffield:

History is the world's collective memory, the explanation of our culture and society. Our degree in history will also equip you with skills in argument, presentation and data selection. You will learn to exercise independent judgement, to be critical of accepted opinion and to sustain a convincing argument both verbally and on paper. These are skills highly valued by employers.

(Sheffield, *Prospectus*)

They are equally the desiderata of cultivated intellect and informed citizenship.

The comment presented in this section gives a clear demonstration of the perception from within the history teaching profession that skills have a central claim for inclusion in degree-level work. Moreover, as is appropriate with students' interests in mind, the development of skills is being viewed from a broad perspective, seeking to enhance both cognitive abilities and employability. To do otherwise is to miss opportunities to add to the relevance of history as a degree-level subject and hence to its appeal for prospective students. Additionally, because skills development is strongly associated with the use of primary evidence, encouragement is given to forms of learning that require active participation by students and in-depth investigation of issues. What remains, of course, is to consider precisely how skills are developed in undergraduate history programmes and the issues that arise from developing different skills in various ways.

TEACHING DISCIPLINE-SPECIFIC SKILLS TO HISTORY STUDENTS

If the craft of history, culminating in the apprentice's masterpiece, is so central to higher education history, what measures are taken to train students in the mystery? Since the emergence of the academic discipline, this training has been achieved primarily through a structured and iterative programme of different types of course units that seek to expand students' historical horizons and experience (Slee, 1986). As discussed in other chapters, a diet of broad chronological surveys, thematic reviews and optional specialist subjects, with a general trend from relatively broad-ranging to increasingly specialist course units, gradually inculcates in students a deeper sense of historical understanding. There is much to be said for this basic approach, since, to a large extent, doing history successfully is a matter of judgement born of experience. How to assess and assign weight to different kinds of evidence, or how to balance alternative arguments, depends on appropriate contextualisation of sources and the depth of one's comprehension of particular instances. Thus it is through the regular practice of studying actual historical episodes that students acquire an appreciation of how to do history and sufficient experience to apply themselves to novel situations. It is obvious that this view is central to degree-level history in that, to an overwhelming extent, history degree programmes consist of a series of content-based course units in which students study particular areas of history and demonstrate their historical competence through a variety of assessments.

This perspective could be taken to argue that any attempt to instil historical skills independently is consequently artificial and unnecessary. Yet, in recent years, there has been a definite trend towards offering dedicated course units concerned with the development of historical skills. These units model aspects of historical thinking and practice, breaking them down into manageable components that students can address directly and practise under structured and supervised conditions. Such exercises might be oriented primarily towards conceptual thinking skills, or towards practical methodologies, although the two are essentially interrelated. Since our concern in this chapter is to discuss ways and means of skills' development, we will focus on the contours of this trend and its implications, but we will return to the counter-argument at the end of the section.

Developing conceptual thinking skills

If historical judgement arises mainly from experience, is it possible actively to promote it? What can be done to enhance students' 'intellectual maturity', empathy or 'imaginative insight'?

A number of British higher education institutions now use introductory core modules of deliberate, even jarring, diversity to extend historical awareness.

- At the University of York, first-year students encounter course units in *Historical Perspectives* and *Historical Topics*. The former aims to encourage broad and conceptual thinking while the latter provides an 'intensive introduction to unfamiliar periods, subjects and/or approaches to the study of history' (York, *Overview*).
- Reading University has paired course units of *Landmarks in History*, which provides a thematic introduction from the birth of Islam to the twentieth century, and *Approaches to History*, which comprises a focused study of two historical texts in their contemporary and later contexts (Reading, *BA History*).
- Taking a deliberately tangential view of the past, the University of Newcastle has modules that juxtapose contrasting periods, places, events, topics and issues around the organising themes of *Encounters in World History* and *Identities in World History* (Newcastle, *History*).
- At Hull University, a new first-year course unit was reported in 1999 entitled *What If – Exercises in Virtual History*, the aim being to look at problems of causality and determinism in history using a counterfactual approach (Bates, 1999: 55–6).

Designated core units of this type can undoubtedly help new undergraduate students to experience the cultural shock of encountering the otherness of the past to which the *History Benchmarking Statement* refers, helping to shake them out of any complacency or limited perspective. And encountering something consciously surprising, unusual or controversial may well help to encourage new patterns of thinking and persuade students that there are other topics worth studying besides Nazi Germany, a matter that has come to greatly concern historians teaching British undergraduates (Bates, 1999: 55; Pearce, 2003: 55–6; Booth, 1997: 215).

Breadth of experience is inevitable in the United States system of majors and also underlies the general educational programmes in which students are required to study a diversity of arts, science, social science and humanities subjects, albeit at an elementary level. Noticeably, history is a common feature of core programmes and, in an interesting perspective on the topic of this chapter, can itself be seen as an educational skill. Montana State University – Billings lists history as one of nine categories of skills which the general educational programme is supposed to cover and spells out six abilities within the category that students are supposed to acquire:

- recognition of processes of continuity and change;
- identification of the characteristics of a major era of world history, 'thereby providing a framework for comprehending aspects of human experience';
- explanation of human agency;
- analysis of factors leading to dominance or suppression of different groups;
- analysis of the role of individuals in influencing events;
- use of factual and interpretive data (Montana, *Requirements*).

Developing practical skills

General historical awareness is probably something that requires practice more than anything, and can only be actively promoted to a certain extent. In contrast, the practical skills of historical craftsmanship are more amenable to explicit honing, and dedicated course units on methods seem to be proliferating rapidly. In their survey of English higher education institutions, reported in 2000, Hitchcock et al. found that 39 per cent of their respondents offered some kind of compulsory introductory course unit in skills or methodology (Hitchcock et al., 2000: 51). Yet an availability sample we recently undertook into the extent and nature of skills-orientated course units, based mainly on the publicity literature relating to 33 institutions in the United Kingdom and Republic of Ireland, revealed only four that do not make a specific reference to a methods-based course unit, albeit with varying emphasis on the extent of engagement with primary evidence (Appendix 1).

Obviously, the fundamental skill that methods units seek to develop is the analysis of primary sources of evidence, the foundation of all historical practice. There are different ways by which this process is achieved, however, and, arguably, there are other important skills that are neglected. These points must now be considered and, in the process, an important question emerges about when in a programme it is appropriate to introduce skills.

A recent survey by Aldous and Hicks into how sources are used in undergraduate history in Britain has revealed tremendous variety in what is understood by sources and how to use them. It is now widely agreed that a crucial element of historical education is allowing and encouraging students to engage with primary sources of evidence. Most programmes include a diversity of sources, including visual and oral material as well as field evidence. The survey also confirms the tendency for more primary source work to take place in later years of study, culminating in the special subject or dissertation. There are differences, though, as to the length of source extracts used, whether short gobbets or extensive selections from original material, on how much independence or direction students receive in how to approach them and in how far and in what ways source work should be assessed. The authors conclude that tutors within a department, let alone in separate institutions, may be doing quite different things under the rubric of source work, perhaps even producing different kinds of historian, although the complexity of the issues permits of no ready answers (Aldous and Hicks, 2003).

The survey by Aldous and Hicks considers approaches that extend across the range of course units that are included in history pro-grammes. For our purposes the question is more one of how to instil and enhance the skills of undertaking source-based work in dedicated course units. The basic technique, of course, is to persuade students not to accept things at face value, but to interrogate a source with the essential questions of who it was produced by, when, why, and for whom. On the basis of the interrogation, and a consideration of the context of the source, some assessment can be made as to what evidence can be gleaned and how it might be used in historical analysis. Precisely how these tasks are undertaken within methods course units is not always evident from the detail we have been able to secure, but there seems to be two basic approaches:

1. Pursuing a mini case study, in which a range of sources are brought to bear on a topic. This approach has the virtue of allowing students to juxtapose different pieces of evidence, perhaps of different kinds,

and is close to actual historical practice. There is a danger, though, that the topic becomes the main focus of attention and the wider lessons of how to use sources may not be appreciated.

2. A focus on different kinds of evidence and on questions of what their relative advantages and disadvantages might be in relation to investigating particular historical themes. This approach at least puts the source at the centre of attention, although perhaps in slightly artificial situations.

What becomes apparent from examining the provision of skills-based modules is that both these approaches are pursued, commonly at different stages in programmes. Accordingly, the question arises of when to introduce students to historical methods units, a matter that extends our discussion on progression in Chapter 2. In our sample of skills-based provision in United Kingdom and Republic of Ireland history departments, 13 out of 33 (39 per cent) appear to offer methods course units in the first year only, with titles such as *Doing History* or *Introduction to the Study of History*, raising concerns about the continuity of provision leading up to final-level work. Four programmes seem to begin consideration of methods only in year two, while several Scottish universities include methods course units in the third of a four-year programme. On the other hand, eleven of the institutions feature methods course units at both introductory and later stages. The inclusion of skills course units at more than one level no doubt reflects a strong orientation towards skills-based approaches, which may well be strengthened by the inclusion of additional primary source work in more general provision.

At first-year level, methods are often combined with the study of historical themes and general study skills, which are considered more fully below. At Queen's University, Belfast, for example, a core lecture programme deals with different approaches to history – political, social and so on – and is supported by a range of tutorial course units on more specific topics such as *Early Irish Society, c.AD400–800* and *The Spanish Armada*. Part of the aim is to promote such skills 'as researching, note-taking, essay-writing, and oral participation in tutorials'. Moreover, one lecture considers the ways in which historians use documentary sources and how the scope of documentary research has expanded, while consideration of primary sources is evident in a number of the seminars (Queen's, Belfast, *History*). Yet more specialised units are also provided, an example being that offered to single-honours history students at Canterbury Christ Church University College, which features group research activity.

> Students will be divided into small groups in term 1, with each group allocated a tutor to act as supervisor. The groups will then be set research tasks related to a number of historical issues; normally, one group will endeavour to build a case for, and another against, a given assertion. At the end of term 1, each group will present its case and defend its findings before the full course cohort and supervisors. Each group will be assessed on the quality of its presentation, its ability to uphold its findings in the face of questioning, and on the content of a research log and portfolio constructed during the preparatory period.
>
> (Canterbury, *Year 1*)

Such course units provide a counterpoint to broadly-based content courses offered at introductory level, adding to the variety of teaching approaches as well as helping to lay a firm foundation for subsequent research-orientated activity.

Methods course units beyond first-level usually focus directly on the use, advantages and disadvantages of a range of different kinds of evidence. There might also be specialist course units, for example, in history and computing or oral history, which have a heavy skills orientation, though are still based on the use of a certain type of source. These kinds of unit are often regarded as providing preparation for independent work in projects or dissertations. The *Research Skills in History* course unit at University College, Northampton, for instance, is billed as having this as one of its main functions.

> This module analyses the use of history sources within historical theories. It aims to develop practical skills of using archival collections. The general aim is to equip students with the knowledge, skills and confidence to proceed to a research dissertation at level 3.
>
> (Northampton, *Modules*)

A variation is offered in the economic and social history degree at Edinburgh, where there are required classes in *Dissertation and Project Preparation*. The dissertation element occupies 24 hours' class time, and though it is not directly examined, class exercises have to be submitted. The provision is intended to help students acquire a wide range of skills they need for dissertation preparation, including:

> Information about information and how and where to find it and how to use and present it; introduction to archives and archival research; historical and scientific method and research design; use of artefacts and representations in Economic and Social History; ways of summarising and presenting data in numbers and in graphs; some basic skills of data analysis through spreadsheets and databases; do's and don'ts of oral presentation and the use and abuse of visual aids; a basic facility with text processing and the integration of non-textual material into report writing.
>
> (Edinburgh, *Courses*)

The University of York also offers a dissertation preparation course unit giving a systematic introduction to dissertation sources and leading to a dissertation proposal (York, *Overview*).

While discussing historical skills, it is worth returning briefly to the topic of historiography, for course units dealing with methodology, especially at second- or third-year level, commonly refer to the conceptual concerns of the nature of history. At least 19 of the institutions we sampled with regard to methods modules made clear reference to issues of historiography alongside consideration of methods. It is not surprising that such elements have become a growing feature of undergraduate curricula given the amount of debate that has emerged among historians. And addressing research methods leads naturally to the nature of the discipline in that the rather loose and ill-defined character of historical methods arises from the uncertainty of historical knowledge. Research methods course units raise the issue of how historians know about the past as an introduction to the centrality of primary sources in historical investigation. Differing interpretations of evidence are also, of course, the foundation of historical controversy and debate.

Our discussion so far has focused on British experience, but what of that overseas? As in the case of the dissertation, with which they are generally associated, methods are also addressed at the honours level in Australian universities and historiography may again be considered alongside. At the University of Western Australia, for example, honours students prepare a dissertation of up to 15,000 words, take a compulsory course unit on historiography that addresses different ways of 'knowing' history and select two from a variety of seminars, at least some of which require the analysis of primary evidence (Western Australia, *Discipline*). It seems unusual, however, to find methods-based course units forming part of the Australian ordinary degree. As to the United States, evidence of methods course units in the undergraduate major is mixed. The bachelor's degree there is not intended to provide discipline-specific training – a feature of graduate programmes – but is more generally educational. Yet examples can certainly be found. Thus at the University of Mary Washington, Virginia the long-established *Introduction to the Study of History* course unit emphasises research and writing, as well as thinking and speaking. And no doubt to strengthen the research dimension, one of the University's librarians acts as a member of the course teaching team (Ferrell, *Method*). At the State University of Virginia, distinguished history majors are required to take a seminar course unit that focuses on research matters during the spring term of their third year. To illustrate the type of approach taken, the unit entitled *The United States Confronts the Middle East: Strategy, Diplomacy and Culture* is quoted.

> After a month of preliminary readings, each student will identify a research topic to pursue for the remainder of the semester. The student will then propose a research paper topic and compile a tentative bibliography of primary and secondary sources on that subject. After 'pitching' his or her project to the class and receiving constructive criticism and suggestions from classmates and professor, the student will research and write a 25–30-page critical paper grounded in primary sources. Each student will be assigned to read and critique the draft of one of his classmates. In the last two classes of the semester, students will present the drafts of their papers to the seminar and comment upon the work of one other student.
>
> (Virginia, *Websites*)

If the experience of Central Connecticut State University is anything to go by, skills course units may become increasingly important in the United States. Faculty there found 'that some students entering 400 level courses are not adequately prepared in terms of writing and research skills, as well as the ability to analytically evaluate various materials'. Consequently, a new course unit entitled *The Historical Imagination* was introduced in the Fall of 2001 to help major students acquire the skills required in advanced-level work (Central Connecticut, *Imagination*).

A fairly clear pattern emerges from this discussion, of course units at first-year level in the United Kingdom introducing students to the basic tools of historical analysis while those at later levels are more concerned with preparation for the advanced work of dissertations. Despite the different forms they take, however, it seems that methods course units serve a fundamentally similar purpose. Research methods, commonly combined with historiography, form a rite of passage into serious study in the discipline. Some institutions evidently feel that this ritual is best performed at the outset, others after a period of acclimatisation. In the United States and Australia, methods units naturally come later in the programme, being provided for those students who want to specialise for honours degrees. What is perhaps most problematical about either of these patterns of provision, however, is the temptation to fit everything into one course unit. Thus there may be too much for first-year students to take on when they have as yet little experience of higher education history, while it is odd to offer training in how to do the subject part way through a programme. Increasingly, this point seems to be recognised, for there is a growing pattern in the United Kingdom of building a progressive spine of skills units throughout a programme. Introductory course units initiate students into the basics of historical enquiry and higher education generally, while intermediate units develop more sophisticated skills, leading to the final-year dissertation. This approach gives more opportunities to practise and reinforce essential historical skills and avoids ghettoising them into a single curricular slot.

Developing other advanced historical skills

With regard to more advanced research methods units, the question arises as to whether there are other higher-level skills that might not be receiving the attention they deserve in undergraduate history programmes. Two in particular present themselves, namely problematising and project management.

A key historical skill which many students find particularly difficult is the ability to problematise an issue. Most finalists can tackle a set question but even very able students can find formulating and articulating their own questions excruciating matters. Yet the ability to recognise how a historical topic can be addressed and how to negotiate between what an historian wants to do and what the sources will allow him or her to do are crucial to historical practice. Arguably, these skills are too advanced for many undergraduates to acquire, but they are nonetheless central to completion of a dissertation or independent project in history. Hence they need to be addressed at some point in the curriculum, ideally as a general issue to provoke students into thinking about them and as a key element in follow-up discussions in relation to individual projects. Maybe, too, the challenge of problematising should be built into notions of progression, with students being encouraged or even required to devise their own essay titles in the later stages of their studies.

With regard to project management, finalists often seem to be overwhelmed by the scale of a dissertation and uncertain how to deal with it. Their previous experience might have run to essays of between two and three thousand words, but a dissertation is often of the order of 10 to 15,000 words, bringing new concerns about how it should be approached, the form it should take and how its preparation can best be managed in the time available. Some methods course units, including that provided at Worcester University College, do include consideration of the kind of planning that students need to undertake for project work, the themes covered including:

- identifying and supplying a rationale for a research project;
- devising a research programme;
- identifying and addressing the particular requirements of a project;
- writing a research proposal (Worcester, *Descriptions*).

Of course, much support on dissertation preparation is given to students by means of handouts and individual tuition, but the key point to address as regards curriculum planning is how far the support students need in managing dissertation projects should be made available as part of the provision offered them in core course units. Also entering into consideration here is the need to ensure that the very practical demands involved in dissertation work are taken into account, including locating sources in the first place, navigating an archive, extracting and interweaving different kinds of source material, and relating secondary and primary sources.

The value of skills-based course units

Issues of historical problematising, advanced techniques of manipulating sources and project management may well deserve more attention in sessions on dissertation preparation than they appear to receive. How and where they are included in the curriculum, and how far they should comprise compulsory elements, are plainly important considerations. Yet the question remains as to whether these and other initiatives in skills development really do enhance students' historical competence. It might still reasonably be asked whether attempts to model historical processes lead only to artificial situations. Since the analysis of evidence varies from one kind of source to another, and is dependent on considerable background knowledge for its contextualisation, how far can historical methodology be acquired independently of particular historical cases? Can historical judgement, so dependent on accumulated experience, really be taught and learnt? In this vein, a major problem with the teaching of methodology in a dedicated course unit is persuading students to transfer the techniques to their other course units. Given an exercise in source analysis, a student will typically be excessively critical and reject most pieces of evidence as unconscionably flawed with bias and partiality. When presented with an essay to write, some students have a depressing tendency to cling to the infallibility of any evidence from even the most unreliable of sources.

To acknowledge these criticisms, however, does not support the alternative scenario of not dealing directly with issues of methodology. Course units on methods, as with historiography, help students to stand apart from routine activity and give a breathing space in which they can assess and reflect upon what they are doing. If students are not exposed to the fragmentary, contradictory messiness of evidence and the circumstances of historical study, it is difficult to see how they can ever fully appreciate how history works, assess confidently the status of what they read in secondary texts or apply themselves to their own historical writings. Analysing and practising complex tasks in a structured and supportive environment promotes the active learning and reflective practice that builds sophisticated understanding. It seems simple justice, moreover, that if the ability to do history is valued, there should be some effort to teach students what is involved. Hoping that an appreciation of historical practice will be absorbed by osmosis is hardly a sound educational strategy. By the same token, hiving off consideration of methods into a separate component is no panacea. Methods course units do have a degree of artificiality, and skills, whether conceptual or technical, still have to be applied appropriately and iteratively in the run of ordinary activity if they are to have any real meaning and any chance of becoming internalised.

TEACHING GENERIC SKILLS TO HISTORY STUDENTS

Since higher learning in history usually culminates in a piece of advanced work demonstrating the capacity actually to do history, then it is difficult to object to teaching some of the practical techniques which could help develop that capacity. Moving beyond the immediate confines of the discipline to teach generic skills is much more contentious, however, though a sliding scale can be identified. Thus acquiring skills in the course of disciplinary study, which happen also to be generally useful, may be more acceptable to academics than exercises devoted to skill acquisition that are more or less independent of learning the discipline.

To consider the question of generic skills, as noted in introducing this chapter, three rough categories are identified, namely key or basic study skills, skills of wider applicability acquired in the course of disciplinary learning, and overtly workplace-oriented skills. While each is discussed in turn, there are few hard and fast distinctions between them, particularly in the case of basic study skills which overlap substantially with the kind of introductory research methods discussed above.

Basic study skills

'Study skills' is another disparate term, embracing a multitude of abilities. It can refer to basic educational capacities of literacy and numeracy, personal attributes of time-management and organisation, information collection and collation, or communication in a variety of forms. Some study skills, such as literacy, are genuinely generic across academic and non-academic situations; others, like the conventions of historical referencing, are clearly disciplinary in nature. Many, including essay writing, have features of both; written communication as expressed in an essay can be applied in many contexts, but there are qualities peculiar to a piece of effective historical essay writing. Study skills are no doubt addressed in all history programmes, if only in the form of a course or subject guide distributed to students that contains advice and suggestions on how to prepare, write and present an essay.

Many higher education history departments, however, are devoting class time to study skills. The introductory *Historical Topics* course unit at York University assists students in acquiring techniques of seminar presentation and essay writing (York, *Overview*), and the *Making History* course units at Sheffield Hallam University consider the skills of essay writing, library use, group work and IT (Sheffield Hallam, *History*). To take an Antipodean example, the objectives of Stage I at the University of Auckland include imparting skills of effective use of a library, obtaining information from textbooks and monographs and taking notes from lectures and books (Auckland, *BA*). References to study skills in United States history major programmes, however, are not common. Most of the requirements are addressed under the general educational programmes, where detailed agendas of various skills are set out and often assigned to different subjects. Upper-level history course units are often designated as writing-intensive, where the requirement to demonstrate that a student has the capacity to write coherently at some length can be assessed. The senior seminars offered at the University of Utah provide examples (Utah, *Requirements*). However, it is not clear where or how the demands of extensive essay writing are introduced in order that they can be displayed. As already noted, the diffuse nature of United States' degree programmes makes it difficult to ensure clear lines of progression that enable foundations to be laid before student assignments are assessed. Where there are undergraduate methods course units, study skills can be incorporated, as at the University of Southern Maine where history students are introduced to fundamentals specific to history.

Three approaches to introductory study skills teaching are exemplified by the course units run at the Universities of Nottingham, Dundee and Central Lancashire.

- The introductory course units in *Learning History* at Nottingham deal with basic skills of using booklists and reading effectively, discussion skills in seminars, writing essays and delivering oral presentations (Booth, 2001: 491–4). There is also an element of historiography, with discussion of the challenges of postmodernism and an essay on the nature of historical writing. In the second semester, students work on group projects, which seek to develop research skills and teamwork. These modules make up about a quarter of a BA History student's timetable.

● A recent initiative at Dundee has introduced a study guide and workbook to operate in conjunction with, but separately from, the first-year survey course unit. A discrete seminar series takes students through a carefully worked out programme of study skills from definitions of lectures and seminars to analysis of primary sources and an independent project. Class contact time comprises a one-hour seminar per week.

● At Central Lancashire, two compulsory modules, *Modern World History*, and *Understanding History*, are run together. A series of lectures, primarily devoted to modern world history, is complemented with seminars that seek to develop a range of skills, including study skills, and an understanding of the nature of history via exercises on topics relevant to the lecture programme, thereby trying to make the skills relevant to a content-based programme. The two modules constitute one third of a first-year timetable.

In favour of the Central Lancashire approach is that the skills elements are considered both in their own right and are also integrated with the subject matter, perhaps helping to overcome the potential resistance of students to study skills work. Explicitly skills-based course units, however, may afford skills even greater significance in the curriculum, allowing essential skills to be addressed directly. In this respect, the Dundee study guide is extremely practical, while the Nottingham version has the advantage of providing students with an intellectually challenging historiographical dimension. Moreover, both the Nottingham and Dundee approaches do not occupy a very significant proportion of a first-year student's time, perhaps making them more acceptable overall.

With regard to content, all three of the units offer new students the opportunity to attempt practical exercises concerned with using the library, footnoting and essay writing, as well as with presenting seminars in a specially supportive and formative environment that allows general issues to be raised. For example, students might be given essay-marking exercises requiring them to judge essays of varying quality against the marking system used. Offering students advice on essay writing, referencing conventions or exam technique is not new, of course, but addressing these skills directly in dedicated course units is a more recent innovation, in part a response to the changing nature and dimensions of the student population, particularly in the United Kingdom. As is frequently pointed out, a great many more students, commonly first-generation and often with less secure general educational backgrounds, are entering higher education. When student numbers were such that individual tutorials were a much more viable proposition, it may have been possible to instil basic study skills informally, or simply to assume that they would be acquired along the way. Larger numbers entail a more overt, mass approach, however. Equally, it surely ought no longer be assumed that students will simply absorb essential study skills by osmosis.

Nevertheless, there is a legitimate question to ask as to how far study skills should be incorporated into higher education history programmes. Is it the proper task of academics trained in history to deal with such matters as basic literacy, reading and note taking, use of the library, how to perform in seminars, what lectures are for, and time management? Should historians attempt to teach students how to write, even if an engaging and literate written style may considerably enhance a student's ability to communicate historical arguments? In addressing these matters we should not underestimate students' ignorance of how higher education works, its complex structures, arcane terminology, obscure marking systems, and just what is required from a history undergraduate. Nor is this an issue only for marginal students. Booth's substantial survey of history students, who could be counted among the 'successes of the English school system', found a significant lack of confidence arising from the narrow range of experience they had gained as a preparation for undergraduate work (Booth, 1997: 207–9). Students coming straight from secondary education, and non-traditional students coming from work, are likely to be completely unused to the minimal class contact time and the very considerable demands of self-management in degree-level work. Few will be experienced with a large academic library and extensive reading lists. School leavers are often unused to the idea that their views are welcomed and can be very reluctant to articulate questions and concerns. There are no reasons for assuming that new students instinctively know what is expected of them. Since it is widely recognised that the transition to higher education is a major, frequently unsettling, life event, introductory course units that try to address the issues involved may do much to smooth the process. Moreover, the central point remains that if the ability to perform certain tasks is regarded as important, then it is not unreasonable that some effort be made actively to develop those abilities within the curriculum.

Skills of wider applicability

Information collection and collation, bibliographical skills and the ability to write effectively are clearly essential for adequate performance in a history degree, as well as being of value in other contexts. To this extent, potentially transferable skills have been, and have long been recognised as, features of studying history. As we have seen, evidence from prospectuses and websites indicates that such skills are being increasingly highlighted and promoted more directly in undergraduate history programmes. Yet, until very recently, many students were unaware of what skills they were capable of developing and how their skills might be applied to other contexts. And this point extends to postgraduates, too (Cryer, 1998). Actually drawing students' attention to the skills they are acquiring through degree study is a useful first step in addressing the problem.

There are other skills, frequently promoted via the study of history, that also have wider applicability and it is to these that we now turn. They are oral communication skills, group work skills, ICT skills and language skills.

Oral communication is eminently transferable; most graduate-level employment probably entails oral presentations at some stage. There are also educational grounds for encouraging effective oral capability. Presentations can help enhance student participation in seminars, and some students may be better at oral than written communication. Yet it might be argued that the ability to speak well is not itself relevant to historical understanding and therefore has no legitimate place in a history curriculum. The problem of what to do with a historically astute but preternaturally shy student is pertinent and applies to many of the skills considered here (Woollard, 1995: 322–5). Logically, however, the same argument applies with equal force to written communication and, even more so, to the highly peculiar skill of being able to perform under examination conditions. Some students are better at oral than written communication so, if nothing else, natural justice demands that they be given an opportunity to show their understanding to best advantage. In fact, oral presentations are becoming pervasive features of history degree programmes and some preparation is often provided in study skills modules, although probably not to the same extent as written communication.

Being able to work cooperatively and cohesively as part of a group is frequently cited by employers as a desirable attribute and also has relevance to the process of historical research (Winstanley, 1992: 57). Yet group work grates against the notoriously independent practices of historians. Students, too, are often wary of group projects and, where every mark counts towards their degree classification, resentment against non-contributors is not unreasonable. The use of logs that allow an individual record and reflective assessment of individual contributions can help to overcome these concerns. The problem of the shy or insular student, however, again applies to group activity. Certainly, there have to be careful safeguards, but the rewards of successful group projects are often immense. Where co-operation and cohesion do take root, the genuine peer learning that arises can be an extremely fulfilling experience. And more higher education history departments are incorporating some kind of group work activity into their programmes, including the first-year provision at Canterbury Christ Church College, reported above, and the second-year group research project at the University of Birmingham, noted in Chapter 2.

Literacy in ICT is a prime example of both a quintessentially transferable skill and also an increasingly valuable disciplinary skill. There is no doubt that the development of ICT has exercised historians over the past couple of decades, a mid-1990s survey suggesting that all British university history departments seemed to be offering classes dealing with computer studies in history (Fitzgerald and Flint, 1995: 55). No clear pattern of ICT provision for history students emerges from our survey of skills-based units in United Kingdom history departments, and marked variation clearly exists. Thus Bristol University offers a compulsory module of IT skills for historians in year one (Bristol, *IT-One*), training is available for history students to develop their computer skills at University College, London (UCL, *Information*), while Sheffield Hallam University is able to offer a progressive core of ICT provision from introductory to advanced level (Lewis and Lloyd-Jones, 2000: 77–81). The still tentative relationship between historians and computers is captured in the 2002 prospectus for Hull University which, having emphasised the extent of IT facilities available to historians, notes that the first-year introductory module 'makes the experience of coming to terms with this technology as painless and interesting as possible'.

In perhaps no other area than ICT is there such a clear distinction between enthusiasts and the rest, a consideration reflected in the problems of teaching ICT in history programmes. Typically, an introductory class will contain a portion of students that is more advanced than any of the teachers, along with an element that is even more terrified than the most Luddite academic. In planning ICT provision, a distinction should probably be made along the lines of the Sheffield Hallam model, between basic computer literacy, including word-processing and the use of on-line catalogues and the Internet, which might properly be made compulsory at introductory levels, and more advanced research methods, involving statistical manipulations and the use of databases, appropriate for higher-level options. Encouragingly for historical study, Lloyd-Jones and Lewis have noted a tendency to move away from the purely technical aspects of using computers to focusing on the historical questions that are best addressed with the kind of data that a computer can utilise (Lloyd-Jones and Lewis, 1996: 15–16). At the same time on-line approaches to learning and teaching have added a further dimension to ICT provision with which higher education historians and their students have had to contend, a matter which is considered in the following chapter.

One of the most surprising features of history programmes in Britain, conspicuous mainly by its absence, is the requirement to be familiar with foreign languages. It could reasonably be argued that being able at least to read another language is a central historical skill – how can one properly get to grips with a nation's history if one cannot read its national language? Genuine primary source work is almost impossible, yet despite the continual emphasis on analysis of sources, vanishingly few United Kingdom higher education institutions ask for a foreign language, even as an entry requirement. A classical language is demanded in several, but not all, ancient history programmes, however. And where history overlaps with area studies, then language is also an important feature. Languages are commonly available as options for history students and are regularly recommended as desirable, but not to the point of being seen as essential. The situation is better in the United States, where general educational programmes usually include some language proficiency, and some history major programmes, including that at the University of Southern Maine, make a point of requiring it (Southern Maine, *Bachelor of Arts*). Altogether, though, it is remarkable how rarely language features in undergraduate history degrees, to the detriment both of historical expertise and transferable skills.

Workplace skills

Building on the skills inherent in history, or logical extensions of them, is still located safely within the confines of the discipline and the physical space of the institution. Making connections with the world outside the academy raises a whole new tranche of issues. To begin with, it is readily acknowledged that history does not have many immediately vocational career routes and this can inhibit the development of work-related experience in history programmes (Beck, 1996: 243). One obvious avenue, however, is through consideration of heritage or public history, which can operate at the level of academic debate and also create opportunities for employment-like experience or work placement. Public history is a well-established sub-field in the United States and most institutions offer internships in which students can earn credit for relevant employment. At Central Connecticut State University, for instance, BA students can choose a primary or secondary area of concentration that is 'designed to teach students about the way in which history impacts the public sphere' (Central Connecticut, *Concentration*). Moves in this direction are more tentative in the United Kingdom, but appear to be growing. Analysing the relationships between academic history and the public world of heritage is a fairly straightforward way of considering the wider political, cultural, social and commercial pressures on communicating understanding of the past. Historians often have close relationships with museums, archives and libraries and these can lead to placing students in vocationally-relevant situations.

A number of variations around this theme are being pursued in undergraduate history provision.

● Community history projects, where students work on historical topics in liaison with an outside agency, offer an intermediate stage between academic study and work experience. At Lancaster University, community history projects were introduced to help develop a range of transferable skills, including group and IT skills, as well as to gain experience with primary sources (Winstanley, 1992). In terms of community links, these projects also involve liaising with outside bodies, problem-centred historical research and delivering findings to a non-academic audience.

- The next stage involves placing students more clearly in the workplace. Projects run at the University of Staffordshire originate primarily in the museum or archive service, and students are appointed to them (Elkes, 2002). At several institutions, including Manchester Metropolitan University, workplace projects feature negotiated learning contracts as an important element of the experience (Nicholls, 1992: 71–3). A particularly resourceful approach pioneered at Edge Hill University College combines a taught academic component, considering debates around heritage, with placement in a heritage site (Frank, 2002). The projects mentioned generally include both a report on a specific historical topic and some kind of reflective self-assessment about the working situation. Comments from the workplace may or may not be included in assessment.

- An extremely ambitious undertaking at Huddersfield University, introduced in the early 1990s, features a compulsory workplace course unit in the second year, which is not necessarily related to a historical topic. The placement lasts for six weeks with two weeks' induction and evaluation, and takes place at the end of the second year. A lengthy preparation period inducts students and sets up the placements with prospective employers. The placement is simply passed or failed but does involve a continuous record and assessment from the student, the employer and the member of academic staff who acts as mentor during the process (Roberts and Myock, 1991).

The historians who have devised and run these projects are the first to acknowledge the practical, academic and educational problems encountered. Practically, establishing relationships with outside agencies and supervising students while on placements, even on a limited scale, is colossally time-consuming. Negotiating learning contracts and ensuring that proper safeguards are in place for the protection of all parties entails enormous hidden costs both of academic staff time and on the part of employers. Academically, serious issues arise around assessment; if a work placement is not assessed it may not be taken seriously, but assessing non-disciplinary activity as part of a degree may be open to objection. Work placements may also be more valuable in the final year but at that stage may interfere with other studies, especially dissertation preparation. Moreover, there are clear elements of risk around the whole undertaking – whether the work is of a suitable level, whether the student will behave appropriately and whether sufficient support and guidance will be available. In the element of uncertainty, however, lies the opportunity of rising to the challenges and enjoying an enormously fulfilling and rewarding learning experience, besides acquiring insights into a working environment. Feedback from such projects is certainly overwhelmingly positive. A follow-up study of the Huddersfield experiment found that, in general, those who were in the first cohort regarded the experience as useful, either in actually finding a job or clarifying their career aspirations (Roberts and Myock, 1995: 69–71).

On top of these concerns is the question, to what extent is it the responsibility of academic staff in history to try to enhance their students' career prospects? One response is that this is not a bona-fide component of historical education and that trained historians are woefully ill equipped to deal with such matters. Work experience may be something that employers look for in applicants, but this is something that students can and generally do (indeed increasingly are forced to) acquire for themselves. With increasing numbers of non-traditional students having gained some experience of employment or wider life-skills, creating work experience opportunities in higher education might be thought unnecessary. It could also reasonably be argued that most history students do not have clear vocational aims, and choose to study history out of interest in the subject, perhaps consciously rejecting a career-oriented experience of higher education. Indeed, non-traditional students are often actively seeking a break from a lifetime of work experience! And some maintain that a good degree from an elite university is still the best passport to a job (Barker, 1997: 59).

Is it permissible, though, for academic staff simply to ignore what happens to their students after graduation? It is salutary for academics to be aware of their limitations, but to insist on addressing nothing that is not strictly within the confines of the discipline is surely too blinkered. All history tutors are aware that few of their students go into a directly history-relevant occupation, but presumably want them to go into useful and rewarding occupations. Assisting in this process is simply an integral part of helping to nurture an individual through a course of learning and onto new pastures, one of the privileges of being a teacher. Nor is attention to work-related skills inimical to historical learning; most of the projects considered above are based on real historical study, but conducted in a different context and bringing out alternative aspects of the nature of the subject. Placements in the community can bring to life issues of the social context of history and give rise to genuine reflection on historical understanding and personal experience. Even the Huddersfield scheme quickly moved to an emphasis on work-based learning, with the onus not so much on simply gaining experience of a working environment but on the skills that can be acquired for graduate employment. The move reflected concern about the potential resistance to the scheme from mature students who had already gained work experience. Particularly pleasing in this respect was the response from one such student who found the experience helpful in restoring confidence after a period out of work (Roberts and Myock, 1995: 63 and 67). Similarly, supercilious complacency about the ability of supposedly superior institutions to grease their students' paths into employment may well be misplaced. Elitism might yield an interview, but if candidates have no more than knowledge of a discipline to support their case, they are unlikely to be viewed favourably by an employer.

To finish on a cautionary note, a particularly irritating feature of skills development is the paradoxical resistance of many students to the language and pedagogy of skills. Skills teaching is now pervasive throughout school years and some students seem to feel that they have been skilled to death. We have periodically raised the question of compulsion in history programmes and there is often great resistance to compulsory course units dealing with skills. If new students expect content-driven course units, introductions to skills and methods may seem a distraction or, again paradoxically, either too trivial or too challenging. It is noticeable, however, how optional skills sessions often attract the more able students who need them least but are more aware of their importance. Yet attitudes are not always consistent and when deadlines approach there is a general thirst for information on how to write essays or improve examination techniques. Skills course units are often also appreciated more in retrospect, especially when it comes to preparing a dissertation or finding a job. These considerations do not make the task of teaching skills any easier, as each cohort has to rely on the promise that they will appreciate the value arising one day! Reassuringly, surveys of new students do show that there are significant areas in which they want advice and guidance, particularly about how higher education works and what is expected of them. This is a fundamental message; we need to know much more about what students themselves feel they need, as well as what we know they will require, and then build our understanding into a meaningful and respected component of the degree programme.

CONCLUSION

It is clear that skills have come to play a very important role in history degree programmes. To a considerable extent, historians have acknowledged that to operate effectively and demonstrate one's ability within the discipline requires certain practical and conceptual expertise, which it is only reasonable to seek to promote for undergraduates in an overt and explicit way. Course units on research methods are becoming common in undergraduate programmes and there is evidence of increasing moves to develop a progression from introductory study skills and historical practices that ease the transition into history at degree level (and improve retention rates), to more advanced research skills needed for dissertation preparation. Higher-level historical skills, however, seem to be interpreted overwhelmingly in terms of analysis of primary sources of evidence, perhaps ignoring other valuable aspects. Such a progression is easier to achieve in the more controlled United Kingdom degree structure or Australian honours programmes, but there are indications of moves towards this situation in the United States as well. Beyond promoting directly disciplinary skills, at least drawing attention to the wider applicability of the skills acquired during a history degree is also coming to be widely accepted. Making directly employment-related skills a featured element in the history curriculum is less widespread, although there are numerous, and increasing, examples, and one can reasonably predict that there will be much greater moves in this direction in the future as the notion of enhancing employability in the undergraduate curriculum gains ground. The potential benefits to students are enormous but considerable concerns remain in terms of implementation.

This chapter has urged that it is vital to develop a wide range of skills within history degree programmes, indeed that skills, appropriately conceived, may constitute an essential core to the discipline of history. It is important to re-emphasise, however, that attention to skills does not have to be mechanistic or reductive, and it is helpful to rethink the language of skills in the more holistic and educational terms of student-centred learning. After all, the underlying purpose of skills development is to promote reflective practice and critical thinking, applicable as much within a degree programme as in the outside world. Many historians, however, may still be uncomfortable with the notion that skills acquisition and enhancement are principal objectives of a degree. The danger is that history as a study of and attempt to understand the past becomes merely a vehicle for other priorities, and some kinds of externally imposed pressures do need to be resisted. However committed they may be to their students' welfare, most tutors of history would also maintain that there must be something about history itself that has particular value and significance. Thus it is essential to keep in view the historian's distinctive qualities of mind – an appreciation of diversity, of complexity, of the 'always different context of the past', of the influence the past exerts on the present, of the need to understand people and situations on their own terms and to forbear from value judgement. Students are drawn to history by its endless fascination and enduring importance. The reflective practice and critical thinking that skills development promotes should encourage a more sophisticated, informed and engaged study of the human past that helps students appreciate history's unique dimensions.

Key references

Aldous, C. and Hicks, M. (2003) *A Survey of Historical Source Work in Higher Education*. Winchester: King Alfred's College.

Bennett, N., Dunne, E. and Carre, C. (2000) *Skills Development in Higher Education and Employment*. London: Society for Research into Higher Education and Open University Press.

Booth, A. (2001) 'Developing history students' skills in the transition to university', *Teaching in Higher Education*, 6: 487–503.

Hitchcock, T., Shoemaker, R.B. and Tosh, J. (2000) 'Skills and the structure of the history curriculum', in A. Booth and P. Hyland (eds) *The Practice of University History Teaching*. Manchester: Manchester University Press, pp. 47–59.

Roberts, B. and Myock, M. (1995), 'Work-based learning on an Arts degree course', *Journal of Further and Higher Education*, 19: 62–72.

Winstanley, M. (1992) 'Group work in the humanities: history in the community, a case study', *Studies in Higher Education*, 17: 55–65.

Websites

QAA (2000), *History Benchmark Statement* at http://www.qaa.ac.uk/crntwork/benchmark/history.html

Learning and teaching

INTRODUCTION

This chapter focuses on the methods of learning and teaching used by higher education historians. It draws strongly on the literature dealing with the theme, both in relation to history teaching specifically and, to provide context, in relation to undergraduate teaching more generally. The approach is mainly one of considering reported examples of the methods employed, along with the reflective comment that practitioners have made on them, in order that key issues arising can be identified and discussed.

Implicit in the discussion is the importance of developing methods that promote more active forms of learning. Based on the notion that people learn best by doing, active learning moves the emphasis away from didactic teaching to the creation of learning situations. As far as history at undergraduate level is concerned, the approach often involves students being required to use primary source material to enhance their understanding of the content covered, with the expectation that, as a result, they gain sufficient competence increasingly to set their own work agenda. Accordingly, an independent approach towards studying is encouraged, with an emphasis on students learning how to learn. Studying in depth is also promoted, with students being able, not least through reflection, to explain the understanding they have reached rather than merely demonstrate what they know. Other advantages that active learning is seen to bring include the development of a range of intellectual skills, with problem-solving and critical thinking to the fore among them (Mitchell, 2002).

The adoption of active approaches to learning does not require an abandonment of traditional forms of teaching. As far as history undergraduate programmes are concerned, lectures and seminars can, and no doubt will, remain the major means of delivering programmes, even though some changes to the form they take are likely to be required to accommodate more active forms of learning. Furthermore, the *History Benchmarking Statement* is unequivocal in its support of lectures and seminars, regarding both as essential parts of the undergraduate experience. And this is so despite the barrage of criticism that educationalists have brought to bear on them as methods of teaching and learning, at least in their more conventional forms.

Given the widespread usage and the strong and continuing support given to lectures and seminars, the form that they take, and the concerns to which they give rise, provide the focus of this chapter. Discussion of them is set in the context of history benchmarking requirements, as well as the changing circumstances in which history learning and teaching is taking place at undergraduate level. Of particular importance in this respect is the growing use of ICT approaches, especially web-based provision, a matter about which higher education historians often seem to express interest but, as far as application is concerned, tend to see as the province of others. Even so, the work of the enthusiasts in this area is as instructive as it is impressive, not least with regard to the promotion of active learning. A major section of the chapter is therefore devoted to examination of the work they have undertaken and reported.

The chapter begins with a brief discussion of the history benchmarking requirements as far as learning and teaching matters are concerned, noting the kinds of challenge arising from them. A section dealing with the vital role of the teacher in promoting effective learning follows. Further sections are devoted to lectures and seminars, considering the general advantages and disadvantages associated with them, as well as the approaches to them that higher education historians have adopted. Discussion of these themes is continued in the final section, which is concerned with ICT applications, especially in the form of web-based provision.

BENCHMARKING AND HISTORY LEARNING AND TEACHING

In teaching and learning, as with other matters it considered, the group responsible for compiling the *History Benchmarking Statement* refused to be prescriptive, insisting that teaching and learning are evolving processes and that their intention was not 'to freeze the teaching of history in a particular model'. What the group has done, however, is to offer recommendations with regard to how teaching and learning might usefully be approached, especially with quality of provision in mind. These recommendations are summarised in Table 5.1 (QAA, *History*, 2000: 1, 5–6).

As with other elements of the *Benchmarking Statement*, there is much in the list that reflects existing practice and with which disagreement is unlikely. Even so, issues arise from the recommendations that have profound importance as regards how students learn, especially in an active manner. Take the advocacy of lectures and seminars, for instance. Both have stood the test of time in history undergraduate programmes and remain of fundamental importance in the learning and teaching process, a situation that the *Benchmarking Statement* clearly seeks to reinforce. Yet support for lectures might be seen as incongruous, given the heavy assault that has been made on them by educationalists, some of whom consider that lecturing has little if anything to offer learners. Likewise, finding ways of engaging students in seminars will be seen as a laudable ideal, but no sooner has the statement been digested than the all too familiar image of the unresponsive seminar student springs to mind. How often is the complaint made that, despite the best endeavours of the tutor, a sizeable minority of students in history seminar groups are reluctant to make a contribution, with the implication that the silent students are at fault?

THE ROLE OF THE HISTORY TUTOR IN LEARNING AND TEACHING

From the student's perspective, the quality of teaching provided remains pivotal to a successful learning experience, and it is to a brief consideration of the influences that affect the teaching quality experienced by history undergraduates that our discussion turns.

The relationship between teacher and taught

A survey undertaken by Alan Booth into history students' perceptions of their undergraduate courses at two different types of British higher education institution reveals that they see tutors as 'overwhelmingly the most important influence in their development' and that they compare the anonymity they experience in higher education unfavourably with the supportive relationships they enjoyed at earlier stages of their studies. The survey has yielded a list of the particular characteristics valued by the students in their tutors, as follows:

TABLE 5.1 *History benchmarking teaching and learning recommendations*

Teaching and learning element	Summary of comments
Documentation for students	Course guides should detail outcomes and how they are to be achieved, along with details of course structure and assessment and a bibliography.
Formal contact for students with tutors and other students	Regular contact of this type is seen as important in terms of deepening students' research, oral and communication skills and inculcating the qualities of self-discipline.
Opportunity for students to experience lectures or lecture type arrangements	These should be designed to capture interest and excite curiosity, a key function being to 'provide a broad framework which helps define the course, while also introducing students to its main themes, debates and interpretations'.
Opportunity for students to experience seminars	It is suggested that group discussion should be 'aimed at improving students' understanding rather than the acquisition of knowledge *per se* and should be structured in such a way as to maximise effective student participation'.
Encouraging students to use information repositories imaginatively	Objectives here are to get students to expand their knowledge base and their range of historical approaches.
Students undertaking a wide variety of assignments	A key point is that the assignments used should be appropriate to the aims and outcomes of the course.
Critical and constructive feedback for students	The stipulation here is that there 'should be adequate discussion of, and response to, a student's individual work'.

- approachability: accessibility and willingness to help students;
- enthusiasm for the subject matter;
- expertise (most often mentioned by first-year students);
- communicates ideas clearly and cogently;
- makes the subject 'come alive';
- encourages and respects students' views;
- knows how to encourage active student participation;
- gives clear guidance on reading;
- provides clear, constructive feedback on assignments;
- has an obvious commitment to teaching.

As Booth observes, the quality of tutor–student relationships expressed in the list shows that effective learning 'is felt to occur as much through interaction with others as from a one-to-one relationship between student and text' (Booth, 2000: 32–3, 35–6). How far students perceive such interaction to be more effective when it occurs face-to-face rather than in a virtual learning environment raises a further matter to consider, but, on the basis of the Booth evidence, students clearly place high value on the guidance and support they receive from their teachers, as well as on the expertise and enthusiasm that their teachers display.

Engaging in reflective self-criticism

Booth and Hyland argue that teaching and learning practices in history need constantly to be reviewed by the teacher, for example, 'keeping a journal or portfolio of teaching experiences, using self-evaluation questionnaires on particular aspects of teaching, using student feedback, informal or formal discussion with colleagues, peer observation schemes or, more ambitiously, researching one's own teaching using action-research methodology' (Booth and Hyland, 2000: 9). Furthermore, it has been suggested, if students are to be placed at the centre of the learning process, history tutors need to recognise

> the importance of understanding the ways in which students learn in their subject, of understanding their perspectives on learning, and of encouraging them to explore their own conceptions of teaching and learning so that they can become more effective critical thinkers of the sort most valued in a History education.
>
> (History 2000, 1977: 1)

In helping to achieve such ends, the type of reflective questions that Booth and Hyland have enunciated are highly pertinent:

- What kinds of things do we want students to learn (*knowledge, skills, concepts, methodologies, etc.*)?
- What opportunities are provided for students to learn (*lectures, seminars, fieldwork, etc.*)?
- What kind of assessment tasks are used to test the achievement (*essays, exams, posters, project, reports, etc.*)?
- Who assesses the learning (*tutor, self, peer, public audiences, etc.*)?

- What do students think are the most important things that they learn from a history education?
- How does the department review its practices and keep abreast of learning and teaching innovations? (Booth and Hyland, 2000: 9).

Reflection on such matters involves an investment of time and intellectual energy, of course, but, as has been pointed out, improved practice depends upon 'examining what we are actually doing to encourage student learning in the light of what we *think* we are or should be doing, and then changing or adapting our practices in the light of what we have learned' (*History 2000*, 1977: 2). And even if great teachers are born, maintaining pedagogical excellence clearly requires sustained commitment and hard work. It requires, too, a willingness to adapt to the changing circumstances in which learning and teaching take place, not least the emergence of bigger classes at higher education level and an increasing emphasis on ICT applications.

Linking teaching and research activity

The growing interest in teaching and learning in higher education has contributed to a debate about whether pedagogical issues are complementary to, or a diversion from, the 'traditional' academic role of researching and publishing. Yet Booth and Hyland have pointed out that the 'dominance of research over teaching, administration and public service is itself only a recent phenomenon' (since the 1950s), but subsequently the research model has become the norm (Booth and Hyland, 2000: 1). Writing in 1967, however, Elton maintained that the trend was in the opposite direction at Cambridge University, with teaching taking up more time than had previously been the case and sometimes distracting from the real business of research and writing. But he did defend the notion of the lecturer devoting time to teaching on the grounds that 'it makes him a better historian', remarking, too, that 'the teacher who has ceased to take part in the work of exploration, discovery and restatement is very unlikely to remain a useful instructor' (Elton, 1967: 178–9). As far as he was concerned, therefore, research and teaching were complementary, with the latter flowing naturally from the former.

In 1998, the History in Universities Defence Group confirmed that higher education history teachers in Britain were drawing heavily on their research interests, in the belief that excellent teaching arose from excellent research (HUDG, 1988: 10). During the 1990s, however, one strand of educational literature rejected the notion that being a good researcher necessarily meant being a good teacher. Thus Graham Gibbs strongly challenged 'the research myth', that is 'the notion that teaching excellence flows primarily from research excellence', which he believed was 'demeaning and damaging to teaching'. He argued that while teaching can be enhanced through research, 'teaching excellence involves a scholarship of its own' (*Guardian*, 3 June 1997). Moreover, much has been made of the need to foster the link between research and teaching, which is seen not to occur naturally. One suggestion for achieving this end at course unit and programme levels is to enhance students' understanding of the role of research by, for example, designing the curriculum to incorporate consideration of research developments and by creating awareness of how students can learn from staff involvement in research. A further suggestion is to promote students' ability to carry out research within their discipline, ways forward here including the development of the curriculum to reflect the research process and to encourage students to critique staff publications from a research perspective (Jenkins and Zetter, 2003: 6–8).

What is quite evident from this brief discussion is not only that the history tutor has a crucial role to play in helping to ensure that effective student learning takes place – a point that is developed more fully in the following sections of this chapter – but that the role is a complex and demanding one. At its heart lies the notion of the reflective practitioner who is not only prepared to think long and hard about learning and teaching matters, but also to translate thought into action with a view to enhancing the students' learning experience. Such a perspective highlights the role of tutor as learner, perhaps expanding learning into new types of research activity that centre on scholarship associated with teaching and learning history, as well as with the subject matter of history itself (Booth, 2004: 251–8).

LECTURES

At the beginning of the twentieth century, Booth has observed, history teaching was mainly concerned with the transmission of an agreed body of knowledge to students who would often themselves become history teachers. Assessment, therefore, tested little more than the ability to remember and reproduce given information. Such approaches may have become discredited but, Booth contends, 'what is actually practised in lectures and seminars is not always so dissimilar to the transmission model' (Booth, 2000: 31). Even so, there has been a growing emphasis on promoting active forms of learning in lectures and seminars alike. And this development has been accompanied by a rejection of surface approaches to learning and a move towards deep learning (a tendency noted in Chapter 3) where students not only memorise, but also seek to understand and apply their knowledge. These new orthodoxies have profound implications for the role of the lecturer as a learning facilitator and the students' understanding that they are central to the learning process rather than simply passive receptacles of information.

Criticisms of lecturing

While varied approaches to teaching and learning in history have been adopted, the lecture remains a ubiquitous feature of undergraduate programmes. Yet lecturing has been castigated as a method of teaching, especially when it takes the form of uninterrupted exposition. Its shortcomings are not always perceived to arise from the inadequacies of lecturers. Of greater concern is the lack of effectiveness that lectures are believed to have in the learning process, a matter that has certainly concerned historians. Thus Peter Stearns argues that lectures are seen 'to impose a rather passive learning mode on the audience' (Stearns, 1993: 97), while John Cannon suggests that they 'make extremely heavy demands upon the audience, which are rarely met', singling out in this respect the idea of the lecturee as a critical thinker 'about what is being said, and what is not being said' (Cannon, 1984: 18–19). Lack of effectiveness is also evident in the contention that, as a lecture takes place, there is a marked decline in the amount of information the student can recall and that what can be recalled is soon forgotten unless it is quickly applied. Moreover, lectures are believed to have little value in stimulating thought, changing attitudes, promoting interest in a subject or in teaching various types of skills. Nor, it has been suggested, are they any more effective than other methods of transmitting information (Light and Cox, 2001: 97–8).

Advantages of lecturing

Faced with such criticisms, it might appear that lectures should not have a particularly strong role to play generally in higher education, let alone in teaching history. Yet lectures do offer considerable advantages, a fact that is recognised by the *History Benchmarking Statement*. In advocating that all history students should experience lectures, the *Statement* puts forward a number of supportive reasons.

- By stamping 'an imprint of personality' on a course unit, lectures can enable students to reflect on, and respond to, the individual interpretations that arise.
- Lectures can provide a broad framework for a course unit, introducing students to its main concerns and providing a range of ideas and information which students will be unlikely to derive themselves.
- Lectures should enable students to develop skills in listening, note taking and reflection (QAA, *History*, 2000: 5).

Other arguments in support of lectures include the economies they bring in staff time, that they can provide an up-to-date view of the subject matter under consideration, and that good lectures (and lecturers) can inspire students. They have been seen, too, as adding 'zest and pace' to a course (Cannon, 1984: 18). Furthermore, as Peter Frederick of Wabash College, Indiana has pointed out, 'it is wrong to assume that students listening to a lecture are necessarily inactive' (Frederick, 1991: 70).

The role of lecturing: interactive approaches

Given the differing viewpoints that educationalists hold about the value of lectures, the question arises as to the role lecturing should play in undergraduate history teaching. One approach to the question draws on the idea of seeing lectures more in terms of engagement than transmission (Light and Cox, 2001: 101–3). In essence, rather than merely purveying information, the lecturer engages in dialogue with the students during lectures, the intention being to promote and deepen their understanding through active learning. These ends can be achieved in a number of ways and are implicit in Gill Nicholls's recommendations regarding the way in which history lecturing might be approached:

Students' motivation can be greatly increased if lectures are made more informal and loosely organised, so that discussion is included. This gives students responsibility to raise questions and be involved in their learning. In this type of approach the conclusion of the lecture is very important. It should have a punchy, well-structured conclusion. This will give the students the feeling of a memorable session.

(Nicholls, 2002: 84)

The inclusion of discussion in lectures goes beyond the idea of engaging with students through the lecturing technique employed, though this consideration remains important, as historians have observed. Thus Elton argued that the lecturer '*must* endeavour to be new, even original, even wild, at all costs' and that, in terms of engaging students' interest, 'wit, humour, savagery, even obscenity can be justified at times' (Elton, 1967: 205–7). Again, Robert Blackey of California State University contends that the key to any teaching, including lecturing, is 'the ability to *engage* students, to get them involved intellectually' and that students can be motivated and inspired, as well as having their curiosity aroused, if lecturers are 'enthusiastic, dynamic and passionate' (Blackey, 1997: 3–7).

Higher education historians have reported a variety of ways in which they incorporate interactive approaches in their lectures. Examples include the following.

Asking questions

Stearns argues that routinely asking questions to large student audiences brings 'real exchange and the passive mould is broken not only for participants but for at least some others who are thinking through their own responses even if the setting inhibits their explicit involvement' (Stearns, 1993: 101). Myra L. Pennell of Appalachian State University argues for the use of low-level questions that require information recall as well as higher-order questions that require analysis. She sees the former as being a powerful learning tool, not least because they can be used to help students make successfull responses at an early stage (Pennell, 2000: 31). And Peter Frederick suggests the use of an emotionally powerful slide, such as one depicting events at Pearl Harbor, with the lecturer asking students first to describe what they see – a low-order activity – and then to move to 'higher-order "why?" and "what do you think about it?"questions' (Frederick, 2000: 104).

Answering questions

Questions may also be invited from students at various points in a lecture to ensure they understand the issues being considered. In other words, the students question the lecturer as well as the lecturer questioning the students. Again, interaction between teacher and taught occurs, while the type of questions asked can be helpful in revealing where clearer exposition is required on the part of the lecturer. The technique can even expose the limits of the lecturer's knowledge of what is known!

Small-group discussion

Frederick notes various means of introducing group work into lectures, the most dramatic being that involving classroom intruders.

> *Halfway through the first day of a history course, as the class is discussing the purposes and significant issues of studying history, two (prearranged) intruders burst into the class, shout some angry words at the teacher and students, and then storm out of the room.*

This intrusion is used as the basis for small-group discussion of the validity of historical sources, the students being asked to write their accounts of the incident, to read each other's accounts and then to write a short history based on the primary evidence they generate (Frederick, 2000: 101).

Brainstorming

One approach here is to write the title of the unit on the board at the outset of the lecture and then to invite students to call out words, feelings and images that they associate with the title. Apart from promoting active learning, such an activity allows students to divulge what they already know about the topic and what they do not (Frederick, 2000: 101–5). Booth points out that using a brainstorming approach, especially during the first session with a new class, can help to generate the sense of ownership and community on which critical discussion depends (Booth, 2003: 95).

Polling students

The idea here is that students are asked to vote on key questions that arise during lectures. The vote could follow from a class debate

(Stearns, 1993: 102; Frederick, 2000: 106–8). It might also arise from the lecturer presenting possible responses to a question he or she poses. For example, at the University of Central Lancashire, a course unit entitled *Privies, Privacy and Privation: the House and Home in Lancashire, c1600–1939*, incorporates a slide presentation analysing the design characteristics of Victorian working-class houses. Students are shown slides of two-up two-down dwellings and asked which rooms had fireplaces, when, as indicated by chimney pot numbers, only two fireplaces per house were provided. Logically, as a moment's thought will show, the students have six combinations from which to choose. Each possibility is offered to them in turn for voting purposes, adding a 'don't know' choice as well. In practice, and understandably, the students tend to choose the two downstairs rooms, but, in fact, the normal pattern, as further slides reveal, is for the downstairs and upstairs front rooms to have been equipped with fireplaces. The vote results offer further scope for interactive discussion between teacher and taught.

Drawing on students' own experiences
Frederick provides an interesting example of this approach using the autobiography of Two-legging, a Crow warrior. He explains how his students listed similarities and differences between heroic acts that they and Two-legging undertook in order to determine aspects 'unique to Crow culture, their own, and universal human qualities' (Frederick, 2001: 113–22).

Despite the criticisms made of them, it is quite evident from this discussion that lectures have a major role to play in undergraduate history teaching. Yet it is equally evident that careful thought is required as to how they are presented if students' best interests are to be served. The indications are that history lectures are at their most effective when they are lively in presentation, rooted in scholarship and incorporate ways to involve students actively in the learning process.

Preparing lectures

Stearns gives useful advice on preparing history lectures (Stearns: 1996, 103–6) which reflects that given in the general education literature (Brown and Race, 2002: 125–8, for example). Undertaken properly, the task is complex and demanding, but three considerations are particularly important, each of which can be briefly rehearsed.

The first concerns the structure of lectures. Provision of an outline framework for each lecture conveyed to students helps them to follow the course of the lecture and to organise note taking. How full this outline should be is debatable, though it may be that, with progression issues in mind, fuller outlines are offered in the earlier than in later stages of study. But very full outlines might raise concern about spoon-feeding students, encouraging them to rely on the information being given to them rather than encouraging them to gather material for themselves. Clearly, a balance must be struck here.

The well-tried tripartite division into introduction, main body and conclusion provides an obvious structure for a lecture, with the main body being subdivided into key themes. Such a structure allows opportunity to demonstrate to students how they might structure their assignments, highlighting the importance of handling introductions and conclusions in appropriate ways. The introduction might briefly recapitulate what has gone before, perhaps with a reminder of the course unit objectives, as well as outlining the main points to be covered in the lecture. The conclusion might draw out the main points established during the lecture, linking them to the major themes and outcomes of the course unit as a whole.

The second consideration in lecture preparation concerns the amount of material to be included. Stearns reasons that, within a 50-minute history lecture, three or four basic points that are 'diversely illustrated and sometimes subtly repeated' is sufficient (Stearns, 1996: 104). Accordingly, only about ten minutes or so will be available to cover each main theme in the lecture. It must be remembered, too, that the greater the amount of coverage that is planned for the main part of the lecture, the less time there is to develop key points in depth as well as to allow for interactive elements, planned or otherwise, and to introduce and conclude adequately.

The point about not including too much in a lecture extends to interactive elements. Thus, unintentionally or otherwise, student questioning cannot always be relied on to remain strictly within the main line of discussion, while organising group work and obtaining responses from each group can easily prove more time-consuming than anticipated. Indeed, the inclusion of active learning elements can be seen to inhibit the ability to cover the required amount of material. Yet this view raises the question of what the required amount of material actually is, bearing in mind that lectures are not intended to cover everything the student will need to learn. In part, the issue may be seen to revolve around the nature of the course units being planned, with those that are broadly based in content terms perhaps being seen to provide less opportunity for incorporating active learning elements than those dealing with topics in depth.

One other major consideration in lecture preparation concerns the way in which the lecture is to be delivered. To prevent the 'deadly effect on an audience', as Stearns puts it (Stearns, 1996: 95), preparing copious lecture notes and simply reading them out should be avoided. Stearns observes that the use of minimal, well-organised notes facilitates contact with students, including eye contact, as the lecture progresses. Such notes, which might be displayed to the students as the lecture progresses, are often used effectively as prompts for the lecturer.

How far oral delivery is to be accompanied by the use of visual aids is a major consideration. The old pedagogical adage that 'one in the eye is worth two in the ear' is a crude generalisation, but at least it makes the crucial point that providing visual images alongside oral commentary can have a strong impact, both assisting and reinforcing understanding. Presenting historical data as graphs and features of historical buildings in slide form provide examples. In some cases, it is possible and desirable to build entire history lectures around visuals, each one of which as it is displayed perhaps being used as a prompt instead of notes. Furthermore, there is much to be said in favour of the view expressed by Larry J. Easley that bringing a wider variety of visual, audio and computerised methods into the history classroom will form a bridge to more interactive teaching approaches (Easley, 1998: 70).

The location of interactive elements needs thought in relation to aiding student's concentration. One approach is to include such elements towards the middle of the lecture when concentration may be thought likely to flag, though they may easily be included more frequently by means of inviting questions and comments. What must be borne in mind, however, is that very few students will be able to ask questions within the time span of a single lecture unless the class size is small. And it is likely that the same, more confident students will be involved in questioning as the lecture programme proceeds, unless steps are taken to encourage the more reticent without embarrassing them. One way of doing so is to build an element of group work into the lecture series, though not necessarily into every lecture, on the grounds that students will be more prepared to speak in small groups than in large groups.

What is clear from the considerations outlined above is that the preparation of history lectures requires a good deal of careful thought that must be firmly rooted in the learning needs of students. In order to pitch the lecture at an appropriate level, account must be taken of their likely levels of understanding – which may often be lower than anticipated – and of how their understanding will be enhanced by experiencing the lecture. The challenge is not only to engage student interest at the outset, but also to maintain it as the lecture proceeds, if necessary making adjustments to the planned approach. While lecturer enthusiasm is of great importance in achieving these ends, so too is the inclusion of interactive approaches, the extent and form of which may vary considerably from lecture to lecture.

SEMINARS AND GROUP WORK

Since seminars are the other major means by which history undergraduates are taught, the possibilities and problems they offer also need our attention. As with lectures, using them in ways that are best calculated to aid student learning is by no means easy to accomplish, and careful planning and execution are again required.

Advantages of seminars

The types of advantage that seminar and group work can bring are neatly encapsulated in the *History Benchmarking Statement*. In the context of deepening students' understanding and developing their oral communication skills, the *Statement* suggests that such teaching:

- encourages a critical, as well as a self-critical but tolerant, approach to historical discussion and builds students' self-confidence;
- improves students' abilities to:
  - marshal historical evidence;
  - summarize historical arguments;
  - think quickly on their feet;
  - communicate articulately and persuasively with others;

– recognize the value of working closely with others. (QAA, *History*, 2000: 5)

As is evident from the list, the advantages are as much rooted in promoting social and personal qualities as they are intellectual qualities, especially by bringing students and staff together in a way that encourages interaction and informality, a consideration that has profound implications for the approaches adopted. Thus notions of working closely with others imply the inclusion of opportunities for students to undertake some seminar activities working in pairs or small groups rather than as whole groups, while developing a self-critical approach to discussion suggests the need to incorporate reflective elements, perhaps concerned with how and why students' views might have changed as a result of their studies. It is also evident from the list that seminars and small-group teaching focus on enhancing students' understanding rather than on the transmission of knowledge, giving them great potential for promoting in-depth learning.

There are, of course, concerns about students being required to speak in seminar situations, particularly if, as Jennifer Rogers and others have suggested, evidence is lacking to link participation in discussion with learning achievement (Rogers, 2001: 221). And investigation by Moust and associates among a group of health science students adds a different dimension to this issue. The results they obtained failed to demonstrate any relationship between the students' achievement and their participation as measured by the number of utterances made in group discussion. A possible explanation, they suggest, is that those students who do not participate in group discussion, or who do so to a limited extent, may 'elaborate as much as those who do participate, without verbalising their elaborations to the same extent as the latter'. They conclude that 'not only the talkers benefit from their efforts, but also the listeners, because both groups are cognitively active' (Moust et al., 1987: ch. 13).

Difficulties in achieving seminar advantages

Achieving the advantages that seminars offer is by no means straight-forward, with several inhibiting factors arising. Key among them are:

Participants' shortcomings

With reference to history seminars, John Cannon advances three considerations under this heading. His first point is that, compared with lecturing, leading seminars makes more demands on the teacher, with the result that mistakes are more easily made. Of particular concern in this respect are intervening too soon and speaking too much, both of which bring the risk of killing off discussion. Secondly, he suggests, 'an ideal seminar discussion depends upon rough parity of knowledge, which is hard to attain in universities'. At issue here is not only the difficulty of ensuring that all students prepare themselves adequately for seminars, but also problems of getting students to criticise each other's contributions. Cannon's third point is that seminars rely on inexperienced people to carry out the bulk of the discussion. Accordingly, if the introductory paper is not well focused or of an appropriate length, it can prove a delicate matter to take remedial action without embarrassing the student concerned (Cannon, 1984: 21).

Perceptions of the purposes that seminars fulfil

In this context, Light and Cox point to the dangers of taking too limited a view. For instance, seminars might be seen primarily as a means of helping to ensure that students understand the material that has been covered in lectures, perhaps with the tutor asking questions of them. But to take such a view misses other opportunities for students to benefit from seminar work, especially in terms of expressing their own views. Moreover, there can be missed opportunity for tutors to benefit from seminar discussion, not least in discovering how students are responding in general to the educational experiences they are receiving (Light and Cox, 2001: 116–18).

The growing size of seminar groups

Research by John Davis (Kingston University) and Patrick Salmon (Newcastle University) reveals that, in many British higher education institutions, the size of undergraduate history seminars had reached between 15 and 30 students by the end of the 1990s, representing an increase of between five and ten students (Davis and Salmon, 2000: 125, 131 and 135). Accordingly, how to ensure that seminars meet the ideals of all students participating, and do so to a significant degree, have become matters of increasing anxiety. Of particular concern is to prevent the seminar from becoming similar to a lecture, with a high degree of tutor dominance occurring.

Examples of seminar approaches

Historians have noted a variety of techniques that can be used to deal with large seminar groups, most involving the creation of smaller groups within them (Davis and Salmon, 2000: 127–8; Barker et al., 2000: 66; Booth, 2003: 97–8 and 104–5). They include:

- fish-bowls, which involve small-group discussion observed by the rest of the class;
- student role play;
- presentations by groups or individuals, with tutor involvement;
- pyramiding/'buzz' groups, where a small group discusses ideas and then shares them with others;
- syndicates, where students work in parallel groups;
- formal debate, with teams arguing a particular line;
- creating texts, such as propaganda statements;
- workshops, with students undertaking a collaborative project.

Examples of how these approaches are used include:

Role play

One of the simulation exercises devised by W. Gregory Monahan of Eastern Oregon University centres on the German election of 1932, using characters who seek action – the representatives of various political parties – and other characters who are able to act, including faction leaders (Monahan, 2000: 12). At San Diego State University, Eve Kornfeld has used role-playing debates for both pedagogical reasons (in that adopting a role can free timid or shy students from their normal inhibitions) and for academic reasons (particularly that of helping students to appreciate the complex nature of history and historical interpretation). Varying degrees of sophistication are incorporated into these debates, with, for example, students on a survey course unit simply taking a Federalist or an Antifederalist position, while upper-level students, either as groups or individuals, might adopt the stances of particular characters, such as Madison, Hamilton or Mason (Kornfeld, 1993: 147–51).

Advocates of role playing point to a number of requirements for a successful outcome, including careful preparation, allowing sufficient time (Monahan takes a minimum of three, 50-minute class periods per simulation), strong direction from the tutor and an emphasis on debriefing. And Kornfeld reasons that debates are best held towards the end of a course unit to give students time to familiarise themselves with the material. It may be noted, too, that requiring students to adopt views differing from those they normally hold can add to the effectiveness of role-playing activity (Booth, 2003: 98).

Pyramiding

George Preston of Bath College reports success in encouraging students to speak in seminars by means of 'pyramiding'. Using this approach, students discuss a topic or task for ten minutes in pairs, then for a further ten minutes in groups of four, and finally in plenary session. Interestingly, Preston allows five minutes at the start of seminars for students to work on their own, 'so as to give the more reticent an opportunity to prepare their contribution' (Preston, 1996: 119–22).

Syndicates

This approach can take many forms using various types of primary and secondary evidence. For example, Peter Davies and associates describe a seminar in which small groups of students identify and discuss gaps in numerical data relating to the 1992 General Election in Britain. Plenary sessions are used to introduce the seminar and to fill the gaps, as well as for further discussion (Davies et al., 2000: 115–18).

Workshops

At the University of Central Lancashire, in seminars on a third-level history course unit dealing with Lancashire's industrialisation, small groups of four or five students investigate limited amounts of printed parish register data to determine occupational structures in different parts of the county. The results they obtain are written on the board as each group reports its findings. Discussion is focused on comparing the results and assessing the value and limitations of the evidence used.

Group presentations

George Preston describes an approach which involves small groups of students working together on a topic over several weeks before they make a presentation. Work allocations made by the students to draw on their particular strengths could mean that not all members of the group are as equally involved in actually giving the presentation, an approach that can help any group members who are anxious about so doing (Preston, 1996: 124–5). In contrast, the approach taken by Victoria Gunn required small groups of students to prepare and present mini essays on topics received in advance. Each group member contributed a paragraph, which had to have an agreed critical stance or hypothesis (Gunn, 2000).

By no means all the comments that higher education historians have made about seminars are concerned with teaching large groups. Other practices they report are equally instructive in helping to plan successful seminars, as the following examples reveal.

Multi-session seminars

A seminar might occupy several sessions. Thus the Salem Witch Trial seminar mounted by Simons and LaPotin at the State University of New York involved students in intensive investigation of primary evidence over four seminars. During the first, they studied differing interpretations of the trial, as well as an information pack comprising 15 primary extracts, and then discussed the material working in small groups. The following week they were shown an edited version of a film (*Three Sovereigns for Sarah*) depicting the trial. In week three, the two tutors debated the topic in front of the students giving conflicting interpretations before allowing open discussion. In the fourth session, the students formulated their own interpretations based on all the work already undertaken (Simons and LaPotin, 1992: 52–7).

Encouraging students to prepare for seminars

In grappling with this perennial problem, Preston finds it useful to spend some seminar time discussing the material that will inform the following week's deliberations. Reading might be allocated to students, perhaps with a variety of works being set to allow different perspectives to be explored, or students might be left to find their own material, an approach that has obvious possibilities in terms of progression and differentiation (Preston, 1996: 121). The nature and amount of material students are expected to read can also be crucial in encouraging their interest. Thus instead of relying solely on large chunks of written material, discussion based on the analysis of visual, oral and physical evidence can be usefully introduced. And Stearns reports success with frequently repeated homework exercises that guide students in focusing on such techniques as comparing social, cultural, political and economic practices within different countries (Stearns, 2000).

Students helping each other

This commonly arises when students make joint presentations in seminars, though there are variations around the theme. At the University of Southern Maine, for example, Diana Long breaks students into smaller groups in her *Reference, Research and Writing* course unit, but she also requires each student to choose a partner. The partner acts as editor and commentator for research papers that are jointly presented to the whole group towards the end of the semester. In part, the editor's function is to keep the paper within manageable bounds and that of commentator to help stimulate discussion.

It is evident from our discussion in this section that, just as with lecturing, there is much concern among higher education historians to develop more active approaches to learning in seminars, and that, in so doing, a varied range of innovative techniques is being applied. Again the emphasis is one of moving away from the lecturer as the source and dispenser of knowledge to the lecturer as facilitator of student learning. Implied in such an approach is not only the notion of students assuming greater involvement in, and ownership of, the learning process, but also that lecturers adapt their teaching methods so that, overtly at least, they come to play a less dominant role in seminar proceedings. Crucial here is the need to encourage students to speak by making them feel secure about doing so. Often this end can be achieved by division into small groups for part of the seminar. But there is also a need to be encouraging about the responses students may make in plenary session, finding at least something to praise even in the less penetrating observations that are offered. Preston's idea of responding 'Yes and . . .' rather than 'Yes but . . .' is helpful in this regard (Preston, 1996: 125). And giving hints and clues can also prove highly effective in provoking a desired response. Equally, there is a need to be firm with students who try to dominate proceedings, especially by ensuring that others who wish to respond are given the opportunity to do so and, over a series of seminars, by encouraging the more reticent to contribute, perhaps asking them where they stand on an issue once it has been discussed.

Using ICT in undergraduate history teaching

The *History Benchmarking Statement* says relatively little about the role of ICT within undergraduate programmes, even though the use of ICT constitutes one of the most significant changes in teaching and learning in the last decade or so and is likely to have a growing and marked impact. In the section of the *Statement* dealing with teaching and learning, comment is confined to the recommendation that, among several other types of provision, history departments should consider the use of ICT in 'learning or analysis' and that, as part of the range of assignments made available to them, students might undertake C and IT projects (QAA, *History*, 2000: 3 and 5). That undergraduate history programmes do not offer students the opportunity to engage with ICT, however minimally, seems unlikely, though the extent to which students should be expected to engage with it is another matter and one that is of growing importance as regards curriculum planning.

General approaches

In making its recommendations on ICT, the *Benchmarking Statement* reflects Donald Spaeth's observation that computers can be used to support learning and teaching in two ways. The first way he terms the 'workshop' approach, where 'students learn to use general purpose programs to explore and analyse historical data derived from primary sources'. Database and spreadsheet programs seem to be used particularly in this respect. The other way he identifies is that using the computer as an instructional medium which supplements or replaces other means of instruction, lectures and seminars among them. The essays and accompanying source material that form the History Courseware Consortium's hypermedia tutorials, available on CD-ROM or via the Internet, provide a good example (Wissenburg, 1996). (The Consortium formed part of the Teaching and Learning Technology Project or TLTP, a government-funded initiative dating from the early 1990s aimed at enhancing teaching efficiency in a wide range of subjects through the use of ICT.) As Spaeth points out, though, the use of such hypermedia packages, which allow students to work in their own way through various types of source material as well as to explore historical data, is bridging the two approaches (Spaeth, 1996: 155–6).

The focus of our discussion is on the use of ICT as an instructional medium. The reasoning is twofold. Firstly, the workshop approach is well covered in existing texts (Lloyd-Jones and Lewis, 2000: Schick, 1990; Trinkle, 1998). Secondly, the use of on-line teaching techniques is being increasingly reported by higher education historians and to review a selection of their recent contributions enables the kinds of approach they adopt to be illustrated and the learning and teaching issues that arise to be considered.

Approaches to on-line history teaching

The overview provided by Guinevere Glasfurd and Michael Winstanley of how the Internet might be used in teaching and learning provides a useful starting point (Table 5.2). As the table demonstrates, the use of ICT as an instructional medium offers rich opportunities for developing approaches to teaching history undergraduates, especially with active and independent forms of learning in mind. Not only do students have massive amounts of additional resource material made available to them, albeit of varying use value, but they can also explore new means of communicating with one another and of presenting their findings. Of course, effective exploitation of on-line facilities can pose substantial challenges for both teacher and taught, not least in terms of the time investment that may be required to develop the necessary skills and understanding. Yet, as is evident from discussion in the remaining sections of this chapter, some historians believe that the effort involved yields worthwhile results at undergraduate level, especially when on-line approaches are used to supplement more traditional forms of teaching and learning rather than to replace them.

Teaching and learning in the digital age project

To gain some appreciation of how the types of approach noted in the Glasfurd and Winstanley list are being developed in undergraduate history programmes, our discussion turns first to the Teaching and Learning in the Digital Age Project. Sponsored by the American

TABLE 5.2 *Uses of the Internet in learning and teaching*

Internet use	Example
Encouraging active and independent learning	On-line hypertext lectures, with choices of pathways through content
Testing ideas and encouraging critical reasoning	Evaluation of on-line resources
Communicating within and beyond the seminar group	On-line discussion groups
Encouraging subject exploration, information retrieval and network literacy	Effective searching of networked information
Developing creativity with text, pictures and sound	Creating student websites
Developing presentational skills via on-line publishing	Considering how to communicate information via the Internet
Providing understanding between subject areas	Providing links between disciplines
Enabling differentiation	Using hypertext to provide pathways with different learning styles
Opening up learning opportunities to students in under-represented sectors	(Glasfurd and Winstanley, 2000: 89–90)

Historical Association (AHA), this project has funded higher education historians to develop ways of using digitised primary sources in teaching surveys on American and world history, a key outcome being the provision of models for others to follow. Some of the models offer 'post-hole' opportunities, providing further examples of how in-depth learning can be achieved in teaching broad survey course units, a matter raised in Chapter 3. In the words of the AHA, the 'topics of the models vary, as does the technological sophistication' (AHA, *Survey Course*).

Accompanying the models are short reflective essays written by participants in the project. These essays are designed to 'allow the user to see how faculty have thought about the challenges involved in using the Internet and primary sources in their courses' and to explain what worked for them and what did not. To give some idea of the flavour of the essays, and of the considerable use value they have, two examples may be considered briefly.

Mary Beth Emmerichs, at the University of Wisconsin-Sheboygan, approaches her teaching on the basis that 'students learn more, retain more, and understand more when they are directly and actively involved in the learning process'. She describes how, in teaching the course unit *US from the Civil War to the Present*, she posts a set of documents on her website each week and asks the students to read them before they next meet. She notes how group discussions of the documents have come to reduce the time she spends on lecturing. One of the benefits she identifies arising from her approach is that students e-mail her frequently with queries relating to the material and as a consequence, she observes, 'we finally have a way to let the shy students express themselves without fear'. However, her experience is that some documents work better than others, with students preferring short articles or those that include visual material. They also favour documents that contain material which 'rarely shows up in the text book', such as Alabama's Literacy Test or the Jim Crow Laws, awareness of which makes the civil rights movement more real for the students. Perhaps the best measure of the success of the approach is that, in the tutor's words: 'Attendance is great, class response is growing . . .' (Emmerichs, *Essay*).

A project undertaken by Daniel Kallgren at the University of Winconsin-Marinette provides the second example. His aim has been to incorporate into a 'second half' United States history survey unit four research-orientated 'modules'. These enable students to study aspects of American society in depth, using various types of web-based primary material. In general, he is pleased with the way the approach works in practice, although he has found that the students dislike the open-ended projects he assigns, preferring those with clear instructions and outcomes. More positively, the students see the role of technology as beneficial because it allows them to deploy their 'Internet savvy' while giving them access to sources that are not available in the library. Moreover, Kallgren has found, technology fosters group work and works well in bringing together a variety of source material – text, images and sound – in a single place (Kallgren, *Essay*).

Coursework for History Implementation Consortium (CHIC)

This project, mounted in British higher education institutions between 1998 and 2001 and sponsored by the Higher Education Funding Council, gives further insights into the way in which ICT can be used as a learning medium in undergraduate history programmes. The remit of the project was both to evaluate the implementation of ICT-based learning and teaching innovations and to disseminate the findings within the higher education sector so as to support change. The project managers worked with 14 higher education history departments in the UK, the first phase concentrating on the TLTP History Courseware Consortium's packages. In phase two, the strategy focused on the development of websites that are specific to particular course units and that bring together student support materials with learning resources. In this way, the project managers sought to promote the creation of websites that offer 'a holistic learning experience, which promotes co-operation, engagement and involvement'. Rather than using ICT within existing teaching approaches, the belief is that ICT should 'help align learning, teaching and assessment' (Hall and Harding, 2001: vii–ix; see also Hall, 2003).

Again, a couple of examples can be cited to illustrate the sort of approaches adopted in phase two of the CHIC project. One is an on-line course unit developed by Graham Rogers at Edge Hill College, Ormskirk (near Liverpool). Using WebCT as its virtual learning environment, the unit is based on an early eighteenth-century enclosure act for Croston, a village near Preston in Lancashire. Not only are students able to use a range of primary material to undertake in-depth investigation into the impact of an enclosure act on the economy and society of a local community, but they also have a means of evaluating the interpretations that historians make about the process of enclosure more generally. Underpinning successful implementation of the module has been the notion that, for the most part, 'the role of the teacher must change from "expert" instructor to facilitator, guide, problem-solver and partner', so that the learning agenda becomes common property. Thus one of the major objectives has been that of 'encouraging purposeful, productive and collaborative engagement between learners, and between tutor and learners'. Key to achieving this objective have been weekly group seminars, which serve as an anchor point of the course, and on-line discussions between students which allow them to post their thoughts and invite responses. At the outset, the seminar series sets out an agreed learning agenda and because, subsequently, the focus is on issues arising with regard to the on-line seminar tasks, considerable immediacy is achieved. The tutor's role extends to that of mediator with regard to on-line exchanges, and that of instructor in order to define 'the context and framework of ideas within the programme . . .' The website is seen not merely as a 'deposit for resources' but also as creating a learning environment that guides students through a structured investigation. To this end, on-line 'task work' is provided. Altogether there are five linked tasks, each self-contained as far as resources and learning objectives are concerned, but with one building on another (Rogers, 2001: 4–5; Hall et al., 2001: 81–95).

The second example demonstrates the approach taken by Jeremy Boulton of the University of Newcastle, who uses the Web to assist in delivering a first-level module *Death and Dying in Early Modern England*. Instead of the 'two lectures a week route', one weekly lecture is replaced by a web-based, interactive workshop. Thus, as in the case of the Croston enclosure module, traditional teaching is by no means entirely abandoned. To support the workshop activities, much use is made of secondary and primary material readily available on the Web and this is supplemented by locally generated resources and by a small amount of customised TLTP material. The students are divided into groups for the workshops and the groups prepare reports on each workshop task, as well as constructing a website to illustrate a module theme. The reports are transmitted to the module leader, in this case using Blackboard rather than WebCT software as a virtual learning environment. Students also take a weekly on-line quiz to test their understanding of the preceding week's lecture (Boulton, 2001: Hall et al., 2001: 76–80; Boulton, 2000).

Advantages of on-line teaching approaches

The experience of using on-line approaches has enabled historians to identify several key advantages that arise from incorporating these elements in their teaching. The advantages are seen to lie principally in facilitating student learning, though the question arises as to how far their realisation might be achieved without the use of on-line provision.

Flexibility in learning

A clear advantage identified in the Newcastle project that arises from including a web-based component in history teaching concerns the flexibility students gain as to when they work and the pace at which they work. A regular timetable slot is made available each week for the workshops to take place, but the evidence obtained so far is that fewer than half the students make use of it, with various times of the week being preferred. That weekly responses that have to be made to the tutor circumscribe the degree to which students can take advantage of flexible learning, as does the extent to which the web-based component within course units replaces traditional forms of teaching. Yet the issue of how much flexibility students should be allowed with regard to on-line learning is a real one.

As has been demonstrated, a feature of the approaches adopted in the Edge Hill and Newcastle modules is that the learning experience is paced for students to a considerable extent. How far a looser rein might be deemed advantageous depends on the objectives in mind. It may be that, as in the examples cited, a different form of learning experience is favoured, which is no less labour intensive than traditional forms of tuition and which extends learning flexibility within a fairly traditional teaching framework. On the other hand, web-based learning may be seen as a means of offering a much greater degree of flexibility, with an associated reduction in face-to-face contact time between teachers and taught. Such an eventuality arises with distance learning, of course. Similarly, on the basis that a tutor devotes a set number of hours to teaching a module, a trade off might be made between reducing contact time through on-line provision and offering course units on campus more than once during an academic year. The rationale here is that students may appreciate, and be able to benefit from, having to respond to tutors less frequently than on a weekly basis and having the flexibility that repeated course units can offer in designing their programmes of study. There is also the point that the notion of flexibility can extend to the content students cover. Thus, in his United States survey course unit, Michael Goldberg of the University of Washington gives his students 'numerous opportunities to explore stories that interest them on their own and report back to the class about where they have been . . .'. In this way, the scope of the unit is broadened and the problem of what content to include and what to leave out is eased (Goldberg, 1996).

Promoting in-depth learning

Web-based approaches are seen to promote learning in greater depth where they reinforce traditional teaching. Tellingly, in this respect, both the Edge Hill and Newcastle projects have reported that, in many instances, deeper learning has been more evident in on-line bulletin messages than in module assignments, with the better quality assignments drawing on the insights provided by the bulletin material. A key factor at work here may be that the approaches employed in the projects, both through group activities and high levels of tutor support, generate active learning responses from students, or at least opportunities for them, on a more sustained basis than would be the case with conventional seminars. Yet students achieving high levels in on-line discussions do not necessarily transfer their deeper understanding to essay work and their achievements may be under-rewarded if their on-line seminars contributions carry only a small proportion of the available marks (Rogers, 2004).

Quality of discussion

Further insights into the benefits arising from on-line seminars are provided by E.L. Skip Knox of Boise State University. He has developed on-line course units that are taught entirely by computer, except for an initial live meeting as a scene setter. In relation to his on-line teaching, he has unexpectedly found that 'the most significant reward is the improved quality of class discussion'. He finds this is so for several reasons, which may be summarised as follows:

- The students are better prepared, since they come to the discussion having read and having something to say.
- The students can be observed thinking as they try to answer one another's questions and to respond to the tutor's comments. The tutor can see where they understand and where they do not and how they try to work things out.
- Tutor responses made to matters raised by individual students in conventional teaching can be relayed to all.
- Discussion is not confined to a limited time period, so that issues students do not understand very well can be more fully rehearsed.
- No student can dominate discussion, while each can contribute at length, taking the time needed to formulate thought.
- Students have access to source materials during discussion and can cite them.
- Every student gets a turn to contribute.
- Several students can respond to a point simultaneously, so that none of them is put off by having to wait and risk the discussion moving on before their contribution can be made (Skip Knox, *Rewards*).

Such observations reinforce the idea that greater opportunities are provided for active learning to take place on-line, in the context of students making contributions from more informed standpoints and with more time to reflect. Furthermore, as T. Mills Kelly of George Mason University, Virginia, has suggested, given that student communication is nowadays mediated by technology to an unprecedented degree, students may actually prefer to use on-line approaches as a means of enhancing collaborative learning (Mills Kelly, *East European*). And students' learning might also be enhanced by on-line approaches, because their contributions can be used to frame the content of class seminars. Thus John McClymer of Assumption College remarks that he is always able to discover what his students know and what is causing them concern from the on-line notes he requires them to make (McClymer, *Inquiry*).

Resource provision

A further advantage of web-based approaches, mentioned with regard to the use of ICT in primary-source-based work undertaken by second-level history students at Glasgow University, is the availability and diversity of computer-based resources. The CHIC evaluation report on the Glasgow project concludes:

> *Not only were the materials more easily available than books from the library, but they provided a stimulating range of sources which would not otherwise have been available. Students enjoyed being able to access images, facsimiles and sound as well as texts, and being able to compare contrasting as well as contradictory evidence.*
>
> (McCormack, 2001: 103)

Moreover, websites can have high use value in enabling students to revisit visual and other materials shown to them during lectures and seminars. The *History Around You: Approaches to Industrial Archaeology* module offered on-line at the University of Central Lancashire is built around some two hundred visuals, mainly showing the physical remains of past industrial activity. Before conversion to web-based form, students could see the visuals only fairly fleetingly during lectures and lecture discussions but now have them available for further reference, as do other students who might find them relevant. It is too early in the life of this project to determine how far such an advantage is being realised. However, Mills Kelly finds that high proportions of his students do return to view the web-based primary sources he has provided for them, leading him to anticipate that, as good historians do, they consider 'many possible meanings of their sources before finally committing themselves to one interpretation' (Mills Kelly, 2000: 3–4).

Drawbacks of on-line learning

The introduction of on-line learning is by no means cost free and historians making use of it have had to come to terms with several perceived drawbacks. These drawbacks relate both to the preparation of on-line elements and their implementation.

Development time

From a departmental point of view, developing e-learning packages can absorb a great deal of academic time, in preparing and updating materials, in acquiring the necessary skills to do so and, at least initially, in devising new approaches to teaching the module. And opportunity costs may be deemed considerable if funding is not available to support training and development work, and still to be on the debit side even if it is. In the light of his own experience, Jeremy Boulton is to an extent reassuring on these matters, however.

> The administrative load for the course leader proved heavier than for an equivalent module, although this was in part due to higher 'start-up' costs. The second year the course ran, the administrative load was significantly lighter, although some time was spent 'bolting' the existing website onto the new course management software Blackboard.

Boulton notes, too, that the techniques developed and tested in his module could be transferred to other modules (Boulton, 2001, *CBL course*). Undeniably, heavy initial demands arise in adopting on-line approaches, though they can be reduced by curbing ambition in the early stages with a view to achieving greater sophistication over time.

Impersonal nature of web-based teaching

Since both the Edge Hill and Newcastle projects are used on campus and permit regular contact between teacher and taught, anxieties that are often expressed about the impersonal nature of web-based teaching are lessened. Moreover, that students work regularly together in small groups provides an alternative focus for face-to-face discussion. As one of the students taking the Newcastle module remarked: 'You would think that because you were working on computers that it would be less personal, but because you are working in a group you can actually "bond" and keep in touch by group discussion' (Boulton, 2001: 3). On-line discussion provides points of contact, too, of course, with tutor feedback being identified as one of the most important benefits arising from on-line working. As an Edge Hill student observed, 'the tutor's responses to the bulletins has given people a lot more confidence and caused them to think a lot more deeply than they would have in the normal lecture and seminar' (Hall et al., 2001: 92). Clearly, strategies can be put in place to reduce the extent of any tendency towards impersonal teaching, especially as far as on-campus provision is concerned.

But the point can be taken further, as is evident from the experience of Skip Knox. Again, putting forward an unexpected line of argument, he suggests that an 'on-line environment is more intimate than the live classroom'. He seeks to explain his position by comparing the one with the other.

Early in my on-line teaching I was asked what were the demographics of the class. I had to laugh because I had no idea how old my students were, their age, race, appearance or even, in some cases, their gender. I was at the same time teaching a live class on the same subject. Those students I knew by sight. I could have estimated their average age and so on. But I did not know the students in my live class as individuals. My only contact with them was a few moments once a week when they might speak up in class, and their exams. In the on-line class, on the other hand, I could say in some detail what sort of students those people were. I could tell which ones understood how to do research and how to do evidence. I knew which ones had a religious prejudice, which ones tended to reductionism, and so on. In short, I knew my virtual students far better than I knew my live students.

This closeness to the students as students is what I value most. In part it is like having a semester-long conversation with each student, but they are conversations in which every student can participate and from which every student can benefit. For a discipline such as ours, anchored in texts and in ideas, this seems to me to be the best teaching medium ever invented.

(Skip Knox, *The Rewards*)

Probably few higher education historians would be prepared to forego face-to-face contact with students to such a degree, let alone be convinced that on-line tuition is generally more intimate than conventional teaching, especially when formal and informal contact with students is taken into account. And fears about providing a lack of opportunity to develop oral skills would certainly arise. But Skip Knox's stance is a sobering reminder that there are students we teach on a regular basis about whom we know all too little in terms of their educational abilities and the learning difficulties they encounter.

Extent of web-based provision

A further problem, and a vexed one, that faces website developers concerns the amount of material that, from an educational point of view, websites for history undergraduates should contain. Skip Knox maintains that the 60,000 or so words that characterise one of his on-line modules, which comprises 15, 20-page lectures, might be doubled in size and still not constitute an excessive work load for his students (Skip Knox, *The Rewards*).

In making decisions on the matter, much depends on the proportion of course unit content that is delivered in web-based form and what range of tasks the students are expected to undertake besides reading web pages. Even so, there are indications from the literature that too much emphasis can be given to 'supply-side' considerations at the expense of those on the 'demand side'. One of the great temptations in developing websites for course units is to keep adding to them in the hope, and probably the expectation, that students will benefit. Is this a case of misplaced kindness, however, the effect being to add to students' burdens in unnecessary ways? Might there be a danger of spoon-feeding students and, by thinking too much in terms of the quantity of material rather than its quality, risk promoting surface rather than deep learning? And, particularly as far as the more conscientious students are concerned, is more being demanded of them than of students who are taught in more conventional ways and, if so, will the overall quality of their work diminish? Maybe to express such fears is to over-react. Yet students' comments with regard to the quantities of on-line material they are faced with is not altogether reassuring. Thus, in the first evaluation of his on-line provision, Jeremy Boulton found 'that respondents mostly objected to the amount of work set in the weekly workshops' (Boulton, 2000, *Evaluation*), while

Roberta Anderson, reporting on her work at Bath Spa University College, noted that some of her students complained that they did not have enough opportunity to explore the on-line resources fully: one of them remarked that 'you can't pop such materials "into your handbag", and you can't read [them] on a train, bus or in bed' (Anderson, 2001: 7). Perhaps, too, students are coping with what they perceive as large amounts of on-line materials, much of it primary material, by neglecting to use books and articles. One danger here, as T. Mills Kelly points out, is that students may fail to contextualise their studies adequately (Mills Kelly, *Marriage*: 4–5).

Advice on developing web-based teaching

For historians wishing to develop web-based approaches to learning, a good deal of advice has become available from the pioneers. Some of it relates to how the on-line material should be presented, and is well encapsulated in the remarks made by John Dunne of the University of Greenwich in evaluating the use of TLPT materials:

> *As one of our students said: 'Nobody actually likes reading from the screen'. Even some students who called for greater use of Web resources stated their aversion to reading large quantities of text on-line. The web is best used as a hypermedium, which makes best use of links, discussion areas, images, and sources, and minimises text-based provision.*
>
> (Dunne, 2001: 4)

Adding to this point, Anderson remarks that students do not like to read text on screens for long periods of time (Anderson, 2001: 7). As a counter to the problem, Boulton suggests the inclusion of graphics and images as a means of breaking up text (Boulton, 2001: 3). In similar vein, Paula Petrik argues that those visiting websites tend to scan materials, printing out what they want to read later. She continues:

> *Transferring hard copy material directly to the Web without giving some thought to altering its format will exasperate visitors because they will be unable to find the information that they need as quickly as they desire. The solution: chunk the information into bite-sized pieces, use shorter lines (10 [to] 12 words), adopt shorter paragraphs, and employ bulleted lists where it is possible.*
>
> (Petrik, *Mistakes*)

Yet such advice, though helpful, does not negate the point that moving lectures and other details of course units onto the Web will not in itself enhance student learning, since the process is essentially one of delivering information rather than promoting interaction in the learning process (Glasfurd and Winstanley, 2000: 89: Booth, 2003: 123).

To advice about presentational issues in on-line learning can be added that concerning asynchronous discussion groups. A key point is how far these groups should be mediated by tutors, even if intervention can diminish as students gain in confidence and experience (Hall, 2003: 165–6). David Sicilia points out that non-mediated discussion groups are more democratic than mediated ones, but that they can easily spin out of control. Thus some of the discussions he has set in train have elicited comments that are merely assertive and lack an historical basis. Sonja Cameron stresses the crucial importance of the tutor both in planning and implementing on-line discussion, not least making regular on-line contact with students to reassure them that progress is being monitored and that intervention will occur should problems arise. Both authors recommend establishing a code of conduct, or netiquette, in order to formulate appropriate ground rules for discussion (Sicilia, 1998: 78–9; Cameron, 'Online').

Further helpful advice on developing on-line teaching is encapsulated in the comments of Gary J. Kornblith of Oberlin College, Ohio. He believes that even 'klutzy folks' such as himself can succeed with web-based provision and, based on his experience in the field and with particular reference to United States history, he offers a number of highly practical suggestions. These can be summarised as follows.

- Explore what the Web has to offer – visit general history sites as well as those that are more relevant to your specific interests.
- Master the mechanics of posting material on the Web – learn to use a web authoring/editing program, befriend computer support personnel in your own institution and obtain assistance from a web-savvy colleague or student.
- Be creative but not fancy in designing your on-line syllabus – copy and save images from existing websites to enhance the appearance of your web pages, but, with download times in mind, don't incorporate too many pictures.
- Bend the technology to suit your purposes, not vice versa – incorporate links to websites you expect students to use, develop an assignment that requires intensive use of a website, and

encourage technophobic students to recognise the creative opportunities that the use of ICT can offer (Kornblith, 1998: 1447–53)

Adding to Kornblith's point about the nature of assignments, Boulton's advice is to make them as simple as possible. Crucial in this
respect, be argues, is to avoid setting tasks requiring 'major computing
ability or statistical awareness' (Boulton, 2001: 3).

What is quite apparent from these suggestions is that, despite the
problems that will arise and the time that will be taken, historians with
limited knowledge of using the Web for teaching purposes can make
progress, as long as a degree of determination is present and help from
the more knowledgeable is sought and obtained. The use of ICT is not
in general being seen as a replacement for the traditional teaching and
learning experiences provided within history departments. And as
Kornblith has concluded following his conversion to using the Web,
technology has not 'radically transformed my pedagogical objectives
. . .'. It is evident, too, that seeking to introduce ICT elements generates
considerable difficulties of both development and implementation.
Even so, the indications are that using ICT as a learning and teaching
medium is being greeted with enthusiasm by a growing band of
higher education historians. Furthermore, despite the reservations
they may have, they see on-line learning as yielding considerable
benefits to their students, not least in terms of enriching the learning
experience.

CONCLUSION

A key point to emerge from our discussion in this chapter is that while
there is no single way to teach history students, or for them to learn,
an important part of the process is understanding the needs and
abilities that they have as individual learners. In this, developing
active approaches to learning is of major importance. In doing so,
traditional teaching approaches based on lectures and seminars retain
their significance, though since opportunities for generating active
learning are probably stronger in the latter than the former, some shift
in emphasis between them might be thought desirable. Furthermore,
the indications that active, deep learning can and does take place when
on-line seminar techniques are used with history undergraduates
raises the possibility that the value of face-to-face seminars can be

overrated. The vital matter here seems to be the manner in which both real and virtual seminars are conducted, with the need to avoid teacher dominance and to provide ways of involving all students, if necessary by non-oral means.

What also emerges from our discussion is that incorporating active learning approaches, while requiring careful planning, need not involve massive inputs of preparation time. Including elements of discussion in lectures and organising small-group discussions in seminars are prime examples. And a varied range of approaches can be adopted in doing so, as a recapitulation of the methods outlined in the chapter demonstrates:

- asking questions;
- answering questions;
- small-group discussion;
- brainstorming;
- polling;
- drawing on students' experiences;
- role playing;
- pyramiding;
- syndicates;
- workshops;
- group presentations.

However, the generation of interactive, on-line learning and teaching presents far greater challenges, which historians, along with colleagues in other subject disciplines, seem generally loathe to take on. In commenting on this matter, Katherine Holden of the University of the West of England notes a tendency among history tutors to see computer-based learning in terms of developing static websites, which simply provide students with additional resources rather than with opportunities for collaborative learning (Holden, 2001: 32). To take the next step certainly requires commitment, perhaps with high opportunity costs, but even to take the first step can represent useful progress and bring substantial advantages to students.

Key references

Blackey, R. (1977) 'New wine in old bottles: revitalising the traditional history lecture', *Teaching History*, 22: 3–25.

Booth, A. (2000) 'Creating a context to enhance student learning in history', in A. Booth and P. Hyland (eds) *The Practice of University History Teaching*. Manchester: Manchester University Press, pp. 31–46.

Frederick, P.J. (1991) 'Active learning in history classes', *Teaching History*, 16: 67–83.

Glasfurd, G. and Winstanley, M. (2000) 'History in cyberspace: challenges and opportunities of internet-based teaching and learning', in A. Booth and P. Hyland (eds) *The Practice of University History Teaching*. Manchester: Manchester University Press, pp. 85–97.

Hall, R. and Harding, D. (eds) (2001) *Chic Project Case Studies: Managing ICT in the Curriculum*. Middlesbrough: University of Teesside.

Hall, R. (2003) 'Forging a Learning Community: A Pragmatic approach to co-operative learning'. *Arts and Humanities in Higher Education*, 2(2): 155–172.

Jenkins, A. (2003) *Linking Research and Teaching in Departments*. York: Learning and Teaching Support Network.

Websites

QAA (2000), *History Benchmark Statement* at http://www.qaa.ac.uk/crntwork/benchmark/history.html

Skip Knox, E.L. *The Rewards of Teaching On-Line* at http://www2.h-net.msu.edu/aha/papers/Knox.html

Cameron, S. *Achieving Online Discussion* at http://hca.ltsn.ac.uk/resources/Briefing_Papers/index.php

6

Assessment issues

INTRODUCTION

This chapter centres on two key issues that arise in assessing the work undertaken by history undergraduates. One concerns the assessment criteria and the statements of attainment (or level descriptors) with which they are associated. The *History Benchmarking Statement* recommends their implementation in British higher education history departments, so we need to consider the problems that arise in their formulation and use, along with the advantages they offer. The way in which assessment criteria are devised is also addressed, drawing on a small-scale survey undertaken by the Student Assessment and Classification Working Group (SACWG).[1] The survey findings amplify aspects of our discussion, as well as provide a checklist of considerations that need to be taken into account when assessment criteria are being devised or refined.

The other key issue to be addressed concerns the types of examination and coursework assignments that are set for history undergraduates. The aims here are to demonstrate something of the wide range of approaches that are adopted and to consider the possibilities and problems they bring. Inclusion of this element in our discussion is again driven by history benchmarking, which recommends that undergraduate history students in Britain should be assessed in a variety of ways, though 'in significant part on their essay-writing skills' (QAA, *History*, 2000: 6). By investigating essay writing alongside other forms of assignment, the case for considering how far undergraduate history students should be assessed by essays can be addressed more meaningfully. The point here is not to advocate blind acceptance of innovation in assessment regimes, but to suggest that, in the changing circumstances in which history undergraduates are being taught, some revision of these regimes will be required if course aims and outcomes are to be achieved successfully.

Discussion is informed by reference to the general literature on assessment matters. This is vast and detailed and does not always make for easy or riveting reading. Nonetheless, in the absence of statements about assessment rationale, it can prove instructive in helping to understand why higher education history departments are taking particular courses of action. And the general literature is also enlightening about the pros and cons associated with various aspects of assessment practice, in terms of both its formative dimension (which advises students) and its summative dimension (which judges student attainment). Additionally, there is useful literature on which to draw that deals specifically with assessing history undergraduates. Though not extensive, this literature does provide valuable insights into current practice as well as raising issues that are highly pertinent to the main themes under consideration. The same can also be said of examples culled from website module descriptors and handbooks, some of which provide a good deal of detail on assessment practices.

A start is made with the question of what is being assessed in history undergraduate programmes. The value of formulating statements of attainment in relation to assessment criteria is stressed, despite the difficulties that arise in their compilation and use. Discussion then moves to the types of assessment that are being employed within history programmes, examining the variety of practice that takes place in order to view essay work in context. In concluding, the two main threads of discussion are drawn together in an attempt to tease out the key considerations involved in devising appropriate assessment regimes for history undergraduates.

ASSESSMENT CRITERIA

Assessment criteria for history programmes arise from statements of programme aims and/or outcomes. Accordingly, they are concerned with enabling judgements to be made about students' skills acquisition as well as their historical knowledge and understanding. Indeed, the skills elements of assessment criteria may commonly have come to the fore in history programmes and are certainly well represented in the examples that have entered the public domain.

In considering the nature of assessment criteria, it is instructive to examine two sets of examples with somewhat different characteristics. One set is taken from the *History Benchmarking Statement*. Linking with

TABLE 6.1   *History benchmarking learning outcomes*

- Command of a substantial body of historical knowledge
- The ability to develop and sustain historical arguments in a variety of literary forms, formulating appropriate questions and utilising evidence
- An ability to read, analyse, and reflect critically and contextually upon historical texts and other source materials
- An appreciation of the complexity of reconstructing the past, the problematic and varied nature of historical evidence
- An understanding of the varieties of approaches to understanding, constructing, and interpreting the past and, where relevant, a knowledge of concepts and theories derived from the humanities and social sciences
- The ability to read, analyse, and reflect critically and contextually upon historical texts and other source materials
- The ability to gather and deploy evidence and data to find, retrieve, sort and exchange new information
- A command of comparative perspectives, which may include the ability to compare the histories of different countries, societies and cultures
- Awareness of continuity and change over extended time spans
- An understanding of the development of history as a discipline and the awareness of different historical methodologies
- An ability to design, research, and present a sustained and independently conceived piece of historical writing
- The ability to address historical problems in depth, involving the use of contemporary sources and advanced secondary literature
- Clarity, fluency, and coherence in written and oral expression
- The ability to work collaboratively and to participate in group discussion
- Competence in specialist skills which are necessary for some areas of historical analysis and understanding, as appropriate.   (QAA, *History*, 2000: 7–8)

the main recommendations that the *Statement* makes about the design of undergraduate history programmes, 16 learning outcomes are suggested that might be used in helping to determine assessment criteria. These are recorded in a somewhat abbreviated form in Table 6.1. The other set, given in Table 6.2, is that devised by the history department at the University of Sydney. The set contains 21 statements divided into the four broad categories of *Content*, *Understanding*, *Independence* and *Style* (Sydney, *Policies*).

The number of criteria

That the number of statements given in the two lists differs at once raises the issue of what the optimum number of statements in

TABLE 6.2 *Assessment criteria for history students at the University of Sydney*

1. *Content*
   a. extent of reading
   b. accuracy of knowledge
   c. breadth and depth of knowledge
   d. relevance of information
   e. sufficiency of evidence and documentation

2. *Understanding*
   a. understanding of problem or project
   b. judgement of significance of material
   c. awareness/understanding of different arguments in reading
   d. recognition of implications of evidence
   e. familiarity with/use of historical concepts (ability to 'think historically')
   f. ability to think critically
   g. grasp of relevant theory
   h. understanding of ethics and values relevant to reading and subject matter

3. *Independence*
   a. judgement and initiative in reading and research
   b. originality in use and interpretation of evidence
   c. development of argument
   d. independence in use of concepts and language

4. *Style*
   a. correctness of grammar and scholarly documentation
   b. organisation and presentation of material
   c. clarity of writing style
   d. originality and creativity of writing style

assessment criteria lists should be. Plainly, manageability must enter strongly into consideration, since the greater the number of criteria that are distinguished, the more demanding the assessment task becomes, both for teacher and taught; to have to consider, say, eight or nine criteria is one thing, but to have to respond to double that number is quite another. In fact, and perhaps with this point in mind, the compilers of the *History Benchmarking Statement* do not envisage that all the learning outcomes they designate will necessarily be used for the purposes of degree classification – that is to say for summative assessment. On the other hand, the Sydney University list is accompanied by the observation that 'individual units are likely to have additional and more specific requirements and criteria'. So, while one set of statements that is quite lengthy allows for the possibility of reducing the range of assessment criteria, thereby assisting manage-ability, the other that is even longer allows for its extension, so that assessment potentially becomes even more demanding. How, then, might the number of assessment criteria for a history programme be kept to a manageable level?

One approach is to focus on the type of broad categorisation devised by the University of Sydney historians. The four group headings they use have particular value in specifying generic assessment criteria that neatly summarise the main requirements of their programme. Further-more, the notion of concentrating on just four main assessment criteria is eminently manageable and is well within the maximum of six or seven that have been advocated as a general guideline (Bull et al., 1997: 50; Freeman and Lewis, 1998: 45). Whether other criteria might be substituted for them, or added to them, is a matter of debate. All four might be seen as vital components of undergraduate history pro-grammes, but other possibilities might also be identified. For example, some of the criteria appearing *within* the four main headings could be seen as significant enough to become generic assessment criteria in their own right. *Relevance of information* and *ability to think critically* are among them. And account may be taken of other generic assessment criteria that are used in history programmes, including *analysis* and *structure*, which appear alongside *knowledge* and *presentation* in one of the history courses at Edinburgh University (Hounsell, 2000: 187–9), and *reading, content, argument, analysis, presentation* and *scholarly apparatus*, which are favoured at the University of Wales, Bangor (Bangor, *Handbook*). For a rather fuller list, the criteria identified by SACWG can be cited (Woolf et al., 2001):

- approach to question/relevance;
- evaluation of/reflection on sources;
- analysis;
- independent thought;
- deployment of evidence;
- range of knowledge;
- range of sources;
- reference to historiography;
- structure;
- style;
- scholarly apparatus.

All such criteria are undoubtedly appropriate in providing guidance on assessing the quality of undergraduate history work and the issue becomes one of deciding which of them best meet the needs of particular history programmes.

The policy of designating a relatively small number of generic criteria still allows scope for including other criteria in assessment schemes, as Freeman and Lewis point out (Freeman and Lewis, 1998: 43). Take content, for instance. The University of Sydney list recognises both quantitative and qualitative dimensions in this area. Each of these dimensions could be seen as separate strands for assessment purposes, the former ensuring that enough sources are consulted and the latter that they are appropriate and used accurately. By focusing in this way, the manageability of assessment is maintained while ensuring that the main dimensions of the generic criteria are clearly identified. The view may be taken, of course, that using just two assessment strands does not allow sufficient precision for assessment purposes in relation to content or to any other generic criteria that are formulated. And more strands may well be required in some instances. The essential point, however, is that while adding to the number of assessment strands may be thought desirable, in practice the manageability of the assessment process acts as a severe constraint on ambitions in this direction. Even designating just six or seven generic criteria with two or three strands in each might still make the assessment task far too burdensome.

The extent of application

A further matter concerning the manageability of assessment criteria is whether those chosen can be applied to all types of students' assignments and to all course units within a history programme. In terms of economy of effort, such an outcome is plainly desirable. Yet some clarification of how the criteria are to be applied within particular course units will still be required. Thus students' ability to analyse may be assessed in every course unit, though only in a few units, if at all, will they be assessed on their ability to do so using, say, computerised databases. Rather than devising a separate assessment criterion relating to this matter, however, the criterion of 'analysis' can still be used. What matters for assessment purposes is that students enhance their ability to analyse in the varying contexts that arise in historical work. Historical databases provide one example, but others might include different types of historical evidence, such as those derived from field investigation and oral testimony, transnational or inter-regional comparison, and change and continuity over long periods of time.

Adapting generic assessment criteria to accommodate specific elements of assessment can prove difficult, however. This is especially so with regard to presentational issues, since assessing written and oral assignments brings quite different considerations into play. In the case of written assignments, emphasis might be laid on achieving grammatical and lucid expression coupled with appropriate use of scholarly apparatus. But with oral assignments, the main concerns might be about engaging an audience and using appropriate visual aids. Other elements in assessing written and oral presentations, such as analysis and relevance of discussion, will remain common, but the marked differences in the nature of oral and written presentations make formulating separate assessment criteria hard to avoid (Allen and Lloyd-Jones, *Groupwork*: App. 1; Booth, 1996a; 279–80, 282 and 290). To an extent, therefore, course units in history programmes will draw on varying assessment criteria according to the nature of the assignments set. And some criteria may be used relatively infrequently, especially when they are perceived to relate to more demanding tasks. The *grasp of relevant theory* included among the University of Sydney's assessment criteria is a case in point, its applicability perhaps being greater in the later stages of study than earlier.

Relative weighting of criteria

At issue here is whether most or all the criteria are weighted equally in assessing students' work or whether some are seen to be more important than others. Presentational skills are a case in point, since it would seem unreasonable to award high marks for a well-presented history essay which shows marked defects in, say, content coverage or analysis. Yet some assignments, because of the form they take, might be assessed by giving higher weighting to certain criteria than to others. Presentational criteria might be among them, as in the case of mounting an exhibition. So, too, may originality of thought, as in the case of the 'applied history' assignments available at the University of Central Lancashire, which enable students to devise classroom activities that meet history National Curriculum requirements. More

generally, the question arises as to how far weak or average perform-
ances in relation to some assessment criteria can secure compensation
by good performance in others.

Clarity of criteria

The question here is how well the terminology used in designating
assessment criteria will be understood by both teacher and taught.
Suppose, for example, one criterion for assessing history students is
that of critical thinking. Peter Knight remarks that this term can have
several meanings (Knight, 2001: 13) and even if a particular definition
is agreed, such as 'passing informed judgement', students will still
need guidance on what is actually required of them when they attempt
to make judgements in historical contexts. Quite plainly, history
teaching teams will need to come to a view on what they think their
assessment criteria mean and students will need to be given full
opportunity to understand this view, perhaps in part through being
involved in the deliberations (Brown, 2001: 16).

Advantages of assessment criteria

Despite the problems with which they are associated, assessment
criteria play a fundamental role in enhancing the quality of students'
work. And they do so in several respects.

Firstly, they promote awareness among students of what is seen as
being important for assessment purposes in relation to the coursework
and examinations they undertake, enabling them to focus their efforts
accordingly. Without this awareness, students may lack direction and
may waste a good deal of time in undertaking activities that are at best
peripheral to the task in hand (Brown and Knight, 1994: 102). The
designation of a clearly articulated and manageable set of assessment
criteria can do much towards enabling students to organise their
learning activities in an efficient and effective manner.

Secondly, assessment criteria help in achieving reasonable levels of
consistency among tutors in grading students' work. Without the
guidance of programme-wide criteria, students are forced to anticipate
the requirements of tutors, which may well differ appreciably, causing
them justified concern (Booth, 1996b: 262–3). Moreover, as Sally Brown
and Peter Knight remark, to have available a mark scheme with the
criteria included is invaluable when more than one tutor is marking

work from seminar groups linked to a particular course unit (Brown and Knight, 1994: 103). Indeed, the point can be made more generally. Students should have confidence that a team of lecturers is assessing their work in relation to an agreed and published set of criteria that are applied consistently.

Thirdly, assessment criteria help to provide student feedback easily and quickly. Sheets listing the criteria can be given to students, the feedback taking the form of ticked boxes – say on a scale of one to five – printed alongside each of the criteria (Rust, 2001: 12). However, while such an approach may be helpful in trying to cope with large numbers of students and in facilitating the speed with which feedback is given, it does not tell students how to improve their work (Brown, 2001: 15). Additional feedback will plainly be required to deal with this matter, perhaps by making brief comments in relation to some or all of the criteria.

Students' attitudes towards assessment criteria

While assessment criteria have become fashionable in higher education history teaching, their use has not always met with student approval, as a survey undertaken in 1995 by Janet Baker reveals. She analysed the attitudes of history students at Monash University regarding their assessment experience as first-year undergraduates and in the Victorian Certificate in Education (which gives qualification for university entrance). Assessment criteria were used for the Certificate course, but not for the first-year undergraduate programme; instead, some guidance to performance in key areas was offered. Questionnaire responses obtained from the students about whether or not they preferred criteria marking showed an even split. Those in favour remarked on the value of the focus and direction assessment criteria brought to their studies. Those against commented unfavourably on the restrictive nature of the criteria, which they saw as curtailing the scope for individuality. Notwithstanding such markedly opposed views, in-depth interviews revealed that most students in the survey felt uncertain about precisely what was valued in assessment terms at university level (Baker, 1995). On this evidence, the indications are that students do appreciate guidance on how they will be assessed, though they do not wish to have too much prescription imposed on them. This point is picked up by Peter Knight, who observes:

the more that criteria are used to identify what is to be valued, the more they constrain learning processes and outcomes to divergent paths. Powerful though this learning may be, there is a view that higher education should be about more besides . . .

(Knight, 2002: 111)

To summarise the discussion in this section, decisions about the number and importance of assessment criteria that should feature in undergraduate history programmes are complicated because of the tension between what might ideally be assessed and the practical difficulties of realising the ideal. The development of assessment criteria provides a useful way forward, though not one that is problem free, either in terms of planning or implementation. Yet the process is vitally important in helping to ensure that balanced and consistent assessment regimes are implemented and that students have a clear understanding of what assessment regimes expect of them.

STATEMENTS OF ATTAINMENT

Identification of assessment criteria may be seen as a first stage in establishing an assessment regime. However, the further problem arises of devising descriptors, or statements of attainment, that relate to each assessment criterion and that enable the level of performance achieved by students to be assessed. These statements must:

- correspond to degree classifications;
- be applied to all types of assessment;
- provide the basis both for judging and guiding performance;
- prove time efficient and effective in operation;
- be fair and reasonable to students in terms of expectation;
- provide the type and amount of feedback students need to enhance their achievement.

Furthermore, as the *History Benchmarking Statement* recommends, descriptors for all levels of classification

should give predominance to positive achievement, although below the first class they should also indicate the kinds of limitations which disqualify a candidate from achieving a mark in a higher class.

(QAA, *History*, 2000: 7)

TABLE 6.3 *Selected statements of attainment used at the University of Sydney*

Level	Statement
High pass 60–64%	*Work has considerable merit, though Honours is not automatically recommended.* Written work contains evidence of a broad and reasonably accurate command of the subject matter and some sense of its broader significance, offers synthesis and some evaluation of material, demonstrates an effort to go beyond the essential reading, contains clear focus on the principal issues, understanding of relevant arguments and diverse interpretations, and a coherent argument grounded in relevant evidence, though there may be some weaknesses of clarity or structure. Articulate, properly documented.
Low credit 65–69%	*Competent work, demonstrating potential to complete Honours work, though further development needed to do so successfully.* Written work contains evidence of comprehensive reading, offers synthesis and critical evaluation of material on its own terms, takes a position in relation to various interpretations. In addition, it shows some spark of insight or analysis. Demonstrates understanding of broad historical significance, good selection of evidence, coherent and sustainable argument, some evidence of independent thought, grasp of relevant historiography.
High credit 70–74%	*Highly competent work, demonstrating clear capacity to complete Honours successfully.* Evidence of extensive reading and initiative in research, sound grasp of subject matter and appreciation of key issues and context. Engages critically and creatively with the question and attempts an analytical evaluation of material. Makes a good attempt to critique various historical interpretations, and offers a thoughtful contribution to an existing historical debate. Some evidence of an ability to think theoretically as well as empirically, and to conceptualise and problematise issues in historical terms. Well written and documented.

(Sydney, *Policies*)

Formulating statements of attainment

Statements of attainment can be presented in generalised form covering the range of assessment criteria at each level of degree classification. This approach is used in the history department at the University of Sydney, and examples of the statements that have been formulated there for a selection of levels are given in Table 6.3. The alternative is to present the statements of attainment separately for each of the assessment criteria at each level. Table 6.4 provides examples, which, although used in the English Department at Queen's

TABLE 6.4 *Selected statements of attainment, Queen's University Belfast*

Criterion	Upper second class	Lower second class	Third class
Relevance	An answer which is directly relevant to the question.	Some attempt to answer question; may drift away from the question into broad generalisation.	Some significant degree of irrelevance is common.
Knowledge	A sound and substantial familiarity with the material showing awareness of the issues raised.	Adequate knowledge of a fair range of material.	Basic understanding of a limited range of material.
Analysis	A good analytical treatment of the evidence.	May show some analytical treatment, but tends towards description.	Largely descriptive with little evidence of analytical argument.
Argument and structure	A generally coherent and logically structured argument.	Some attempt to construct a coherent argument, but tends to be superficial or predictable.	Basic argument may be evident, but tends to lack clarity and coherence.
Originality	May contain some distinctive or independent thinking; may begin to formulate an independent position.	Sound but derivative thought and approach.	Largely derivative in thought and approach.
Presentation	Well written, with standard spelling and syntax, in a readable style and with appropriate documentation.	Reasonably well written, with standard spelling and syntax, in a readable style and with appropriate documentation.	Some deficiencies in written expression.

(Belfast, *Criteria*)

University, Belfast, are highly instructive in considering statemennts of attainment that can be used in assessing history undergraduates.

In analysing the two approaches, several issues arise. One is the number of attainment levels that are determined and the mark range that each level covers. In the University of Sydney's scheme, eight levels are defined ranging from fail (below 50 per cent) to high distinction (85 per cent and above). Between the two extremes, levels of attainment are defined at 5 per cent intervals. In contrast, the Queen's Belfast scheme distinguishes just five levels of attainment ranging from fail to first class and each level covers intervals of 10 per cent. Whether there would be any value in seeking to create more and finer divisions than in the Sydney University scheme, or fewer and wider divisions than in the Queen's Belfast scheme, is highly unlikely. Attempting the former would be highly challenging and the end product would be extremely difficult to use, while attempting the latter would not create statements of attainment fine enough to relate to each of the main degree categories in question.

A further matter to consider is the degree of differentiation that is to be made between the levels of attainment. This differentiation has to be extended to each of the assessment criteria and is underpinned by notions of above average, average and below average performance at undergraduate level. In other words, what might be seen as being above average for undergraduates in relation to any assessment criteria might be regarded as being only average or even below average for postgraduates. Commonly, expressions of differentiation within assessment criteria can be expressed as positions along continua, such as description/analysis and derived ideas/original ideas. The challenge thus becomes one of framing statements so that reasonably clear differentiations are created which correspond to the expectations at particular levels.

This task is far from straightforward, however, and the kinds of problems that arise can be illustrated from the published examples. Among them is the terminology employed. In the Queen's Belfast scheme, for instance, that the attainment of 'some distinctive or independent thinking' at the upper second class level is permissive rather than required – the word 'may' appears – does not necessarily mark a clear advance from the level below, though one is certainly implied. Nor in the University of Sydney scheme is the difference made plain between the 'articulate, properly documented' responses that characterise the high level pass and those that are 'well written and documented', the requirement at high credit level. Taking a broader perspective on the matter, Harvey Woolf has drawn attention to other problems with terminology in attainment statements, including giving common-sense words uncommon meanings, an example being the description of a first-class response as 'broad, deep and assured', and the inclusion of tautologies, as in the description

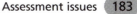

'outstanding work of excellent quality'. He argues that a shared vocabulary is needed, so that teacher and taught are clear about the meaning of the language used for assessment purposes (Woolf, 2002).

Apart from matters arising in relation to devising statements of attainment are those concerning their implementation. They are:

● *Where does the precise grading lie within each attainment level if the mark range is fairly wide?*

In the Queen's University scheme, some guidance is given on this matter. For example, a grade at the higher end of the range would need to show 'an abundance of class criteria with perhaps some elements of the next class up'.

● *How is feedback relating to the attainment statements best given to students?*

Ideally, feedback should be given in relation to each of the statements, perhaps using a standardised sheet. The sheet might list just the assessment criteria, with a space next to each one for a comment about the attainment level achieved. Another possibility is for the sheet to give both assessment criteria and statements of attainment in matrix form (as in the Queen's University example), so that the appropriate boxes can be highlighted in making the assessments. But whatever the form in which feedback is delivered, markers will need to be familiar with the statements of attainment they use and to consider them carefully in grading students' work.

● *How are the attainment statements applied at different programme levels?*

A key issue here is whether or not to be more lenient in interpreting the statements during the early stages of undergraduate work compared with later on and, if so, to what extent. Certainly the Sydney University scheme operates 'with due consideration of the standards likely to be achieved by Junior and Senior students' (Sydney, *Policies*). And a linked matter is whether, at a particular level, compensation should be allowed for assignments that are thought to be more demanding in some respect (Ecclestone, 2001: 308). An example might be where, in one course unit, students are required to analyse primary evidence provided by the tutor and, in another, to gather the primary evidence as well as undertake the analysis.

Advantages of statements of attainment

A major advantage of using statements of attainment is that they add greatly to the transparency of assessment, enabling students to see more precisely what is required of them in achieving a particular standard than is evident from the assessment criteria alone. Indeed, without them it is hard to realise the expectations concerning transparency in assessment that, Phil Race suggests, students should have:

> *You are supposed to know what is being looked for in each element of your assessment. You should not have to resort to guessing what's in the mind of the lecturers who assess your work. They are supposed to be using clear criteria to apply to your work, and they're supposed to make sure that you know exactly what these criteria mean.*
>
> (Race, 2001: 4–5)

Rust notes, however, that merely giving out assessment criteria without finding ways for students to interact with them may have little impact on the quality of their work (Rust, 2001: 9). To facilitate this interaction, one approach is to give students marking exercises as a seminar activity. Referring to the statements of attainment, they can grade essays of varying quality that tutors write specially for the purpose or perhaps grade an anonymised essay written by a previous student (Light and Cox, 2001: 173–4). Such exercises should ideally occur at an early stage in their programmes and might well be repeated as they progress, both to demonstrate why marks are awarded at a particular level and to consider the nature of improvements that could be made to achieve higher grades. The inclusion of peer assessment in history programmes should also help students to appreciate the requirements of assessment criteria and statements of attainment (Higgins et al., 2002: 62), as should explanation of the purposes of the assessments that are devised for each of the course units they take and the feedback they receive on assignments.

One other point concerning the transparency of assessment criteria relates to external examining. External examiners can all too easily be left in the dark as to why particular grades have been awarded. The matter tends to arise more with examination questions than with coursework assignments, probably because comments on examination scripts are not generally relayed back to students and are not, therefore, seen to have a substantial formative role. Yet if external examiners are to help in ensuring that marking is appropriate, they need clear guidance on how the grades awarded were seen by internal markers to relate to assessment criteria both for examinations and coursework. Indeed, there must be concern about how effectively an external examining system can operate unless this matter is addressed, especially where a high proportion of the summative assessment is by examinations.

A further advantage of using statements of attainment is that, compared with using assessment criteria alone, they aid consistency in assessing students' work. Statements of attainment have the potential to enable course tutors to reach a collective view on what, in relation to each assessment criterion, constitutes a given level of performance and to ensure that, across the programme as a whole, grades are awarded in relation to the agreed statements. In practice, of course, the degree of consistency that can be achieved among course tutors will vary, much depending on how closely individuals take account of the statements and on how they interpret them in relation to set assignments. Even so, statements of attainment are still likely to reduce inconsistency between markers across a range of course units and between first and second markers within particular course units.

Taken together, the advantages to be derived from using assessment criteria and the statements of attainment associated with them are compelling. Not only are they key to enhancing the reliability and quality of grading students' work, but they are fundamental to ensuring that both formative and summative assessment stimulate student learning in appropriate ways. Without them, the assessment process becomes too much of a lottery, with neither teacher nor taught being able to work as purposefully as they might.

DEVELOPING ASSESSMENT CRITERIA: A SMALL-SCALE CASE STUDY

Undertaken by SACWG, this case study is concerned with how five higher education history departments in Britain developed their assessment criteria. The approach adopted is considered, the findings are summarised and discussed and, drawing on these findings, several suggestions are offered that need serious consideration in helping to ensure that criterion-referenced assessment delivers its full promise.

Context and approach

Behind the case study lies earlier research showing, disturbingly, that assessment criteria are variously interpreted within the same department (Woolfe et al., 1997). If such criteria are the product and object of departmental discussion, however, this divergence would be expected to narrow, bringing benefit to students, teachers and external examiners alike. If, on the other hand, the criteria are merely conjured up, then problems of interpretation, application and meaning can be anticipated and the basic conditions for effective criterion-referenced assessment will be missing.

To some extent the focus of the case study divorces the process by which assessment criteria are produced from how the curriculum in general, and assessment regimes in particular, are designed. However, the approach adopted aimed to ensure that respondents concentrated on assessment criteria and avoided describing wider curriculum development processes.

SACWG members carried out semi-structured interviews with the head of history in their own institutions using, for consistency, a series of agreed prompts. Interviewees were invited to add comments on any aspects of the subject that they felt were appropriate. Responses were collated and analysed under the following headings:

- Institutional requirement to produce assessment criteria
- Responsibility for producing the criteria
- Internal discussions about the criteria
- External examiner involvement
- The reference points used to devise the criteria
- The formal procedures to agree the criteria
- Dissemination to students (other than publication in subject or module guides)
- Process to ensure a shared understanding among the subject team
- Review of the criteria
- Other observations.

Discussion of findings

The findings are set out in Table 6.5. Responses to each of the interview headings are noted and, where appropriate, comments are added. Under some headings more than five responses are given because respondents made several points in answer to some questions.

Even though the case study reflects different institutional cultures, structures and procedures, it is striking that, in all five departments, the need to provide assessment criteria had been recognised and, more importantly, acted upon (*Item 1*). The diverse drivers here include the requirement of the Higher Education Funding Council for England that higher education institutions should produce learning and teaching (and assessment) strategies, the Quality Assurance Agency's assessment/review/audit of learning and teaching, the curriculum responses to widening participation in higher education and the use of performance indicators more generally in higher education. The causal and temporal relationships between these external drivers and the production of assessment criteria vary from institution to institution, of course, and are worthy of investigation to illuminate the ways in which 'high' strategy and policy influence departmental practices.

Wherever the *formal* responsibility for the production of assessment criteria rests, the evidence from the survey suggests that, in practice, they are usually drawn up by one person, with, at best, limited discussion taking place among the subject team and no consultation with students (*Items 2 and 3*). This approach might have the virtue of consistency in, for example, language or style. However, it is unlikely to generate a sense of shared ownership and a common understanding or interpretation of what the criteria mean. No department sought the views of its external examiners (*Item 4*), who could have served as a valuable testing ground for the clarity and meaningfulness of the proposed criteria.

It is perhaps surprising that not all the respondents identified the QAA *History Benchmarking Statement* as one of the reference points for the creation or modification of their criteria (*Item 5*). Possibly the Departments' criteria pre-dated the publication of the *Statement* or respondents overlooked the role that it played. However, their silence might also reflect the extent to which the *Statement* is perceived essentially as process – rather than outcome-orientated and thus as unhelpful in translating QAA theory into curriculum practice, despite offering a set of exemplar criteria and associated grade (or level) descriptors as an annex.

TABLE 6.5 *SACWG survey on assessment criteria: results and comments*

Item	Responses		Comment
1. Institutional requirement	Required by institution	2	
	Required by department	1	
	No requirement (self-generated)	2	
2. Responsibility	A senior member of department	3	In 1 case, Departmental Learning and Teaching Co-ordinator with Subject team and Departmental Academic Standards Committee (DASC).
	Subject team	2	In 1 case, module leaders for their own modules.
			In 1 case, formally subject leader.
3. Preparatory discussions	Informal discussions within team	2	In 1 case, subject leader's draft accepted 'unanimously'.
	At DASC meeting	1	
	None	2	
4. External examiner involvement	None	5	
5. Reference points	Subject Benchmark Statement	3	In 1 case, 'greater relevance at overall subject/programme points level'.
	Other institutions	2	In 1 case, reference to the History Learning and Teaching Support Network.
	Existing departmental criteria	2	
	Other departments	1	
	None	1	
6. Formal agreement	Yes	2	At validation in both cases.
	No	3	

7.	Dissemination to students	Written feedback with coversheet	3	(Coversheets list the assessment criteria.)
		Written feedback, no coversheet	1	Tutorials do not *necessarily* encompass discussion of criteria.
		Pre-assignment tutorial	1	
		Post-assignment tutorial	1	In 1 case, 'formal discussions with students'.
		Year 1 Induction	2	
		Handbooks only	2	
8.	Shared understanding among tutors	'Away days'	3	In 1 case, 'essay marking exercises' included.
		Annual monitoring/review	1	
		Assessment board discussion	1	
		Double marking	1	
		Standard feedback sheet	1	
		Two tutors at presentations	1	
		Nothing	1	
9.	Review processes	Quinquennial review	2	
		Annual monitoring	1	
		Staff/student liaison meetings	2	In both cases students have not raised criteria as an issue.
		Assessment boards	2	
		Nothing formal	1	
10.	Other observations	One respondent felt a much sharper categorisation of criteria was needed. See comments for an example.		(a) Knowledge, understanding and analysis demonstrated; (b) use of secondary and primary sources; (c) structure, communication and presentation of the work.
		One respondent noted that in practice the term 'criteria' is used/applied very loosely. See comments for an example.		(a) Generic grade criteria generated at level of modular scheme; (b) assessment feedback sheets; (c) assignment-specific criteria relating to an assignment – relatively recent development.
				Feedback sheet and grade criteria not differentiated by level.

In disseminating assessment criteria to students (*Item 7*), the reliance on a subject or module handbook without any systematic explication being given of the meaning that should be attached to the criteria assumes that students share the subject team's understanding of the vocabulary used. In some departments, pre- or post-assignment tutorials were identified as vehicles for explaining how the criteria are applied to a specific assignment. Yet there is no way of knowing how explicitly or how extensively assessment criteria are addressed in these tutorials. And such findings need to be set in the context of British history students in general receiving limited feedback on their assignments (Hyland, 2000: 237; Woolf and Cooper, 1999: 50).

On the whole, the respondents anticipated greater consistency in grading students' work as a consequence of applying published assessment criteria. However, despite employing a range of strategies to promote shared understanding of the criteria among subject teams, including away-day discussion, standard feedback sheets and double marking (*Item 8*), there remain doubts about how far all tutors interpret the criteria in the same way when marking assignments. Moreover, tutors may be using unarticulated criteria, such as literacy, or tacitly weighting some of the published criteria. This tension between 'espoused theories' and 'theories in use' is well known (Ecclestone, 2001: 305), but can militate against students understanding why they have received a particular grade or how to develop their work in appropriate ways.

With regard to reviewing the assessment criteria (*Item 9*), formal procedures were reported in all but one instance, suggesting that considerable scope exists for external comment to be provided on how effectively the criteria operate in practice. Yet how far there is opportunity for student opinion to aid systematically the formal review of assessment criteria must be a matter of concern. Only two instances were reported of assessment criteria being discussed at staff/student liaison meetings and in neither case were students the instigators.

Other comments made by respondents (*Item 10*) may be briefly noted. The criteria discussed in the interviews were mostly designed for use in assessing written assignments. The respondents, though, have acknowledged that, as one of them reported, 'there are ... non-standard tasks – study logs, presentations, map exercises, web design, exhibitions, gobbets – which have non-standard criteria'. This observation reflects our earlier discussion on the need for specific as well as generic assessment criteria. It also serves as a reminder that the broadening of assessment approaches brings the need at least to consider whether changes to the criteria in use are needed.

A further point to note is that there is no evidence that the departments surveyed have addressed the issue of differentiating their assessment criteria by level of academic study. Nor have they explicitly ascribed weightings to these criteria. The indications, there-fore, are that the criteria are not embedded in a programmatic approach to assessment, which would see the same criteria being used to inform judgements and formative feedback throughout the degree programme thus serving as a structural device to stimulate pro-gression and learning. If that is the case, then the opportunities for students to be 'knowing students', that is students who understand the goals, expectations and standards of the programme as a whole and who are able to represent fluently their achievements in respect of the identified outcomes, are likely to be significantly reduced.

The overall impression arising from the survey is that, among the five departments, there is variety in the intensity of engagement with the assessment criteria they had produced. At one end of the continuum, departments use the criteria as the basis for developing detailed specifications for individual modules and individual assignments; at the other end, the criteria provide a broad framework for grading assessments. At both ends of the continuum, though, it is apparent that the criteria are not simply showpieces, put on display when required by the institutional quality system or by an external body.

Future practice: a checklist for action

The previous sections of this chapter provide an overview of the development of generic and specific assessment criteria and of statements of attainment within them, noting, with regard to both matters, the problems associated with devising appropriate terminol-ogy. Drawing on the practices identified in the SACWG case study, the issues that need to be considered in designing and revising assessment criteria for higher education history courses can be articulated with more precision. They are presented in Table 6.6 as a checklist.

Having considered the difficulties that arise in deciding on, and articulating, precisely what is being assessed in history undergraduate programmes, and having pointed to ways forward in dealing with these matters, the remaining sections of this chapter turn to examine the means by which history undergraduates are assessed. To provide

TABLE 6.6 *Assessment criteria checklist*

In determining assessment criteria, there is a need for:
- Clarity about the purpose of, and audience for, the criteria and the type(s) of assessment to which the criteria will be applied.
- Selection of reference points, such as the *History Benchmarking Statement*, that derive from the decisions about purpose, audience and assessment methods.
- Involvement of all members of the history team and history students in formulating and revising the criteria, since it is easier to obtain a common understanding during the drafting phase than trying to divine what someone meant after the criteria have been published (Elwood and Klenowski, 2002: 251–2). More generally, such involvement can contribute to the development of a 'community of assessment practice' (Hall and Harding, 2002: 1–15).
- Formulation of the criteria in language that is sufficiently precise to allow for a consistent interpretation among tutors and students, yet is not so prescriptive that the criteria become straitjackets for either assessors or assessed (Brown, 2001: 7).
- Seeking the views of external examiners and colleagues from other departments.
- Legitimisation of the criteria initially through validation and subsequently through (annual) review and monitoring.
- Briefing students regularly about the criteria, perhaps using 'marking' exercises to familiarise them with how criteria are applied. Also, making assessment a standard item on the agenda of student–staff liaison meetings can provide students with both an opportunity to comment on the consistency with which the criteria are being applied and to acquire a wider understanding of the assessment process.
- Ensuring feedback methods relate directly and specifically to the published criteria.

context, discussion begins with some general observations in relation to coursework and examinations and then moves to consider specific examples of assessment practice used by higher education historians, seeking to demonstrate both the rationale for the approaches they adopt and the sort of difficulties they encounter. The main aim is to stimulate thought not only about the extent to which there should be variation in the types of assessment included in history undergraduate programmes, but also about whether too great a burden is being placed on writing essays, especially conventional essays based on secondary material alone.

ASSESSMENT BY COURSEWORK AND EXAMINATIONS: GENERAL CONSIDERATIONS

Undergraduate history programmes in British higher education institutions vary markedly in the extent to which examinations are used to assess student achievement. In some cases, examinations are absent, or virtually absent, altogether. Thus at Bath Spa University College, the pattern of assessment for history course units is:

- Years 1 and 2: 30 per cent seminar/project work; 40 per cent essays and reports; 30 per cent special assignment
- Year 3: 50 per cent essay; 50 per cent project (Bath Spa, *History*).

In other institutions, examinations may comprise a small proportion of the assessed work that counts towards the final degree classification because they are phased out after the first or second year. At the University of Central Lancashire, for example, single-honours history students are typically assessed by examinations in three of the six units they take at level 2, but in none of those they take at level 3. The examinations account for 40 per cent of total unit assessment in each case, the eleven highest grades being used to determine degree classifications.

Shortcomings of examinations

The varying amount of summative assessment contributed by examinations in undergraduate history provision reflects a decline in their relative importance during recent decades, as is the case in other subject disciplines. This trend strongly reflects the shortcomings of examinations as a means of assessment, a matter that can be explained in several ways.

One concerns the type of coursework elements widely introduced into history courses that cannot meaningfully be assessed by traditional written examinations. The final-year dissertation provides the most notable example, but the argument can be extended to cover smaller-scale projects (undertaken by both individuals and groups) including those associated with work placement units. Additionally, the oral contributions made in a series of seminars, along with the delivery of seminar papers and the handling of responses made to them, can be added to the list. It also appears that examinations held in British higher education institutions are not adequately testing skills acquisition. Thus, in her analysis of overview reports arising from subject review in Britain from 1993 to 1999, Angela Glasner found that, in history, 'the assessment of certain transferable skills at undergraduate level was not always evident, particularly where assessment was based largely on written examinations' (Glasner, 1999: 18).

A second consideration is the unfairness that is seen to arise for those students who, for whatever reason, tend to perform less well in examinations than in coursework. Mature students, who may have experienced failure or limited success in school examinations and who, in consequence, may lack confidence in taking examinations at a higher level, are a case in point. Moreover, unfairness is seen to arise in cases where coursework is used to provide formative assessment alone. From the teaching point of view, such an approach can be seen as highly desirable, especially if examinations, which may comprise a substantial proportion of the total assessment, are used solely for summative purposes. From the learners' perspective, however, the use of coursework for formative purposes alone can be seen to deny them the opportunity of gaining credit for the work undertaken. Not only is this a matter of concern to those who do better at coursework than examinations, but also to those who take the view that all coursework assignments undertaken should count towards summative assessment.

Other perceived shortcomings of examinations have also been raised. There is space to mention them only briefly, though they add weight to the argument for devising assessment regimes that do not depend primarily on examinations. They are as follows:

- too much emphasis is placed on memory and factual knowledge and on experiencing pressure of a kind seldom found in later life;
- insufficient scope is given for originality and sustained writing, nor enough opportunity for constructive feedback;
- too great a reliance is placed on speed of writing and thinking and on an element of luck;
- encouragement is given to rote learning;
- advantage arises to those better able to withstand acute stress (Light and Cox, 2001: 171–2: Brown, 2001: 20).

The shortcomings associated with examinations have as much, if not more, resonance when applied to history undergraduate provision than to that of other disciplines. Underpinning them is a sense that examinations have a stronger role in assessing students' knowledge of content as opposed to their acquisition of skills, so that, as the latter has gained considerably in importance at undergraduate level, examinations have become of lessening significance.

Coursework as an element in progression

How far the growing trend towards coursework has been seen as a way of achieving progression and differentiation in assessment is unclear. That coursework can be so used is evident from our discussion in Chapter 2, though the impressions are that, for the most part, any tendency in this direction arises principally from a need to accommodate the final-year dissertation. Yet the scope for using coursework as a means of making students' work more challenging as they progress through their programmes of study is considerable. Thus, as a general principle, students might be presented with the challenge of demonstrating that they are increasingly able to inform their understanding of the secondary literature by deploying primary material in coursework assignments. Final-year dissertation preparation provides one element in progressions of this type, but the principle can be implemented more widely and in a staged manner. Various models are possible, including that requiring students to use primary material in some major coursework assignments in the penultimate year and in all major coursework assignments during the final year. Assessment progressions with other types of coursework can also be incorporated into history programmes, including, for example, oral assessment. Possibilities here include a move from giving brief presentations for formative purposes only to longer presentations that contribute to final degree gradings. Peer and group assessment (considered in the next section) might also be introduced at a later stage, when academic skills are more developed, though, in their project based at Sheffield Hallam University, Julia Allen and Roger Lloyd-Jones found that while 77 per cent of their level 2 respondents would have valued provision for developing group work and presentational skills at level 1, 83 per cent were against continuing assessed group work at level 3 (Allen and Lloyd-Jones, *Guidebook*: 3).

Persistence of examinations

In spite of the advances made by coursework as a form of assessment, examinations remain a major component in assessing undergraduate history students, though the proportion of marks that students derive from examinations varies markedly from institution to institution. Moreover, appreciable choice may be permitted within history departments for tutors to decide how far the course units they offer should be assessed by examination. Thus, at James Cook University, Queensland, examinations for most second-year history course units comprise 40 per cent of the assessment, but in the case of the *Australian Society and Culture* unit the figure is as high as 50 per cent and for the *Strangers in the South Pacific* unit as low as 30 per cent (JCU, *Handbooks* 2004). And at the University of Warwick, the assessment pattern in many of the second- and third-year history course units allows students to make the choice as to whether they are assessed by a timed examination paper or by a combination of examination and coursework (Warwick, *Study – Arts*). Both approaches allow a considerable degree of individual preference to be exercised, but the latter avoids the danger of students selecting a course unit according to the assessment requirements rather than their academic preferences.

Examinations remain a favoured means of assessment in history undergraduate programmes for several reasons. One is that the criticisms made of them are seen to be overstated. For example, the notion that examinations put too much emphasis on factual recall is questionable, much depending on the form the examinations take, a matter that is considered in the following section. And while examinations can pressurise students, so, too, can coursework, especially if deadlines become bunched (Booth, 1996b: 264). It may also be the case that examinations are still regarded as a useful means of promoting desirable accomplishments among students, those of committing knowledge to memory and of thinking quickly among them. Furthermore, examinations can be adapted to meet some of the criticisms levelled against them. Thus the charges that examinations are too much of a memory test and are too reliant on luck and on speed of thinking may be countered by offering open an examination, with students receiving the question paper some time before they sit it. And reducing the length of examinations and having fewer of them can in general lessen the intense pressure with which they are generally associated.

Advocacy of examinations can also be advanced. One argument concerns the safeguards that examinations offer against plagiarism and collusion (Brown, 2001: 20; QAA, *History*, 2000: 6). At the heart of this issue is concern that allowing appreciable elements of coursework assessment leads to a weakening of control against both these practices. And it does so at a time when the knowledge explosion, intensified by the vast and ever-growing amount of historical information available on the Web, including the sale of student essays, makes tracing plagiarism a matter of growing concern (Van Hartesveldt, 1998: 52–3).

It is noted above that coursework can be used to enhance progression and differentiation in history programmes. But so, too, can examinations. As with coursework, the extent to which examinations are seen as having value in this respect is unclear, though the potential is considerable. One possibility might be to expect more in the way of critical awareness of historiographical issues in final year examinations than in earlier years, perhaps coupled with the ability to contextualise extracts of primary evidence as well as to demonstrate awareness of their value and limitations. Maybe, too, there might be a shift towards fewer questions needing to be answered in order to achieve greater depth of coverage, towards synoptic questions being set in order to test students' cumulative understanding of the knowledge and skills they have acquired, or towards requiring responses rooted in comparative analysis.

ASSESSMENT IN PRACTICE

Types of essay assessment

The *History Benchmarking Statement* emphasises using essays as a form of assessment because of the 'integrative high-order skills which they develop'. It recommends that single-honours students in British universities 'should be assessed in significant part on their essay-writing skills' and that the essays used for this purpose should be varied in type. The examples cited are: 'long' essays, which are linked with assessing depth of scholarship; 'short' essays, which are concerned with assessing precision of focus; and essays dealing with such historical concepts as change, similarity and difference, and causation. The *Statement* also recommends giving 'serious consideration' to requiring that some essays should be written under examination conditions (QAA, *History*, 2000: 6).

In advocating essays as a prime means of assessing students, the *History Benchmarking Statement* strongly reflects long-established practice, though, as part of coursework, essays have come to play a stronger role in summative assessment. For the most part, short essays continue to fulfil their traditional role as a major component of examinations, providing a convenient means by which understanding of particular aspects of the material covered in course units can be tested. Yet they can do so in enterprising ways, as the following examples reveal.

1. The 'notional scenario' essays required in *The Vietnam War* course unit offered at Ohio State University. These comprise one of three, one-page essays that students write under examination conditions, putting themselves in the place of a historical actor in order to 'describe his or her circumstances and reaction to them'. The actors are 'ordinary citizens and combatants, male and female'. Typically, the one-page essays are selected from 12 to 15 options, the wide choice providing an incentive for students to increase their depth of knowledge and understanding by directing effort to those aspects of the course unit in which they have a particular interest (Ohio, *History 308*).

2. Martha Feldman's approach to formulating questions for the final examination on a *World Civilisation since 1500* course unit dealing with the major themes of nationalism, liberalism and economic development. Aiming to encourage students to link the present with the past, her practice has been to give them copies of current newspaper articles relating to the main themes of the course unit. For the Spring 1993 examination, for example, she chose articles dealing with nationalism in different parts of the world, including bombings of Muslim holy places in India and the Serbian attack on the Bosnian town of Srebrenica. The task for the students was to trace the developments reported in the articles historically, and to discuss them in terms of nationalism in the twentieth century. To give time for preparation, students receive the extracts two weeks before the examination takes place, a procedure that makes the students 'feel that they are being treated more fairly and that the instructor is interested in their success' (Feldman, 1997: 33–6).

Short essays up to, say, 1,000 words in length, can also be used as a means of assessing history coursework. However, longer essays of a few thousand words are generally favoured, especially because they allow students the opportunity to examine specific elements of course units in far greater depth. Implicitly at least, both short and long essays are designed to test the type of conceptual understanding noted in the *History Benchmarking Statement*, though, as a rule, they do so in different ways, most notably with regard to the use of primary evidence. The type of distinction that is drawn in this respect is well illustrated by the assessment strategy used for a third-level course unit *The Holocaust* offered in the department of history at Monash University. The coursework component of the assessment comprises two essays, one a short historiographical essay of 1,000 words and the other a much more substantial research essay of 2,500 words, the former counting for 20 per cent of total assessment and the latter for 40 per cent. In undertaking their research essay, students are required to make substantial use of primary source material, restricting the scope of their analysis in order to explore issues in depth. In their historiographical essay, they not only deal with differences occurring between schools of interpretation at any one point in time, but also with shifts in historical understanding that arise over time (Monash, *Handbooks*).

Longer essays are by no means confined to coursework assessment and can be associated with highly innovative practice, as in the case of the two-day *Comprehensive Examinations* used by historians at Wabash College, Indiana. On the first day, the students prepare an essay of up to 2,500 words in length dealing with an aspect of history or with historical approaches or theories. The essay, which is written on a take-home basis, requires students to synthesise, drawing on the knowledge and understanding they have acquired from all the course units they have taken. Freed from the confines of a traditional three-hour exam, students are able to consult the range of sources and texts they have used and have more time both to reflect on what they are writing and to make revisions. On the second day, students work with a varied range of primary material to address set questions, taking up to three hours to produce a further essay, a key aim being to assess their understanding of the Department's core goals (Wabash, *Curriculum*).

Problems with essay assessment

While there is an emphasis on essay writing for both the summative and formative assessment of history undergraduates, concern arises about the different ways in which students perceive essays. A small-scale research project undertaken by Dai Hounsell has identified three distinct perceptions that students have about the nature of the essays they are asked to write. These are:

- *as argument* – an ordered presentation of an argument well supported by evidence;
- *as viewpoint* – an ordered presentation of a distinctive viewpoint;
- *as arrangement* – an ordered presentation embracing facts and ideas.

Plainly, perceiving the essay as argument provides opportunity for a more sophisticated approach than perceiving it as viewpoint or arrangement. But what is particularly disturbing about the findings, with assessment in mind, is Hounsell's contention that the limited understanding of academic essays evident in the viewpoint and arrangement perspectives may be 'resistant to conventional remedies'. At issue here, Hounsell suggests, is whether students are prepared to learn how to think as well as to write as historians, and whether the feedback they receive is couched in terms that are meaningful to them (Hounsell, 2000: ch. 14; Richardson et al., 1987: ch. 14).

There is also concern about how different styles of essay writing submitted by history students are rewarded. Research undertaken by Robson, Francis and Read, based on 87 undergraduate essays, makes it 'clear that "good" writing in history is a very finely judged thing'. The indications from their research are that history students should write assertively, but not too assertively; should show caution, but not too much caution; and should balance and evaluate arguments, but should not do so to too great an extent. 'As teachers', they urge, 'we need to be precise and helpful about what is required, about what tone is appropriate and what we mean when we ask for "argument", for example' (Robson et al., 2002: 360).

Two other concerns that have been expressed with regard to essay assessment for undergraduate history students are worth mentioning. One is the limited use value that essays may have for students as a means of communication outside the academy. The matter is of particular concern with regard to employability, raising the question of how far such capabilities as report writing and web page preparation should form part of the assessment procedures in undergraduate history courses. The other is the heavy demands that can be made on students to produce quite a number of essays during a semester (often at least half a dozen) while being expected to maintain a high degree of quality (Detroit Mercy, *Assessment*).

Other forms of assessment

Although the assessment of history undergraduates depends heavily on their performance in essay work of one type or another, they are commonly judged by other means, albeit to a varied extent. Examples include:

Examination 'gobbets'

These involve the analysis of short extracts of primary source material. They are often associated with special-subject assessment at final level in British universities, giving the impression that they are seen as particularly demanding, not least because they involve students in the contextualisation of primary material. At the University of Durham, a special subject gobbet paper is set for the course unit *From War to Cold War: United States Foreign Policy, c.1944–1948*. It is divided into three sections, the students being required to select from each so that, in line with a key advantage of examinations, they are challenged to demonstrate breadth as well as depth of understanding (Durham, *Gobbet*).

'Identification' questions

As far as testing students' factual understanding is concerned, the 'identification' questions used in the *World War II* course unit at Ohio State University are noteworthy. These require students to define a term and/or to discuss briefly its important features and then to link it with one or more conceptual issues covered in the unit. Barbarossa is given as an example, the term itself to be defined in two short sentences and, with brevity emphasised, its significance considered in just five more. Identification questions also extend to maps, with students being asked to locate strategic places and explain their significance. A feature of both mid-term and final examinations, each identification question is worth 12.5 per cent of the total marks available for the unit (Ohio, *History 307*).

Quizzes and multiple-choice questions

Examinations based on brief responses are also used to test students' factual understanding. In the case of the Ohio University course unit cited above, a short quiz, lasting thirty minutes, is included as part of the assessment, counting for 15 per cent of the marks. The quiz has a similar format and function to the other examinations by which the students taking the unit are assessed, though it is included at an early stage in order to accustom them to the assessment approach. As to multiple-choice questions, the example reported by Susan Bosworth and her colleagues at the College of William and Mary in Virginia is instructive on several counts. The report gives insights into the way the questions were derived as a means of testing 'basic historical information appropriate for graduates to know as citizens in a democracy'. It also notes the problems that can arise with this type of test. In particular, females scored less well on average than males, a reflection of the gender bias in relation to quite a number of the questions that were set (Bosworth et al., 2000: ch. 17).

Oral assessment

Oral contributions made in seminars are commonly assessed in undergraduate history courses, providing the means by which outcomes dealing with, among other things, verbal communication skills can be tested. A recent survey undertaken by Susan Doran and associates, which analysed the approaches to seminar assessment in 18 of Britain's higher education history departments, has revealed three main ways in which students' oral seminar contributions are being assessed, namely:

1. presentations by individuals or groups;
2. student managed seminars;
3. general contributions made in each seminar of a course unit.

The survey found that major features of these types of assessment were that, in summative terms, they carry a relatively low weighting, the average being 10–15 per cent of the total marks available; that only in a minority of cases, albeit a sizeable one, were students provided with published, grade-related assessment criteria; and that, while peer assessment of oral contributions was by no means uncommon and self-assessment might also be used, the responsibility for grading lay in most cases with the course unit tutor. Advantages that were seen to arise from implementing oral assessment included the enhancement of students' employability through developing their oral and presentational skills, the encouragement given to students to take seminars seriously and contribute more fully to them, and the opportunity provided to extend student-centred learning, with the tutor playing a less prominent role in seminar delivery and organisation. But problems were also identified. From the teaching perspective, there was concern about tutors' competency in assessing and moderating oral seminar performance. From the learning perspective, there was anxiety about students experiencing 'presentation overload', arising from having to give too many presentations and from having to listen to too many presentations given by fellow students (Doran et al., 2000).

Group assessment

As Tony Nicholson and Graham Ellis of the History Department at Teesside University neatly observe, group assessment brings difficulties by creating 'a collective exercise within a culture of intense individualism' (Nicholson and Ellis, 2000: 215). As a result, both teacher and taught are led to question the fairness of marking. Not only might the marks of 'freeloaders' and 'weaker' students be raised to undeserved levels, but those perceived as being diligent and more able might receive less than their due deserts. In addressing the problem, the Teesside approach has been to award an overall mark to the group, to multiply this mark by the number of people in the group and then to allocate the product according to the varying contributions made by group members. Nicholson and Ellis also note the difficulties that arise in assessing process – such as the management and delivery of group-based projects – rather than product, and they discuss ways forward, including the use of student diaries (which provide a work record) and e-mail seminar responses (which can be printed off for assessment and moderation purposes) (Nicholson and Ellis, 2000: 208–19).

Despite the problems encountered, the advantages that group work can bring are considerable. Key among them are enhancing transferable skills by enabling students to work in a way common in professional life, providing a good way of enabling students to get to know each other, and enabling students to obtain support from peers, with discussion and pooling of ideas enabling more material to be covered and the quality of work to be enhanced (Allen and Lloyd-Jones, *Groupwork*; Detroit Mercy, *Assessment*).

Peer assessment

In peer assessment, groups or individuals rate their peers, advantage being seen to arise through enhancing student involvement and the provision of formative assessment (Dochy et al., 1999: 337–400). The Doran and associates' survey of history courses reveals many examples of peer assessment being used in oral seminar presentations, even though, in some cases, tutors have found it necessary to moderate the results and discount 'rogue' marks (Doran et al., 2000: 197). To illustrate the types of approach adopted, which can differ markedly, two examples may be cited.

Example 1: Crime and Punishment in Britain, 1690–1800

Offered at Oxford Brookes University, assessment for this module comprises an essay counting for 60 per cent of the total mark and a group seminar presentation counting for the remainder. The seminar presentation has three elements, each equally weighted. One is a mark awarded by the tutor for the group presentation, another is a peer mark calculated as an average from marks given by seminar members, and the third is a tutor mark obtained for writing up the seminar. Enterprise in the form presentations take is encouraged, adding considerably to student interest and enthusiasm.

Example 2: Community History

This module forms part of the provision at the University of Central Lancashire, the peer element of the group assessment counting for 30 per cent of the total marks, the remaining 70 per cent being available for a group project, marked by the module tutor. The project has to make use of primary material and students are required to produce a display, booklet, exhibition or other appropriate assignment that 'articulates and portrays key historical ideas that will appeal to non-specialists outside the university'.

One difficulty that arises in implementing peer assessment is the opposition of students. Their attitude is well exemplified in the results of a survey on group work undertaken by Julia Allen and Roger Lloyd-Jones. Sampling history students at Sheffield Hallam University, they found that no fewer than 86 per cent of their 90 respondents strongly opposed a variant of the Nicholson and Ellis approach, with student groups rather than tutors allocating marks for individual contributions (Allen and Lloyd-Jones, *Groupwork*: 10–11). And the survey undertaken by Doran and colleagues discovered that a number of peer assessment schemes used in higher education history departments had been abandoned because of their unpopularity with students. Reasons for such resistance include students' dislike of judging others and the belief that expertise in assessing lies with tutors (Brown with Bull et al., 1997: 172–3). In seeking to counteract such attitudes, elements of peer assessment tend to carry a relatively small proportion of the available marks and, as in the Oxford Brookes example, the averaging of marks awarded by peers safeguards against 'rogue' marks having an untoward impact. Persuading students of the benefit of peer assessment in terms of their personal development can also be effective (Fallows and Chandramohan, 2001: 235), while the option is available of keeping peer-group comments and marks anonymous, at least to the recipient if not to the tutor (Brown with Bull et al., 1997: 171). There is the possibility, too, of reducing student anxiety by using peer assessment for formative assessment alone (Booth, 1996a: 280).

Self-assessment

Self-assessment involves students in making decisions about their own learning and is mainly used for formative assessment to encourage reflection on the learning process and its outcomes. Students engaging in self-assessment are seen to become more active learners and to achieve outcomes at a higher standard (Dochy et al., 1999: 334–7). The survey undertaken by Doran and colleagues found that, with regard to summative assessment, tutors have found self-assessment helpful in demonstrating to students the fairness and accuracy of other means by which they are assessed (Doran et al., 2000: 197). Moreover, the Nicholson and Ellis experience is that their students were prepared to take part in 'very searching forms of self-assessment' despite their unwillingness to give marks to their peers (Nicholson and Ellis, 2000: 216). How far self-assessment has value for summative purposes, though, has been questioned, the view of Brown, Bull and Pendlebury being that both peer- and self-assessment should be seen mainly as learning tools (Brown with Bull et al., 1997: 179). And where self-assessment in undergraduate history provision does have a summative dimension, the marks awarded may well comprise only a small proportion of the whole. Thus in teaching an upper-level history course unit on *Witchcraft, Magic and Science* during the spring of 2003, Brian W. Ogilvie of the University of Massachusetts/Amherst incorporated a mid-term self-assessment exercise worth only 5 per cent of the total mark. Yet that he required students to reflect on what they had so far put into the course and what they had gained from it can be viewed as a vital part of the learning process, helping them to set clearer and more purposeful learning agendas (Massachusetts, *Guidelines*).

It is quite evident from this brief survey that undergraduate history students are being assessed by a wide variety of means. It may be that the traditional types of coursework and examination essay, which require students to demonstrate their understanding of secondary material, still hold sway. Yet, in response to the changing circumstances in which undergraduate learning and teaching takes place, especially the need to take account of the key skills agenda, other means of assessment have gained considerable ground. Not uncommonly, these involve students making use of primary evidence and go beyond assessment of written work alone. Concern remains, however, as to how far such approaches are seen as integral components in assessment regimes that are designed to encourage growing competency, as opposed to 'one-offs' that reflect the enthusiasms of individual tutors. How far, in other words, are innovatory approaches to assessment being used to maximum advantage?

CONCLUSION

While attention in this chapter has focused on the key concerns of what higher education historians are assessing and the means they employ to carry out their assessments, other considerations must be taken into account in developing assessment regimes. As follows:

- Anonymous marking, which aims to eliminate any discrimination, intentional or otherwise, that course unit tutors might show, and 'blind' second marking, which aims to add to the thoroughness and independence of the assessment process (Brown, 2001: 17).
- How the declared aims and outcomes of course units are reflected in the type and extent of assessment that is favoured or allowed (the so-called validity of assessment), the need being to determine what functions the various assessment components perform (Brown, 2001: 2–3; Race, 2001: 4 and 8).
- Articulating formative assessment, not only to achieve a reasonable balance between critical and supportive comment but also to ensure that the comment is delivered to students in a form they

understand, a point that links back to the issue of transparency in assessment. With regard to the former, the need is to avoid, in David Boud's words, going beyond 'the realm of valid statements into the world of abusive language' (Boud, 1995: 44). As to the latter, Kate Chanock's finding that virtually one half of a sample of humanities students at Le Trobe University were unclear about the feedback comment 'too much description and not enough analysis' is telling (Chanock, 2000: 100–4).

- The means by which the assessment process fits into quality assurance mechanisms, especially if assessment strategies are to be refined in the light of experience and reflection.
- The use of ICT in assessment, not only in recording and presenting student grades, but also in undertaking various types of summative and formative assessment, including the appropriateness or otherwise of using multiple-choice questions (Yorke, 2001: 13–14; Brown, Race and Bull, 1999).

Viewed from this broader perspective, development of an effective assessment regime for history undergraduates that works in their best interests is a complex and taxing business, as well as one that is ongoing. Yet it is apparent from the evidence presented in this chapter that some higher education historians are responding to assessment challenges in a highly innovative manner, especially with regard to assessing transferable skills. Accordingly, not only has coursework assumed growing significance in assessing history students, but so, too, has the variety of forms it takes. The traditional essay may still hold sway in coursework and examinations alike – and perhaps rightly so – but its hold has been considerably weakened and its form has become more diversified, most notably by informing discussion through the use of primary evidence. As has been demonstrated, a range of assessment strategies are being employed, including:

- gobbets;
- identification questions;
- quizzes and multiple-choice questions;
- oral presentations and contributions;
- peer judgement;
- group evaluation;
- self-grading.

In reviewing the developments taking place in the practice of assessing history undergraduates, several desiderata become evident.

1. *Trying to ensure students appreciate what is required of them for assessment purposes.* Publishing assessment criteria and accompanying statements of attainment can go a long way in helping to achieve this objective. Yet the impact of such guidance is likely to be muted unless students receive feedback that is closely related to the statements of attainment. That a student is regarded as achieving a 'good' or 'fair' analysis, say, is not particularly helpful without further explanation. What students need to be shown is how their assignments have been mapped onto assessment statements so that they can obtain clear insights into where their strengths and weaknesses are seen to lie.

2. *Achieving fairness in assessment.* Much here depends upon the transparency of the assessment process, so that students feel reasonably confident about what is required of them in all the course units they take. In achieving this end, assessment criteria and statements of attainment again have a vital role to play, even if they are seen as a constraint on the freedom of individual tutors to assess as they think fit. To a degree, of course, assessment criteria can be modified to accommodate differing requirements, though students will need to be shown how and why. But a small number of well-chosen generic assessment criteria linked with clearly differentiated statements of attainment should provide the backbone of an assessment scheme that will not only direct students' efforts appropriately, but will also encourage them to reflect on how the quality of their work can be improved. And the notion of fairness includes preventing plagiarism.

3. *Ensuring variety in assessment.* At issue here, in part, is the fundamental point that no one means of assessment can cope with the varied range of outcomes that comprise undergraduate history provision, especially in relation to the acquisition of key skills. But there is also the consideration that adopting too conservative an approach towards assessment can act as an unnecessary brake on innovation. What is clear is that undergraduate history provision will continue to change as new opportunities arise and fashions change, and that initiating revised approaches to assessment, despite the difficulties that might arise, can be used to facilitate the process. Furthermore, the notion of varied assessment links with

the question of fairness. If too wide a variation in assessment patterns is allowed for individual course units, some students may feel that others are given an unfair advantage. Allowing only some tutors to use a 'take-home' examination rather than a timed examination held on campus is a case in point. But the argument can also be extended to any marked variation there might be between course units in the proportion of marks awarded to a particular type of assessment component.

4. *Developing progression and differentiation in assessment*. The matter has been touched on in this chapter, adding to the discussion in Chapter 2. The essential point to reiterate, though, is that of the need to make assessment more challenging as students progress through their programmes of study. A wide range of means exists to achieve this objective, both through coursework and examinations, but all require thought about the manner in which the challenge is perceived to become greater and the extent that it does so from level to level. Thus, to take one example, building up the skills and knowledge that students will require to undertake a final-level dissertation informed by primary evidence can be greatly assisted if both the activities and assessment they experience at earlier stages of their studies are, at least in part, directed towards this end. And the formative assessment they receive on the way can, if phrased constructively, be an extremely effective confidence booster.

Key references

Booth, A. (1996b) 'Changing assessment to improve learning', in A. Booth and P. Hyland (eds) *History in Higher Education*. Oxford: Blackwell, pp. 261–75.

Bosworth, S.L., Gossweiler, R.S. and Slevin, K.F. (2000) 'Assessing learning outcomes: tests, gender and the assessment of historical knowledge', in A. Booth and P. Hyland (eds) *The Practice of University History*. Manchester: Manchester University Press, pp. 220–32.

Brown, G. (2001) *Assessment: A Guide for Lecturers*. York: Learning and Teaching Support Network.

Brown, S. and Knight, P. (1994) *Assessing Learners in Higher Education*. London: Kogan Page.

Race, P. (2001) *Assessment: A Guide for Students*. York: Learning and Teaching Support Network.

Doran, S., Durston, C., Fletcher, A. and Longmore, J. (2000) 'Assessing students in seminars: an evaluation of current practice', in A. Booth and P. Hyland (eds) *The Practice of University History*. Manchester: Manchester University Press, pp. 194–207.

Nicholson, T. and Ellis, G. (2000) 'Assessing group work to develop collaborative learning', in A. Booth and P. Hyland (eds) *The Practice of University History*. Manchester: Manchester University Press, pp. 208–19.

Websites

QAA, *History Benchmark Statement* (2000) at http://www.qaa.ac.uk/crntwork/benchmark/history.html

Note

1 Formed in 1994, SACWG comprises administrators and academics from nine higher education institutions in England who collaborate in order to study assessment and related matters. The group's original interest stemmed from a mutual concern about the way in which assessment outcomes from different subject cultures, and from different institutions, were being cumulated into degree classifications. Subsequently, the group has worked on, *inter alia*, academic benchmarking, grading systems, student coursework and examination performance and assessment criteria. The group has published a number of articles and runs an annual workshop on assessment issues.

Conclusion

The profound changes occurring in higher education during recent decades have raised fundamental concerns about the learning and teaching approaches that should be adopted. Most notable among these changes are the widening base from which students are recruited, the development of more rigorous quality assurance procedures, the growing awareness of how effective learning takes place, the need to address the skills agenda and the desire to exploit opportunities arising from the ICT revolution. Any one of these changes would in itself be enough to prompt higher education lecturers to at least consider how far traditional approaches to planning the curriculum and to devising strategies for learning, teaching and assessment might still be effectively applied. Taken together, they have created a powerful impetus towards developing new approaches from which even the most conservative find it difficult to escape, irrespective of their subject discipline, the type and perceived status of the higher education institution to which they are attached and the level of experience and expertise they can bring to bear.

In addition to these general changes, historians teaching at degree level have had to review their approaches to pedagogical matters because of the marked changes that have taken place in the nature of their discipline. Of particular concern has been the rise of 'history from below', which has impacted powerfully both on the subject matter of the discipline and on the ways in which teaching and learning within the discipline can take place. Course units dealing with the lives of ordinary people have gained a strong foothold in higher education history curricula, often giving students the opportunity to move away from a heavy dependency on a diet of political history devoted to the great events and figures at national and international levels, if not to the extent that social historians would like to see (Stearns, 2003: 13). Furthermore, the 'new' history, with the vast and varied range of readily accessible source material at its disposal, has helped to extend to a marked degree the amount and range of historical investigation that students can undertake, and the ease with which they can do so. Accordingly, students have gained greater opportunity to follow their own interests, as well as to take firmer control over the form their learning experiences take.

Developments of this kind reflect the debate that has taken place, and which still continues, about the role that history as an academic discipline should play. The notions of history having 'use value' and 'vocational significance' have become more strongly embedded in the mindset of higher education historians, whether they approve or not. So, too, has the idea of making their subject relevant to a wide range of individual interests – being 'student centred', in other words – as well as to the interests of employers and government. And the implementation of this objective implies that ongoing dialogue with the interested parties will take place. Moreover, there is the role history should be seen to play in promoting the informed and tolerant perspectives upon which the functioning of democratic societies ultimately depends. The burden of expectations placed on history teaching has thus become heavy, adding further to the demands of designing and implementing the undergraduate curriculum.

Faced with such an unprecedented range of challenges, what are the best ways forward? Our approach has been to seek guidance from the *History Benchmarking Statement* in an attempt to build on a considerable amount of thought that has already taken place with regard to undergraduate history teaching and on which a large measure of agreement, at least among higher education historians in Britain, is evident. Such an approach has enabled us not only to tease out major issues raised in the *Statement*, but also to consider how these issues are being tackled in practice, both in Britain and overseas. Inevitably our selection of illustrative examples can only scratch the surface of the numerous progressive and enterprising approaches that are being implemented, a statement which in itself can only be regarded as encouraging for the well-being of undergraduate history. Certainly, there is a great deal of inspiration to be gained from taking account of, and reflecting upon, the work being undertaken by higher education history colleagues. Moreover, the opportunities to do so have expanded considerably, not least because of the growing attention that

is being paid to disseminating good practice by a variety of means, including on-line essays.

But what are the best ways forward with regard to each of the main areas raised in the *History Benchmarking Statement* and what particular issues need to be addressed? Beginning with the notion of progression, the indications are that some practices are widely favoured, including the move from breadth to depth in content terms and the move towards more independent forms of learning by means of final-level dissertations. Such approaches have much to commend them in terms of providing effective learning experiences that take account of students' needs and of the growing levels of competency that students should acquire as they progress. Yet concerns remain about how clearly schemes of progression are being articulated and about how fully they have been developed in relation to the opportunities that are available. Thus the literature entering the public domain tends at best to be implicit on such matters, leading to concerns about whether or not students have a clear enough understanding of what is expected of them as they move through their programmes from level to level. Moreover, it is by no means evident that full opportunity has been taken to explore and justify how greater challenges can be presented to students as they progress within each curricular dimension considered in the *History Benchmarking Statement*. The means by which students are summatively assessed provides a case in point, with the same or very similar regimes appearing commonly to operate at each level of provision.

As to the question of content, what to include and what to leave out remains the basic issue. Achieving some sort of balance between the general and the particular, one type of history and another, the recent and distant past, and domestic and overseas history poses formidable problems. And they are problems that can only be exacerbated as the knowledge explosion continues unabated. In the early stages of undergraduate history programmes, compulsion or restricted choice is widely practised, largely, it would seem, with a view to achieving broad coverage as a foundation for more specialised work at subsequent stages. But even course units with a broad geographical and temporal coverage may lack range with regard to types of history and the opportunity for in-depth investigation. What is required here is consideration of the precise functions given to broadly-based units that are located in the early stages of history programmes, especially to ensure that too great a burden of scene-setting does not fall on any one of them. One implication of this observation is that several such units might need to be offered, with a significant amount of compulsion and/or limited choice being imposed. Another is that less ambition might be exercised with regard to the degree of geographical and temporal coverage deemed necessary. There is certainly a need to remember that what is thought to be good for students in terms of creating broadly-based foundations may not be viewed by students themselves in quite the same light; the degree of motivation students can achieve from following their choice of interests cannot be lightly discounted, whatever level of study is concerned. A progression that increasingly emphasises choice is certainly one way forward, bearing in mind that the differential between levels in this respect is one of degree.

The question of compulsion in undergraduate history programmes also extends to skills-orientated course units, not least with the demands of final-level dissertations in mind. Indeed, such units can justifiably be seen as forming an integral and iterative component of the curriculum, providing students with direct experience of the processes that historians use and the problems they encounter. Accordingly, the units have a crucial role to play in helping to create graduates who have acquired an informed and sophisticated under-standing of history as an academic discipline and who, if they so wished, would be capable of progressing with confidence into postgraduate work. In addition to teaching history-specific skills, however, history programmes are charged with looking beyond the discipline itself in order to inculcate generic skills, both in terms of the study skills needed for life-long learning and the workplace-related skills needed for career development. This is a role that history shares with other disciplines and is of vital importance when viewed from the students' perspective. It is the case, of course, that the teaching of both history-specific and generic skills need not be confined to skills-orientated units. Yet without them, the importance that history programmes give to skills-oriented teaching becomes harder for students to appreciate. In fact, the tendency may be to leave skills-based provision in the hands of some tutors rather than others, with the result that the extent to which students are able to experience at least some aspects of skills-based provision becomes largely a matter of chance.

A particular advantage that arises with skills-based work is the encouragement it gives to active learning. Our discussion of the

approaches used in lectures and seminars has emphasised the importance that educational theorists attach to active learning and has
demonstrated the sort of imaginative and stimulating approaches that
higher education historians have adopted with active learning in
mind. A key point to emerge is how this kind of learning is being
promoted within the framework of traditional approaches centred on
lectures and seminars. And this is the case whether face-to-face or
on-line techniques are being used. The view higher education historians appear to be taking is that the dissatisfaction they express with
lectures and seminars can be significantly reduced, if not overcome, by
looking for opportunities to incorporate active learning. Probably the
scope for doing so is greater within seminars than lectures, especially
where small discussion groups and practical activities using primary
sources can be incorporated. Even so, it is quite evident from reported
examples that the scope for including active learning experience in
lectures is considerable and can be achieved without sacrificing to any
marked extent the value that lectures have in stimulating interest and
raising awareness.

Lastly, but certainly not least, is the issue of assessing students'
work. Much of our discussion has centred on the importance of
establishing manageable assessment regimes based on the identification of assessment criteria and levels of attainment within them. At the
heart of this discussion is the need to find ways both to ensure that
students know what is expected of them in reaching particular
standards and that history teaching teams achieve reasonable levels of
consistency with regard to the grades they award. But beyond these
considerations are concerns about the means by which history
undergraduates are assessed. As with learning and teaching matters,
it is clear that some innovative means of assessment are being
employed by higher education historians, both with regard to
coursework and examinations. Yet how far assessment innovation is
being systematically applied within programmes, and how far it
should be given the changing circumstances in which undergraduate
teaching is taking place, must remain matters of ongoing debate.

Appendix 1: Sampling approaches

The sample information used in Chapters 2 and 4 are derived on an availability basis, so uncertainty arises about their representativeness. Nonetheless, they provide useful insights into the extent to which various curricular approaches are adopted, as well as providing a basis on which hypotheses requiring further investigation can be formulated (Cohen et al., 2000: 102–3).

We are greatly indebted to the following colleagues for providing us with survey information on progression and differentiation matters: Hannah Barker (Manchester); Colin Brookes (Sussex); Callum Brown (Strathclyde); Simon Ditchfield (York); Martin Doherty (Westminster); Pauline Elkes (Staffordshire); Wil Griffith (Bangor); Sean Greenwood (Canterbury); Paul Henderson (Wolverhampton); Michael Hicks (King Alfred's, Winchester); Janet Hollinshead (Liverpool Hope); William Philpott (London Guildhall); Steven King (Oxford Brookes); Jane Longmore (Greenwich); Roger Lloyd-Jones (Sheffield Hallam); David Nicholls (Manchester Metropolitan); Tony Nicholson (Teesside); Michael Power (Liverpool); Philip Richardson (Bristol); Leonard Schwarz (Birmingham); Adrian Smith (Southampton); Don Spaeth (Glasgow); Liz Tingle (Northampton); Greame White (Chester); Michael Winstanley (Lancaster); Tony Webster (Edge Hill); Chris Wrigley (Nottingham).

The institutions reviewed for our survey on skills-orientated course units were:

Royal Holloway College, University of London; University College, London; Lancaster University; University of Newcastle upon Tyne; University of York; Bristol University; Liverpool University; Birmingham University; Hull University; Sheffield University; Leicester

University; Reading University; Oxford University; Nottingham University; University of East Anglia; Cardiff University; University of Wales, Bangor; Edinburgh University; Dundee University; Aberdeen University; Strathclyde University; Queen's University, Belfast; National University of Ireland, Galway; Trinity College, Dublin; University of North London; De Montfort University; University of the West of England; Sheffield Hallam University; Kingston University; University of Central Lancashire; University College, Worcester; University College, Canterbury; University College, Northampton.

Appendix 2: Websites for learning and teaching in higher education history

AMERICAN HISTORICAL ASSOCIATION

Founded in 1884, the AHA is concerned with learning and teaching in history at varying levels of education. *Perspectives*, the Association's on-line newsletter, deals with a wide range of historical concerns, including teaching matters. Published monthly, *Perspectives* can be viewed without charge on-line. An index is provided. The Association's website also contains a *Resources for Teachers at All Levels* section, which links to the *Teaching and Learning in the Digital Age* project, details of which are given in Chapter 5.

Website: http://www.historians.org/

CENTER FOR HISTORY AND NEW MEDIA

Established in 1994, *The Center* is concerned with the ways in which the digital media can be used by historians to reconsider modes of researching, writing and teaching. Particularly helpful as far as higher education history teaching and learning is concerned are the *Essays on History and New Media*. They can be located and viewed free of charge by visiting the *Resources* section of the Center's website.

Website: http://chnm.gmu.edu/index1.html

H-Net

H-Net aims to foster electronic communication within international communities of scholars in the humanities and social sciences. A key activity is to sponsor on-line discussion networks, which contain a varied range of learning and teaching inputs. To take one example, H-Urban has a *Teaching Center* section, which encourages discussion about teaching urban history and urban studies.

Website: http://www.h-net.org/

ORGANIZATION OF AMERICAN HISTORIANS

The Organization of American Historians, which was founded in 1907, is concerned to promote both the study and teaching of the American past. Its *Teaching History Resource Center* provides links to various types of resources and publications of use in teaching history, while both its quarterly *Newsletter*, which can be viewed without charge on-line, and its quarterly *Magazine of History*, for which a subscription is required, contain articles relating to learning and teaching matters. Indexes to back copies of both these publications are provided.

Website: http://www.oah.org/

SUBJECT CENTRE FOR HISTORY, CLASSICS AND ARCHAEOLOGY

Funded by the Learning and Teaching Support Network (LTSN), the Centre aims to promote high-quality learning and teaching in history at higher education level by supporting innovation and disseminating good practice. Guidance on a wide range of matters is available on the site, especially in the *Case Studies*, *Briefing Papers* and *Tutor and Students Guides*. Reports of sessions at the Centre's annual conference are also posted. The site has much to offer in the way of practitioners describing and reflecting on their approaches to learning and teaching.

Website: http://hca.ltsn.ac.uk/

TEACHING HISTORY – A JOURNAL OF METHODS

This journal began in 1976 with the aim 'of providing history teachers at all levels with the best and newest teaching ideas for their classrooms'. It is published twice yearly at Emporia State University, Kansas. The journal's website contains an index to all the articles published and a free sample copy can be requested.

Website: http://www.emporia.edu/socsci/journal/main.htm

THE COURSEWARE FOR HISTORY IMPLEMENTATION CONSORTIUM (CHIC)

CHIC is concerned with enhancing the quality of student learning in history and associated disciplines through 'an evaluated integration of learning-technology-based materials'. Particularly valuable are the case studies, in which higher education historians reflect on their experiences in using on-line learning and teaching approaches. Examples are considered in Chapter 5.

Website: http://www.chicsite.co.uk/

Bibliography

- Contextual sources
- Historical sources
- On-line sources:
  - College and university websites
  - Essays and reports
  - Other information

CONTEXTUAL SOURCES

Ackerknecht, E. (1967) *Medicine at the Paris Hospital, 1794–1848*. Baltimore, MD: Johns Hopkins University Press.

Allen, J. and R. Lloyd-Jones, R. (n.d.) *The Assessment of Group Work and Presentations in the Humanities: A Guidebook for Tutors*. Sheffield: Sheffield Hallam University.

Anderson, A. and Marshall, V. (1996) *Core Versus Occupation-Specific Skills*. London: HMSO.

Appleby, J., Hunt, L. and Jacob, M. (1995) *Telling the Truth About History*. London: W. W. Norton.

Assiter, A. (1995) 'Transferable skills: a response to the sceptics', in A. Assiter (ed.), *Transferable Skills in Higher Education*. London: Kogan Page, pp. 11–19.

Assiter, A. (ed.) (1995) *Transferable Skills in Higher Education*. London: Kogan Page.

Barnett, R. (1994) *The Limits of Competence: Knowledge, Higher Education and Society*. London: Society for Research into Higher Education and Open University Press.

Becher, T. and Trowler, P. R. (2001) *Academic Tribes and Territories*. London: Society for Research into Higher Education and Open University Press.

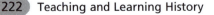

Bennett, N., Dunne, E. and Carre, C. (2000) *Skills Development in Higher Education and Employment*. London: Society for Research into Higher Education and Open University Press.

Boud, D. (1995) 'Assessing and learning: contradictory or complementary', in P. Knight (ed.), *Assessing for Learning in Higher Education*. London: Kogan Page, pp. 35–48.

Bourdieu, P. (1988) *Homo Academicus*. Cambridge: Polity.

Boys, C. J., Brennan, J., Henckel, M., Kirkland, J., Kogan, M. and Youll, P. J. (1988) *Higher Education and the Preparation for Work*. London: Jessica Kingsley.

Bridges, D. (1993) 'Transferable skills: a philosophical perspective', *Studies in Higher Education*, 18: 43–51.

Brown, G. (2001) *Assessment: A Guide for Lecturers*. York: Learning and Teaching Support Network.

Brown, G. with Bull, J. and Pendlebury, M. (1997) *Assessing Student Learning in Higher Education*. London: Routledge.

Brown, S. and Knight, P. (1994) *Assessing Learners in Higher Education*. London: Kogan Page.

Brown, S., Race, P. and Bull, J. (eds) (1999) *Computer-Assisted Assessment in Higher Education*. London: Kogan Page.

Chanock, K. (2000) 'Comments on essays: do students understand what tutors write?', *Teaching in Higher Education*, 5: 95–105.

Clare, J. (1998) 'Curriculum test for universities', *The Daily Telegraph*, 18 March.

Cohen, L., Manson, L. and Marison, K. (2000) *Research Methods in Education*. London: RoutledgeFalmer.

Cryer, P. (1998) 'Transferable skills, marketability and lifelong learning: the particular case of post-graduate research students', *Studies in Higher Education*, 23: 207–16.

Cuthbert, K. (2001) 'Independent study and project work: continuities or discontinuities', *Teaching in Higher Education*, 6: 69–84.

Dochy, F., Segers, M. and Sluijsmans, D. (1999) 'The use of self-, peer- and co-assessment in higher education: a review', *Studies in Higher Education*, 24: 331–47.

Ecclestone, K. (2001) 'I know a 2:1 when I see it: understanding criteria for degree classifications in franchised university programmes', *Journal of Further and Higher Education*, 5: 301–13.

Elwood, J. and Klenowski, V. (2002) 'Creating communities of shared practice: the challenges of assessment use in learning and teaching', *Assessment and Evaluation in Higher Education*, 27: 243–56.

Fallows, S. and Chandramohan, B. (2001) 'Multiple approaches to assessment: reflections on use of tutor, peer and self-assessment', *Teaching in Higher Education*, 6: 229–45.

Fallows, S. and Steven, C. (eds) (2000) *Integrating Key Skills in Higher Education: Employability, Transferable Skills and Learning for Life.* London: Kogan Page.

Fine, P. (2001) 'Academe branded unpatriotic', *Times Higher Education Supplement*, 23 November.

Freeman, R. and Lewis, R. (1998) *Planning and Implementing Assessment.* London: Kogan Page.

Gibbs, G. (1992) *Improving the Quality of Student Learning.* Bristol: Technical and Educational Services.

Glasner, A. (1999) 'Innovations in student assessment: a systemwide perspective', in S. Brown and A. Glasner (eds), *Assessment Matters in Higher Education: Choosing and Using Diverse Approaches.* Buckingham: Society for Research into Higher Education and Open University Press, pp. 14–27.

Graff, G. (1992) *Beyond the Culture Wars: How Teaching the Conflicts can Revitalize American Education.* New York: Norton.

Hall, K. and Harding, A. (2002) 'Level descriptions and teacher assessment in England: towards a community of assessment practice', *Educational Research*, 44: 1–15.

Higgins, R., Hartley, P. and Skelton, A. (2002) 'The conscientious consumer: reconsidering the role of assessment feedback in student learning', *Studies in Higher Education*, 27: 53–64.

Higher Education in the Learning Society. National Committee of Inquiry into Higher Education (1997) Chairman: Sir Ron Dearing. London: HMSO.

Hounsell, D. (1987) 'Essay writing and the quality of feedback', in J. T. E. Richardson, M. E. Eysenck and D. W. Piper (eds), *Student Learning: Research in Education and Cognitive Psychology.* Milton Keynes: Society for Research into Higher Education and Open University Press, pp. 109–19.

Jenkins, A. and Zetter, R. (2003) *Linking Research and Teaching in Departments.* York: Learning and Teaching Support Network.

Jessup, G. (1990) *Common Learning Outcomes: Core Skills in A/AS levels and NVQs.* London: National Council for Vocational Qualifications.

Knight, P. (2001) *A Briefing on Key Concepts.* York: Learning and Teaching Support Network.

Knight, P. T. (2002) 'The Achilles' heel of quality: the assessment of student learning', in *Quality in Higher Education*, 8: 107–15.

Kuhn, T. (1962) *The Structure of Scientific Revolutions*. Chicago: University of Chicago Press.

Light, G. and Cox, R. (2001) *Learning and Teaching in Higher Education: The Reflective Professional*. London: Sage.

Moust, J. H. C., Schmidt, H. G., de Volder, M. L., Belien, J. J. and de Grave, W. S. (1987) 'Effects of verbal participation in small group discussion', in J. T. E. Richardson, M. E. Eysenck and D. W. Piper (eds), *Student Learning: Research in Education and Cognitive Psychology*. Milton Keynes: Society for Research into Higher Education and Open University Press, pp. 147–54.

Moxley, D., Najor-Durak, A. and Dumbrigue, C. (2001) *Keeping Students in Higher Education*. London: Kogan Page.

Nicholls, G. (2002) *Developing Teaching and Learning in Higher Education*. London: RoutledgeFalmer.

Race, P. (2001) *Assessment: A Guide for Students*. York: Learning and Teaching Support Network.

Rawson, M. (2000) 'Learning to learn: more than a skill set', *Studies in Higher Education*, 25: 225–38.

Richardson, J. T. E., Eysenck, M. E. and Piper, D. W. (eds) (1987) *Student Learning: Research in Education and Cognitive Psychology*. Milton Keynes: Society for Research into Higher Education and Open University Press.

Roberts, B. and Myock, M. (1991) 'The experience of introducing work-based learning on an Arts degree course', *Journal of Further and Higher Education*, 15: 76–85.

Roberts, B. and Myock, M. (1995) 'Work-based learning on an Arts degree course', *Journal of Further and Higher Education*, 19: 62–72.

Rogers, J. (2001) *Adults Learning*. Buckingham: Open University Press.

Rust, C. (2001) *A Briefing on Assessment of Large Groups*. York: Learning and Teaching Support Network.

Slee, P. R. H. (1986) *Learning and a Liberal Education: The Study of Modern History in the Universities of Oxford, Cambridge and Manchester, 1800–1914*. Manchester: Manchester University Press.

Swain, H. (1997) 'Things ain't what they used to be', *The Times Higher Education Supplement*, 16 May.

'Trends in higher education' (2000), *Times Higher Education Supplement*, 22 September.

Woolf, H. (2002) *Assessment Criteria: Fuzzy by Design*. Paper presented at the History LTSN Conference, Oxford.

Woolf, H. and Cooper, A. (1999) 'Benchmarking academic standards in history: an empirical exercise', *Quality in Higher Education*, 5: 145–54.

Woolf, H. et al. (2001) *Background Paper*. Presented at the SACWG National Workshop, Wolverhampton.

Woolfe, A. et al. (1997) *Assessment in Higher Education and the Role of 'Graduateness'*. London: Higher Education Council.

Woollard, A. (1995) 'Core skills and the idea of the graduate', *Higher Education Quarterly*, 49: 316–25.

Yorke, M. (2001) *Assessment: A Guide for Senior Managers*. York: Learning and Teaching Support Network.

HISTORICAL SOURCES

'AHR forum: the old history and the new' (1989) *American Historical Review*, 94: 654–98.

Aldous, C. and Hicks, M. (2003) *A Survey of Historical Source Work in Higher Education*. Winchester: King Alfred's College.

Anderson, R. (2001) ' "Into your handbag": implementing web-based learning at Bath Spa', *Chic Newsletter*, Summer, p. 7.

Barker, A. (1997) 'University history 1997', *History Today*, 47: 58–61.

Barker, H., McLean, M. and Roseman, M. (2000) 'Re-thinking the history curriculum: enhancing students' communication and group-work skills', in A. Booth and P. Hyland (eds), *The Practice of University History Teaching*. Manchester: Manchester University Press, pp. 60–9.

Bates, D. (1999) 'Undergraduate history 1999', *History Today*, 49: 54–60.

Beck, P. (1996) 'History, the curriculum and graduate employment', in A. Booth and P. Hyland (eds), *History in Higher Education: New Directions in Teaching and Learning*. Oxford: Blackwell, pp. 242–57.

Black, J. and MacRaild, D. J. (2000) *Studying History*. Basingstoke: Macmillan.

Blackey, R. (ed.) (1993) *History Anew: Innovations in the Teaching of History Today*. Long Beach, CA: California State University Press.

Blackey, R. (1997) 'New wine in old bottles: revitalizing the traditional history lecture', *Teaching History*, 22: 3–25.

Blackey, R. (ed.) (1999) *Perspectives on Teaching Innovations: Teaching to Think Historically*. Washington, DC: American Historical Association.

Bloch, M. (1954) *The Historian's Craft*. Manchester: Manchester University Press.

Booth, A. (1996a) 'Assessing group work', in A. Booth and P. Hyland (eds), *History in Higher Education: New Directions in Teaching and Learning*. Oxford: Blackwell, pp. 276–97.

Booth, A. (1996b) 'Changing assessment to improve learning', in A. Booth and P. Hyland (eds), *History in Higher Education: New Directions in Teaching and Learning*. Oxford: Blackwell, pp. 261–75.

Booth, A. (1997) 'Listening to students: experiences and expectations in the transition to a history degree', *Studies in Higher Education*, 22: 205–20.

Booth, A. (2000) 'Creating a context to enhance student learning in history', in A. Booth and P. Hyland (eds), *The Practice of University History Teaching*. Manchester: Manchester University Press, pp. 31–46.

Booth, A. (2001) 'Developing history students' skills in the transition to university', *Teaching in Higher Education*, 6: 487–503.

Booth, A. (2003) *Teaching History at University*. London: Routledge.

Booth, A. (2004) 'Rethinking the scholarly: developing the scholarship of teaching in history', *Arts and Humanities in Higher Education*, 3: 247–60.

Booth, A. and Hyland, P. (eds) (1996) *History in Higher Education: New Directions in Teaching and Learning*. Oxford: Blackwell.

Booth, A. and Hyland, P. (eds) (2000) *The Practice of University History Teaching*. Manchester: Manchester University Press.

Bosworth, S. L., Gossweiler, R. S. and Slevin, K. F. (2000) 'Assessing learning outcomes: tests, gender and the assessment of historical knowledge', in A. Booth and P. Hyland (eds), *The Practice of University History Teaching*. Manchester: Manchester University Press, pp. 220–32.

Boulton, J. (2001) 'Death and dying on the web', *Chic Newsletter*, Summer, p. 3.

Brooks, C., Gregory, J. and Nicholls, D. (2000) 'Teaching and the academic career', in A. Booth and P. Hyland (eds), *The Practice of University History Teaching*. Manchester: Manchester University Press, pp. 17–30.

Brown, S. and Race, P. (2002) *Lecturing: A Practical Guide*. London: Kogan Page.

Burke, P. (ed.) (1991) *New Perspectives on Historical Writing*. Cambridge: Polity Press.

Cannadine, D. (1987) 'British history: past, present – and future?', *Past and Present*, 116: 169–91.

Cannon, J. (1984) *Teaching History at University*. London: Historical Association.

Collingwood, R. G. (1970) *The Idea of History*. Oxford: Oxford University Press.

Cook, M. J. (1993) 'Finding the layers in your town', in R. Blackey (ed.), *History Anew: Innovations in the Teaching of History Today*. Long Beach, CA: California State University Press, pp. 289–94.

Davies, P., Conneely, J., Davies, R. and Lynch, D. (2000) 'Imaginative ideas for teaching and learning', in A. Booth and P. Hyland (eds), *The Practice of University History Teaching*. Manchester: Manchester University Press, pp. 112–24.

Davis, J. R. and Salmon, P. (2000) ' "Deep learning" and the large seminar in history teaching', in A. Booth and P. Hyland (eds), *The Practice of University History Teaching*. Manchester: Manchester University Press, pp. 125–36.

Dawson, I. and de Pennington, J. (2000) 'Fieldwork in history teaching and learning', in A. Booth and P. Hyland (eds), *The Practice of University History Teaching*. Manchester: Manchester University Press, pp. 166–78.

Department of Education and Science (1990) *History for Ages 5–16: Proposals of the Secretary of State for Education and Science*. York: National Curriculum Council.

Department of Education and Science (1985) *History in the Primary and Secondary Years: An HMI View*. London: HMSO.

'Developing history teaching through reflective practice' (1997) *History 2000 Newsletter*, December.

Doran, S., Durston, C., Fletcher, A. and Longmore, J. (2000) 'Assessing students in seminars: an evaluation of current practice', in A. Booth and P. Hyland (eds), *The Practice of University History Teaching*. Manchester: Manchester University Press, pp. 194–207.

Dunne, J. (2001) 'E(asy)-learning or learning the hard way?', *Chic Newsletter*, Summer, p. 3.

Easley, J. L. (1998) 'The enhanced lecture: a bridge to interactive teaching', in D. A. Trinkle (ed.), *Writing, Teaching and Researching History in the Electronic Age*. New York: Sharpe, pp. 65–72.

Elkes, P. (2002) *Working with professionals: archive and museum-work experience*. Paper presented at the LTSN History Conference, Oxford.

Elton, G. R. (1967) *The Practice of History*. London: Fontana.

Evans, R. J. (1997) *In Defence of History*. London: Granta Books.

Feldman, M. J. (1997) 'Comprehension essays for world history finals', *Teaching History*, 22: 33–6.

Fitzgerald, I. and Flint, A. (1995) 'British history now', *History Today*, 45: 53–6.

Fletcher, A. (1999) 'The making of a history graduate', *The Independent*, 14 January.

Foucault, M. (1973) *The Birth of the Clinic: An Archaeology of Medical Perception*. London: Tavistock.

Fox-Genovese, E. and Lasch-Quinn, E. (eds) (1999) *Reconstructing History: The Emergence of a New Historical Society*. London: Routledge.

Frank, B. (2002) *Developing a History Module with a Strong Work-based Learning Focus*. Paper presented at the LTSN History Conference, Oxford.

Frederick, P. J. (1991) 'Active learning in history classes', *Teaching History*, 16: 67–83.

Frederick, P. J. (2000) 'Motivating students by active learning in the history classroom', in A. Booth and P. Hyland (eds), *The Practice of University History Teaching*. Manchester: Manchester University Press, pp. 101–11.

Frederick, P. J. (2001) 'Learning from inside out', in H. Edwards, B. Smith and G. Webb (eds), *Lecturing Case Studies: Experience and Practice*. London: Kogan Page, pp. 113–22.

Frederickson, M. E. (1992) 'The past meets the present: teaching women's history in the urban south', *Teaching History*, 17: 18–23.

Glasfurd, G. and Winstanley, M. (2000) 'History in cyberspace: challenges and opportunities of inter-based teaching and learning', in A. Booth and P. Hyland (eds), *The Practice of University History Teaching*. Manchester: Manchester University Press, pp. 85–97.

Gunn, V. A. (2000) 'Transgressing the traditional? Teaching and learning methods in a medieval history access course', *Teaching in Higher Education*, 5: 311–21.

Hall, R. (2003) 'Forging a learning community? A pragmatic approach to co-operative learning', *Arts and Humanities in Higher Education*, 2: 155–72.

Hall, R. and Harding, D. (eds) (2001) *Chic Project Case Studies: Managing ICT in the Curriculum*. Middlesbrough: University of Teesside.

Hall, R., Harding, D., Holden, K. and Rogers, G. (2001) 'Supporting students' critical reflection through web-based pedagogical innovation', in R. Hall and D. Harding (eds), *Chic Project Case Studies: Managing ICT in the Curriculum*. Middlesbrough: University of Teesside, pp. 57–96.

Hewitson, R. (1987) *The Heritage Industry: Britain in a Climate of Decline*. London: Methuen.

Himmelfarb, G. (1987) *The New History and the Old*. Cambridge, MA: Belknap Press.

Hitchcock, T., Shoemaker, R. B. and Tosh, J. (2000) 'Skills and the structure of the history curriculum', in A. Booth and P. Hyland (eds), *The Practice of University History Teaching*. Manchester: Manchester University Press, pp. 47–59.

Holden, K. (2001) 'Key issues for effective staff development and training for the use of ICT', in R. Hall and D. Harding (eds), *Chic Project Case Studies: Managing ICT in the Curriculum*. Middlesbrough: University of Teesside, pp. 27–33.

Hounsell, D. (2000) 'Reappraising and recasting the history essay', in A. Booth and P. Hyland (eds), *The Practice of University History Teaching*. Manchester: Manchester University Press, pp. 181–93.

HUDG (1998) *Final Report of Working Party of the HUDG to the QAA. Standards in History*. London: HUDG.

Hunt, L. (ed.) (1989) *The New Cultural History*. Berkeley, CA: University of California Press.

Hunt, L. (1989) 'Introduction: history, culture, and text', in L. Hunt, *The New Cultural History*. Berkeley, CA: University of California Press, pp. 1–22.

Hyland, P. (2000) 'Learning from feedback on assessment', in A. Booth and P. Hyland (eds), *The Practice of University History Teaching*. Manchester: Manchester University Press, pp. 233–47.

Jenkins, K. (1991) *Re-thinking History*. London: Routledge.

Jenkins, K. (1996) 'Teaching history theory: a radical introduction', in A. Booth and P. Hyland (eds), *History in Higher Education: New Directions in Teaching and Learning*. Oxford: Blackwell, pp. 75–93.

Jones, J. A. (1998) 'Constructing history with computers', in D. A. Trinkle (ed.), *Writing, Teaching and Researching History in the Electronic Age*. New York: Sharpe, pp. 83–8.

Jonson, S. and Macintyre, S. (eds) (1988) 'Making the bicentenary', *Australian Historical Studies*, 23, special issue.

Jordanova, L. (2000) *History in Practice*. London: Arnold.

Kaye, H. J. (1995) *'Why do Ruling Classes fear History' And Other Essays*. London: Macmillan.

Kenyon, J. (1993) *The History Men: The Historical Profession in England from the Renaissance*. London: Weidenfeld & Nicholson.

Kornfeld, E. (1993) 'Representations of history: role-playing debates in college history courses', in R. Blackey (ed.), *History Anew: Innovations in the Teaching of History Today*. Long Beach, CA: California State University Press, pp. 147–51.

Kramer, L. S. (1989) 'Literature, criticism, and historical imagination: the literary challenge of Hayden White and Dominick La Capra', in L. Hunt (ed.), *The New Cultural History*. Berkeley, CA: University of California Press, pp. 97–128.

Lee, P. and Shemilt, D. (2003) 'A scaffold, not a cage: progression and progression models in history', *Teaching History*, 113: 13–22.

Lewis, M. J. and Lloyd-Jones, R. (1996) *Using Computers in History: A Practical Guide*. London: Routledge.

Lloyd-Jones, R. and Lewis, M. (2000) 'Integrating information technology into the history curriculum', in A. Booth and P. Hyland (eds), *The Practice of University History Teaching*. Manchester: Manchester University Press, pp. 70–84.

Lowentahl, D. (1985) *The Past is a Foreign Country*. Cambridge: Cambridge University Press.

Lubelska, C. (1996) 'Gender in the curriculum', in A. Booth and P. Hyland (eds), *History in Higher Education: New Directions in Teaching and Learning*. Oxford: Blackwell, pp. 55–74.

McCormack, P. (2001) 'Evaluating the influence of web-based seminar preparation for undergraduate History students', in R. Hall and D. Harding (eds), *Chic Project Case Studies: Managing ICT in the Curriculum*. Middlesbrough: University of Teesside, pp. 97–104.

McCullagh, C. B. (1998) *The Truth of History*. London: Routledge.

Marwick, A. (1989) *The Nature of History*, 3rd edn. London: Macmillan.

Marwick, A. (2001) *The New Nature of History. Knowledge, Evidence, Language*. Basingstoke: Palgrave.

Monahan, W. G. (2000) 'Everybody talks: discussion strategies in the classroom', *Teaching History*, XXV: 6–14.

Munslow, A. (1997) *Deconstructing History*. London: Routledge.

Munslow, A. (2001) 'Editorial', *Rethinking History*, 2: 1–6.

Nash, G. B., Crabtree, C. and Dunn, R. E. (1997) *History on Trial: Culture Wars and the Teaching of the Past*. New York: Knapf.

Nicholls, D. (1992) 'Making history students enterprising: "independent study" at Manchester Polytechnic', *Studies in Higher Education*, 17: 67–80.

Nicholson, T. and Ellis, G. (2000) 'Assessing group work to develop collaborative learning', in A. Booth and P. Hyland (eds), *The Practice of University History Teaching*. Manchester: Manchester University Press, pp. 208–19.

Novick, P. (1988) *That Noble Dream: The 'Objectivity Question' and the American Historical Profession*. Cambridge: Cambridge University Press.

O'Brien, P. (1989) 'Michel Foucault's history of culture', in L. Hunt (ed.), *The New Cultural History*. Berkeley, CA: University of California Press, pp. 25–46.

Pearce, R. (2003) 'University History', *History Today*, 53: 54–7.

Pennell, M. L. (2000) 'Improving student participation in History lectures: suggestions for successful questioning', *Teaching History*, XXV: 25–35.

Peters, J., Peterkin, C. and Williams, C. (2000) 'Progression within modular history degrees', in A. Booth and P. Hyland (eds), *The Practice of University History Teaching*. Manchester: Manchester University Press, pp. 137–53.

Phillips, R. (1998) *History Teaching, Nationhood and the State: A Study in Educational Politics*. London: Cassell.

Plumb, J. H. (1969) *The Death of the Past*. London: Macmillan.

Preston, G. (1996) 'Seminars for active learning', in A. Booth and P. Hyland (eds), *History in Higher Education: New Directions in Teaching and Learning*. Oxford: Blackwell, pp. 111–27.

Ravitch, D. (1999) 'The controversy over national history standards', in E. Fox-Genovese and E. Lasch-Quinn (eds), *Reconstructing History: The Emergence of a New Historical Society*. London: Routledge, pp. 242–52.

Robson, J., Francis, B. and Read, B. (2002) 'Writes of passage: stylistic features of male and female undergraduate history essays', *Journal of Further and Higher Education*, 26: 351–62.

Rogers, G. (2001) ' "Back to the future?" On-line learning in history', *Chic Newsletter*, Summer, 4–5.

Rogers, G. (2004) 'History, learning technology and student achievement: making the difference', *Active Learning in Higher Education*, 5: 232–47.

Schick, J. B. M. (1990) *Teaching History with a Computer: A Complete Guide for College Professors*. Chicago: Lyceum Books.

Sicilia, D. B. (1998) 'Options and gopherholes: reconsidering choice in the technology-rich history classroom', in D. A. Trinkle (ed.), *Writing, Teaching and Researching History in the Electronic Age*. New York: Sharpe, pp. 73–82.

Simons, W. and LaPotin, A. (1992) 'A "Great Issues" format in the American history survey: analysis of a pilot project', *Teaching History*, XVIII: 51–8.

Smith, B. G. (1993) 'Gender, reproduction, and European history', in R. Blackey (ed.), *History Anew: Innovations in the Teaching of History*

Today. Long Beach, CA: California State University Press, pp. 267–72.

Soffer, R. N. (1994) *Discipline and Power: The University, History and the Making of an English Elite, 1870–1930*. Stanford, CA: Stanford University Press.

Spaeth, D. (1996) 'Computer-assisted teaching and learning', in A. Booth and P. Hyland (eds), *History in Higher Education: New Directions in Teaching and Learning*. Oxford: Blackwell, pp. 155–77.

Spaeth, D. and Cameron, S. (2000) 'Computers and resource-based history teaching: a UK perspective', *Computers and the Humanities*, 34: 325–43.

Stearns, P. N. (1993) *Meaning Over Memory: Recasting the Teaching of Culture and History*. Chapel Hill, NC: University of North Carolina Press.

Stearns, P. N. (1996) 'Teaching and learning in lectures', in A. Booth and P. Hyland (eds), *History in Higher Education: New Directions in Teaching and Learning*. Oxford: Blackwell, pp. 97–110.

Stearns, P. N. (1998) 'Goals in history teaching', in J. F. Voss and M. Carretero (eds), *International Review of History Education Volume 2: Learning and Reasoning in History*. London: Woburn, pp. 281–93.

Stearns, P. N. (2000) 'Getting specific about training in historical analysis: a case study in world history', in P. N. Stearns, P. Seixas and S. Wineburg (eds), *Knowing, Teaching, and Learning History: International Perspectives*. New York: New York University Press.

Stearns, P. N., Seixas, P. and Wineburg, S. (2000) *Knowing, Teaching, and Learning History: International Perspectives*. New York: New York University Press.

Thompson, E. P. (1963) *The Making of the English Working Class*. London: Gollancz.

Trinkle, D. A. (ed.) (1998) *Writing, Teaching and Researching History in the Electronic Age*. New York: Sharpe, pp. 65–72.

Van Hartesveldt, F. R. (1998) 'The undergraduate research paper and electronic sources: a cautionary tale', *Teaching History*, 23: 51–9.

Voss, J. F. and Carretero, M. (eds) (1998) *International Review of History Education Volume 2: Learning and Reasoning in History*. London: Woburn.

Watts, R. and Grosvenor, I. (eds) (1995) *Crossing the Key Stages in History: Effective History Teaching, 5–16 and Beyond*. London: David Fulton.

Wilson, A. (ed.) (1993) *Rethinking Social History: English Society 1870–1920 and Its Interpretation*. Manchester: Manchester University Press.

Windschuttle, K. (1997) *The Killing of History: How Literary Critics and Social Theorists are Murdering Our Past*. New York and London: Free Press.

Winstanley, M. (1992) 'Group work in the humanities: history in the community, a case study', *Studies in Higher Education*, 17: 55–65.

Wissenburg, A. M. (1996) 'TLTP History Courseware Consortium: a project report', *History and Computing*, 8: 45–9.

ON-LINE SOURCES

College and university web sites

Australia and New Zealand

James Cook University, *JCU Handbooks 2004: Undergraduate Subject Descriptions* at http://www.jcu.edu.au/courses/handbooks/2004/pt2ugsubj(contxt).html (27.09.04).

Monash University, *2003 Handbooks* at http://www.monash.edu.au/pubs/2003handbooks/units/HSY3580.html (16.09.04).

Murdoch University, School of Social Sciences and Humanities, *Level 1 Units* at http://www.ssh.murdoch.edu.au/curriculum/units/level/1 (17.09.04).

University of Auckland, Department of History, *The BA Degree* at www.arts.auckland.ac.nz/his/theba.html (24.09.02).

—— *Subjects and Courses* at http://www.arts.auckland.ac.nz/subjects/index.cfm?S=S_HISTORY (20.08.04).

University of Melbourne, Department of History, *Subject Information* at http://www.unimelb.edu.au/HB/subjects/131-418.html (16.09.04).

University of New South Wales, School of History, *Honours Study 2004 The Thesis* at http://history.arts.unsw.edu.au/courses_and_study/honours/index.html (17.09.04).

—— *Undergraduate Study 2004: Course Descriptions* at http://history.arts.unsw.edu.au/courses_and_study/undergraduate/index.html (17.09.04).

—— *Virtual Handbook* at http://www.unsw.edu.au/virtualHandbook/courses/HIST1016.html (17.09.04).

University of Sydney, Department of History, *Student Policies* at http://www.arts.usyd.edu.au/departs/history/policies.html (18.09.04)

—— *Handbook, 2001* at http://www.arts.usyd.edu.au/Arts/departs/history/Handbook-2001/handbook2001.html (15.02.02)

University of Tasmania, School of History and Classics, *Honours in History* at http://uniweb.its.utas.edu.au/dev/history_classics/postgrad/honours_information.html (17.09.04).

University of Western Australia, Department of History, *Discipline of History* at http://www.arts.uwa.edu.au/HistoryWWW/honours.html (19.09 2004).

Britain

Bath Spa University College, *History Assessment Methods* at http://www.bathspa.ac.uk/prospectus/undergraduate/undergraduate-courses-2005-2006/history/ (19.09.04).

Birkbeck College, University of London, School of History, Classics and Archaeology, *BA History Degree Structure* at http://www.bbk.ac.uk/hca/timetables/ug.html (19.09.04).

Canterbury Christ Church University College, Department of History, *Year 1 History* at http://arts-humanities.cant.ac.uk/History/year1.htm (16.01.04).

Cardiff University, Department of History and Archaeology, *History, BA (Hons)* at http://www.cf.ac.uk/hisar/history/single.htm (16.09.04).

Kingston University, School of Social Sciences, *BA (Hons) History* at http://www.kingston.ac.uk/~kuweb/undergraduate/courses/v100.htm (1.09.04).

Queen's University, Belfast, School of English, *Criteria for Marking, 2003–4* at http://www.qub.ac.uk/en/resources/marking.htm (25.05.04).

Queen's University, Belfast, School of History, *History at Queen's Year 1* at http://www.qub.ac.uk/mh/mhy%20year%20one.htm (17.09.04).

Royal Holloway, University of London, *Structure of Degree Programmes* at http://www.rhul.ac.uk/History/for-students/undergrad/structure.html (1.09.04).

Sheffield Hallam University, School of Cultural Studies, *BA (Hons) History* at http://www.shu.ac.uk/schools/cs/history/bah1.html (12.09.04).

—— *BA (Hons) History Course Content* at http://www.shu.ac.uk/schools/cs/history/bah_t&l.html (16.09.04).

Trinity and All Saints College, History Department, *Module Catalogue: History Dissertation* at http://www.tasc.ac.uk/modcat0405/viewModule.asp?Ccode=Core;3;130 (16.09.04).

University College, London, Department of History, *Information for Prospective Students* at http://www.ucl.ac.uk/prospective students/undergraduatedegrees/shs/history/department/index.shtml (12.09.04).

University College Northampton, *Prospectus History (BA Honours)* at http://www.northampton.ac.uk/prospective_prospectus_undergsearch.php?courseid=49 (16.09.04).

—— Department of History, *Level 2 Modules* at http://oldweb.northampton.ac.uk/ass/soc/history/courses/leveltwo.htm (16.09.04).

University College Worcester, *Module Descriptions: History BA (Hons)* at http://www.worc.ac.uk/cms/template.cfm?name=history_module (16.09.04).

University of Aberdeen, Department of History, *Guidelines for History Students 2004–2005: Level 1 & 2 Courses 1st* at http://www.abdn.ac.uk/history/resource.shtml (18.09.04).

University of Birmingham, School of Historical Studies, *BA History, Medieval and Modern: The Programme* at http://www.history.bham.ac.uk/umm.htm (18.09.04).

University of Bristol, Department of Historical Studies, *IT-One: Information Technology for Historians* at http://www.bris.ac.uk/Depts/History/ITOne/ (19.08.04).

—— *1st Year Handbook and Unit Descriptions for 2004/05* at http://www.bris.ac.uk/Depts/History/Undergrads/firsthandbook2004.pdf (19.09.04).

—— *2nd/3rd Year Handbook and Unit Descriptions for 2004/05* at http://www.bris.ac.uk/Depts/History/Undergrads/secondhandbook2004.pdf (19.09.04).

—— *Undergraduate Studies in History* at http://www.bris.ac.uk/Depts/History/Undergrads/whyhistory.htm (21.09.04).

University of Durham, Department of History, *On Writing a Gobbet* at http://www.dur.ac.uk/h.j.harris/4CW/howtogob.htm (15.09.04).

University of Edinburgh, Department of Social and Economic History, *Courses for Undergraduates* at www.esh.ed.ac.uk/courses.htm#dpp (19.09.04).

University of Essex, Department of History, *Undergraduate Course Modules, 2004/2005* at http://www.essex.ac.uk/history/courses/ugmodules.shtm (16.09.04).

University of Hertfordshire, Department of Humanities, *History Subject Guide* at http://www.herts.ac.uk/fhle/faculty/humanities/web%20pages/history/resources_his_guide.htm (15.09.04).

University of Leeds, School of History, *Undergraduate Modules, 2003–4* at http://www.leeds.ac.uk/history/modules/undergraduate/Hist_3620.htm (01.09.04).

University of Liverpool, School of History, *Module Descriptors Pages* at http://www.liv.ac.uk/history/courses/index.htm (17.09.04).

—— *History BA (Hons) Programme Content* at http://www.liv.ac.uk/study/undergraduate/courses/V100.htm (17.09.04).

University of Newcastle upon Tyne, School of Historical Studies, *Single Honours History* at http://historical-studies.ncl.ac.uk/degrees/degree_16/index.htm (14.09.04).

University of Northumbria at Newcastle, *Module Descriptor* at http://information.unn.ac.uk/apdb/unitdescriptor.asp?UnitCode=HC512&AcademicYear=2002 (28.09.02).

University of Nottingham, School of History, *Course Information* at http://www.nottingham.ac.uk/prospectuses/undergrad/modules.phtml?code=000720&mod_year=2 (10.09.04).

University of Reading, *2005 Undergraduate Prospectus BA History* at http://www.rdg.ac.uk/ug/courses/128.html (18.09.04).

—— *2005 Undergraduate Prospectus History* at http://www.rdg.ac.uk/ug/subjects/subID34.html (18.09.04).

University of Sheffield, Department of History, *Undergraduate Prospectus, 2005* at http://www.shef.ac.uk/p/prospectus/dept.php?deptid=29&courseid=180 (21.09.04).

—— *Single Honours: History Level 3* at http://www.shef.ac.uk/history/prospectiveug/courses/history.html (21.09.04).

—— *Rethinking History* at http://www.shef.ac.uk/history/current_students/undergraduate/modules/level3_semester2/hst300.html (21.09.04).

The University of Wales, Bangor, Department of History and Welsh History, *Student Handbook, 2003–2004* at http://www.bangor.ac.uk/history/students/student_pages.htm. (18.09.04).

University of Warwick, Department of History, *Undergraduate Study – Arts* at http://www2.warwick.ac.uk/study/undergraduate/arts/history/ (18.09.04).

University of the West of England, School of History, *BA History Optional Modules* at http://www.uwe.ac.uk/humanities/history/optional.shtml# (01.11.03).

University of York, Department of History, *An Overview of the History Course* at http://www.york.ac.uk/depts/hist/undrgrad/overview.shtml (18.09.04).

North America

California State University Hayward, Department of History, *Course Catalogue, 2001–2002* at http://www.csuhayward.edu/ecat/20012002/u-hist.html#section9 (17.09.04).

Central Connecticut State University, History Department, *New Concentration in Public History* at www.history.ccsu.edu/Undergraduate_Info/BA_public_history.htm (19.09.04).

—— *The Historical Imagination* at www.history.ccsu.edu/Undergraduate_Info/Hist_301.htm (19.09.04)

Florida State University, History Department, *Graduate Course Descriptions: European History* at http://www.fsu.edu/~history/courses/gradcourses.htm#european (18.09.04).

Harvard University, History Department, *Undergraduate Handbook: The Senior Thesis* at http://www.fas.harvard.edu/~history/undergraduate/handbook/senior_thesis/length_and_other_guidelines.html (15.09.04).

Merrimack College, History Department, *Catalog* at http://www.merrimack.edu/uploads/Registrar-s_Office/files/Cat34.pdf (8.11.03).

Michigan State University, Department of History, *Undergraduate Course Descriptions, Fall, 2003* at http://www.history.msu.edu/ (23.09.04).

Montana State University – Billings, *General Education Requirements* at http://www.msubillings.edu/catalogs/generalcatalog/Output/chapt12.html (14.01.04).

Ohio State University, Department of History, *History 122* at http://history.osu.edu/courses/syllabi/syllabus.cfm?SYL=hist122.htm (17.09.04).

—— *History 132* at http://history.osu.edu/courses/syllabi/syllabus.cfm?SYL=hist132.htm (17.09.04).

—— *History 307 World War II* at http://history.osu.edu/courses/syllabi/syllabus.cfm?SYL=hist307.htm (17.09.04).

—— *History 308 The Vietnam War* at http://history.osu.edu/courses/syllabi/syllabus.cfm?SYL=hist308.htm (17.09.04).

—— *Undergraduate History Handbook* at http://history.osu.edu/Common/Files/UHObrochure_rev.pdf (17.09.04).

—— *Undergraduate Majors History* at http://www-afa.adm.ohio-
state.edu/u-majors/pdf/history.pdf (21.08.02);

—— *History Courses* at http://history.osu.edu/courses/curriculum/
coursedescription.htm (21.09.04).

Stanford University, Department of History, *History Courses* at
http://history.stanford.edu/courses/65/syllabus (11.11.03).

Stony Brook State University of New York, *Undergraduate Spring 2003
300 Level Courses* at http://www.sunysb.edu/history/courses/
Springund/03Spgund300.htm (18.09.04).

University of California, Berkeley, Department of History, *Course
Descriptions* at http://history.berkeley.edu/academ/courses.html
(12.08.04)

University of California, Riverside, Department of History, *Undergraduate
Information Career Opportunities* at http://www.history.ucr.edu/
academics/undergraduate/index.html (16.09.04).

University of Detroit Mercy, College of Liberal Arts and Education,
Workshop on Assessment at http://liberalarts.udmercy.edu/~riceje/
writing/assessment.html (30.11.03).

University of Illinois, History Department, *Fall 2002 History Courses* at
http://www.history.uiuc.edu/NewCourses/CourseGuides/
Course%20guide-FA02.htm (01.11.03).

University of Massachusetts/Amherst, History Department,
Witchcraft, Magic, and Science: Guidelines for Midterm Self-assessment at
http://people.umass.edu/ogilvie/492H/self-assess.html (25.08.04).

University of Northern British Columbia, *History Program Introduction*
at http://www.unbc.ca/history/index.html (17.09.04).

University of Southern Maine, Department of History, *Requirements for
Graduation for History Majors* at http://www.usm.maine.edu/
~history/Major.htm (10.09.04).

University of Texas, Department of History, *History Honors Programs* at
http://www.utexas.edu/cola/depts/history/undergraduate/
honors/ (18.09.04).

University of Utah, Department of History, *Fall 2003 Course
Descriptions* at http://www.hum.utah.edu/history/Courses/Fall
Description.html (17.11.03).

—— *Requirements* at http://vegeta.hum.utah.edu/history/
Undergraduate/Requirements.html (16.08.04).

University of Virginia, Department of History, *Course Web Sites, Spring
2004* at http://www.virginia.edu/history/courses/spring04/
hius401d/syllabus.html (06.09.04).

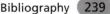

—— *Graduate Courses, Fall 2001* at http://www.virginia.edu/history/courses/fall.01/hiafgrad.html (18.09.04).

—— *Undergraduate Courses, Fall 2004* at http://www.virginia.edu/history/courses/fall04/undergrad.html (10.09.04).

University of Washington, *Course Catalog* at http://www.washington.edu/students/icd/S/hist/112bstacey.html (18.09.04).

Wabash College, History Department, *History Curriculum* at http://www.wabash.edu/academics/history/curriculum (18.09.04).

Essays and reports

Allen, J. and Lloyd-Jones, R. *Assessing Groupwork: Methods and Findings* at http://www.shu.ac.uk/schools/cs/fdtl/grpwk/default.html (04.01.04).

Baker, J. (1995) *The Role of Assessment Practices in the Transition Experience of History Students in First Year at Monash University* at http://www.adm.monash.edu/ched/Awards_Grants/fellow/y1995/1995fellowbaker.html (08.03.02).

Boulton, J. (2000) *Course Evaluation Feedback on HIS104, 8 May 2000* at http://chic.tees.ac.uk/DOCS/eval/Newc/Appendix%20seven%20HIS104%20feedback%202000.htm (23.01.03).

Boulton, J. (2001) *Death and History: The Use of TLTP Modules in a First-year CBL Course* at http://chic.tees.ac.uk/DOCS/eval/Newc/Draft%20evaluation%20document%202001.htm (23.01.03).

Bradney, A. 'Benchmarking: a pedagogically valuable process? An alternative view', *Web Journal of Current Legal Issues* at http://webjcli.ncl.ac.uk/1999/issue2/bradney2.html (20.01.04).

Cameron, S. 'Online discussion groups – how to set them up' at http://hca.ltsn.ac.uk/resources/Briefing_Papers/bp8.php (15.08.04).

Emmerichs, M. B. *The United States Since The Civil War: Reflective Essay* at http://www.theaha.org/tl/LessonPlans/wi/Emmerichs/reflectiveessay.htm (04.01.04).

Ferrell, C. (2002) 'Method in the madness: teaching historical research to majors', *Perspectives* at http://www.historians.org/perspectives/issues/2002/0209/0209teach4.cfm (10.08.04).

Goldberg, M. (1996) *Expanding the Possibilities of the U.S. Survey Through Student-Directed Teaching and Learning* at http://www.oah.org/pubs/magazine/latinos/goldberg.html (04.01.04).

Kallgren, D. *Discovering American Social History on the Web: Reflective Essay* at http://www.theaha.org/tl/LessonPlans/wi/Kallgren/reflectiveessay.html (04.01.04).

Kornblith, G. J. (1998) *'Dynamics Syllabi for Dummies': Posting Class Assignments on the World Wide Web* at http://chnm.gmu.edu/assets/historyessays/dynamicsyllabi.html (04.01.04).

McClymer, J. *An Inquiry Approach to Teaching U.S. History* at http://www.h-net.org/teaching/essays/mcclymer.html (04.01.04).

Mills Kelly, T. *For Better or Worse? The Marriage of the Web and the Classroom* at http://www.h-net.org/aha/papers/Kelly.html (04.01.04).

Mills Kelly, T. *Using New Media to Teach East European History* at http://chnm.gmu.edu/assets/historyessays/usingmedia.html (04.01.04).

Mitchell, L. (2002) *Active Learning and Reflection*, LTSN History, Classics and Archaeology Subject Centre Briefing Paper at http://hca.ltsn.ac.uk/resources/Briefing_Papers/index.php (01.06.04).

Petrik, P. *Top Ten Mistakes in Academic Web Design* at http://chnm.gmu.edu/assets/historyessays/topten.html (04.01.04).

Quality Assurance Agency for Higher Education (2000) *Subject Benchmark Statements*:

—— Archaeology at http://www.qaa.ac.uk/crntwork/benchmark/archaeology.html (14.07.04).

—— *Classics and Ancient History* at http://www.qaa.ac.uk/crntwork/benchmark/classics.html (14.07.04).

—— *History* at http://www.qaa.ac.uk/crntwork/benchmark/history.html (14.07.04).

Skip Knox, E. L. *The Rewards of Teaching On-Line* at http://www2.h-net.msu.edu/aha/papers/Knox.html (09.09.04).

Timmins, G. (2003) *Progression in Higher Education History Programmes: The Conceptual Dimension.* LTSN History, Archaeology and Classics Subject Centre Briefing Paper at http://hca.ltsn.ac.uk/resources/Briefing_Papers/progression.pdf (17.06.04)

Other information

Higher Education & Research Opportunities in the United Kingdom: RAE 2001 at http://www.hero.ac.uk/rae/index.htm

The Quality Assurance Agency at http://www.qaa.ac.uk

QAA (2001) *Framework for Higher Education Qualifications* at http://www.qaa.ac.uk/crntwork/nqf/nqf.htm

Index

Aboriginal rights, 27
accountability, 11
action-research, 136
active learning, 61, 77, 132, 144,
    148–168, 214, 215
African civilisation, 74
Alabama's Literacy Test, 156
Aldous, C., 111
Allen, Julia, 195, 204
American Civil War, 22, 156
American Historical Association, 22,
    154–155, 218
Anderson, Roberta, 165
anonymous marking, 206
anthropology, 19
Appalachian State University, 141
apprenticeship projects, 56
archives, 53, 126
Asian Civilisations, 74
assessment, 8, 42, 58, 127, 135, 136,
    157, 170–209, 211, 215
    checklist, 191–192
    coursework, 62–3
    criteria, 171–175, 176–179, 185–191,
        208
    differentiation, 182–184
    formative and summative,
        184–185, 204–206
    oral presentations, 202–203
    peer, 184, 203–205
    progression in, 195, 209
    self-assessment, 205–206

statements of attainment, 179–182
of students, 155, 170–209
of teaching activity, 31–2
transparency, 207
variety in, 208–209
assignments, 135, 152, 160, 167, 170
    oral, 176
assimilation, 23
Assumption College, 161
atomic bomb, 26
attendance, 156
Australia, 26
Australian Bicentennial, 26–27
Australian Cultural Studies, 27
Australian Historical Studies, 27
Australian universities, 43, 47, 48, 49,
    50, 52, 60, 61, 105, 114, 115, 130,
    178, 196

Baker, Janet, 178
Bath College, 150
Bath Spa University College, 165, 193
benchmarking, 3–5, 8, 33, 71, 72, 79,
    91
    and content, 69–71
    see also, History Benchmarking
        Statement
Birbeck College, University of
    London, 93
black history, 15, 83
Blackboard software, 158, 162
Blackey, Robert, 141

Bloch, Marc, 102
Boise State University, 160
Booth, Alan, 77, 88, 89, 100, 101, 122, 134, 135, 137
Bosworth, Susan, 202
Boud, David, 207
Boulton, Jeremy, 158, 162, 164, 165, 167
Bradney, Anthony, 4
brainstorming, 142
breadth versus depth, 7, 45–50, 68, 77–79, 201, 213
Bristol University, 62
British history, 24, 25
British Empire, 73
Brown, Sally, 177
Bush, George, sr, 22

California State University, 90, 141
Cambridge University, 137
Cameron, Sonja, 166
Cannon, John, 70, 71, 87, 139, 148
Canterbury Christ Church University College, 113, 124
Cardiff University, 104
career routes, 126, 128
Center for History and New Media, 218
Central Connecticut State University, 115, 126
Chambers, Ellie, xii
Chanock, Kate, 207
Cheney, Lynne, 23
citizenship, 17
civic values, 25
civil rights movement, 84
class, 16, 19, 80
Classics and Ancient History Benchmarking Statement, 46–47, 59
classroom approaches, 1
cliometrics, 35
College of William and Mary, 202

Columbus, Christopher, 26
communication, 119
community history, 126–127, 204
comparative history, 83, 85, 176
computers, 145
contemporary sources, 73
content, 67–95, 172, 173, 213–214
controversies, 6, 10, 22–25, 26, 34, 36, 37, 75, 103
Cook, Mary Joan, 85
counter-culture, 14
course units, 49, 50, 51, 60, 64, 68, 71, 72–75, 91, 110, 113, 118–119, 130, 211, 213
coursework, 42, 62, 193, 194, 195, 196, 197, 206
Coursework for History Implementation Consortium, 156–158, 161, 220
Cox, Roy, 76, 148
Crime and Punishment in Britain, 1690–1800, 204
critical reflection, 51, 131, 132, 136, 151, 177
Croston, Lancs., 157
cultural capital, 33
cultural history, 19, 53
Culture Wars, 15, 21–28
curricular dimensions, 6–8, 41–42
curriculum, 42, 70, 86, 87, 121, 138, 211
  choice versus compulsion, 40–41, 47–48, 50–52, 53, 54, 77–79
  content, 45–54, 64, 67–95, 70, 87
  design, 49
  and gender, 82–83
  introductory units, 73
  planning, 2, 5, 63
  specialisation, 47
  race and ethnic history, 83–84
  temporal and geographic coverage, 72, 73
Cuthbert, Katherine, 55–56

Daily Telegraph, 4
data, 3, 145, 150
databases, 153, 175
Davies, Peter, 150
Davis, John, 148
Dawson, Ian, 58
Dearing, Ron, 32
Dearing Report, 32, 33
deep learning, 159–160, 167
deep versus surface learning, 7, 68,
    75–6, 94, 132
Derrida, Jacques, 20
Digital Age Project, 154–156
dissertations, 42, 54, 58, 64, 84, 91–94,
    95, 105, 113, 114, 117, 127, 195,
    214
    see also, extended piece of work
distance learning, 159
diversity of specialisms, 72, 79
Doran, S., 204, 205
Dunne, John, 165

early Irish society, 112
Easley, Larry J., 145
East Asia, 47
East Central Europe, 75
East Oregon University, 149
Edge Hill University College, 127,
    157, 159, 162, 163
Edinburgh University, 113, 114, 174
educational philosophy, 30
elitism, 128, 129
Ellis, Graham, 203, 204, 205
Elton, G.R., 71, 77, 80, 102, 137, 141
e-mail, 156
Emmerichs, Mary Beth, 156
empiricism, 21, 36, 53
employability, 105–107, 130
English history, 13
Enola Gay, 26
environmental history, 86–87
epistemology, 9, 17, 19, 21, 35
essays, 155, 170, 192, 196, 207

assessment of, 197–200
European history, 47, 51
examinations, 42, 63, 185, 192–194,
    201, 206, 207, 209
exhibitions, 190
extended piece of work, 72
external examiners, 184–185
external pressures, 28–29, 131

family and gender history, 82
    see also, gender and women's
    history
feedback, 135, 178, 183, 190, 191, 200
Feldman, Martha, 198
feminism, 53
films, 27
Fletcher, Anthony, 4
flexibility in teaching, 158–159
Florida State University, 75
footnoting, 121
Foucault, Michel, 19–20
*Framework for Higher Education
    Qualifications in England, Wales,
    and N. Ireland*, 41
Francis, B., 200
Frederick, Peter, 140, 141, 142
Frederickson, Mary E., 81, 84
Freeman, R., 175

gender, 16, 202
gender history, 68, 80–83, 94
    see also, women's history
General Election of 1992, 150
geographic coverage, 67, 68, 71, 72,
    75, 77, 94, 214
George Mason University, 161
German Election of 1932, 149
Glasfurd, Guinevere, 154
Glasgow University, 161
Glasner, Angela, 193
Glorious Revolution, 73
gobbets, 190, 201
Goldberg, Michael, 87, 159

graduateness, 32
graphics, 165
Griffith, Wil, 57
group work, 123, 142, 146–152, 156,
    163, 166
  assessment of, 203
Gunn, Victoria, 151

H-Net, 219
Harvard University, 93
heritage, 126
heritage industry, 25, 36
heritage sites, 25, 127
Hicks, M., 111
high order skills, 196, 197
higher education, 50, 122, 137, 140,
    148, 153, 157, 187, 193, 206
  changes in, 1, 10, 11, 211
  expansion of, 14, 28, 29–30, 32, 33,
    37, 122
  progression and differentiation in,
    44
  regulation of, 30–31
  in UK, 37
Higher Education Authority, 32
Higher Education Funding Council,
    156, 187
Historians
  and assessment, 170–209
  in Britain, 4, 6
  common ground, 35–36
  and computers, 124
  divisions amongst, 10, 11–28, 36
  as facilitators, 152
  as lecturers, 139–146
  objectivity of, 21
  skills and qualities of mind,
    96–131
  social profile of, 14
  as tutors, 134–138, 146–153,
    157–162
historical canon, 12, 14, 15–16, 35, 67
historical reconstructions, 25

Historical Theory and Research, 53
historical thinking, 23
historiography, 42, 45, 52, 53, 71, 76,
    81, 85, 89, 91, 94, 114, 197
History, xiv
  as an academic discipline, 11–12,
    21, 34–37, 108, 212
  challenges to discipline, 1
  development of the discipline,
    12–14
  external scrutiny of, 10, 11, 27–28
  non-academic approaches to, 12
  philosophical challenges to,
    17–18
  as progress, 13
  purpose of studying, xiii, 37
  resourcing of, 10
  state of the discipline, 9–38
  teachers of, xiii
  undergraduate curriculum, 36
  and the workplace, 105–107, 212
  see also, Australian and in US,
    benchmarking, teaching and
    learning, progression,
    transferable skills
History Benchmarking Statement, 3,
    5, 33, 39, 42, 43, 67, 68, 69, 70, 73,
    79, 91, 94, 97, 98, 99, 100, 109,
    133–134, 140, 146, 153, 170,
    171–172, 173, 179, 187, 197, 198,
    212, 213
History Courseware Consortium,
    153
history from below, 67, 211
History in Practice, 104
History Teaching Alliance, 22
History Working Group, 24
Holden, Katherine, 168
Holocaust, 199
Hounsell, Dai, 199, 200
Huddersfield University, 127, 128
Hull University, 109, 124
Humanities, 37

Higher Education Research Group, xii
teaching and learning in, xi
Hyland, Paul, 136, 137
hypermedia, 154

ICT, 1, 7, 8, 51, 120, 123, 124–125, 126, 133, 137
in undergraduate teaching, 153–167
see also, web provision and internet
independent learners, 59, 61, 64, 173
industrial archaeology, 161
industrial revolution, 73
information technology, see ICT and web provision
Institute for Teaching and Learning, xi, 32
Institute of Educational Technology, xi
Institute of Historical Research, 5
institutional cultures, 187
interactive discussion, 143, 144, 145, 157
international comparisons, 2–3
internet, 154, 155
introductory courses, 122
Irish Question, 73

James Cook University, Queensland, 196
Japan, 26
Jenkins, A., 89
Jim Crow Laws, 156

Kallgren, Daniel, 156
Kingston University, 148
Knight, Peter, 177, 178
knowledge, 70, 96, 174
knowledge economy, 1
knowledge versus skills, 96–97
Kornblith, Gary, J., 166–167

Kornfield, Eve, 149, 150
Kuhn, Thomas, 9, 10

Lancaster University, 126
LaPotin, Armand, 76, 151
learning environment, 158, 163
learning outcomes, 172
learning and teaching, 132–169
see teaching and learning
lectures, 132–133, 134, 135, 138, 139–146, 158, 164, 215
Leeds University, 81
Lewis, M.J., 175
libraries, 126
Light, Greg, 76, 148
literary reconstructions, 21
literary theory, 19, 20, 35
Liverpool University, 62
Lloyd-Jones, Roger, 195, 204
local and regional history, 79, 84–85, 143
Long, Diana, 152
Lubelska, Cathy, 83

maintenance grants, 29
Malmo, 85
Manchester Metropolitan University, 127
map exercises, 190
mark schemes, 177–178
Marxism, 18, 53
masculine and feminine constructs, 81
mass teaching, 33–34
McClymer, John, 161
medieval history, 51
Merrimack College (US), 73
methodologies, 9, 34, 35, 50, 76, 118–119
Michigan State University, 80, 82
Mills Kelly, T., 161, 165
module descriptors, 171
Monahan, W. Gregory, 149, 150

Monash University, 178
Montana State University, 110
Moust, J.H.C., 147
multiculturalism, 23, 25
Murdoch University 88
museums, 27, 126

nation, national identity and national values, 13, 80, 198
National Archives, 13
National Center for History in the Schools (US), 22, 23
National Curriculum, 41, 43, 176
National Endowment for the Humanities, 23
National Standards, 22, 23, 36
nationalism, 25
native history, 87
Nazi Germany, 109
netiquette, 166
New Historians, 20
New History, 17, 18, 22, 27, 36, 211
    see also, Old and New History.
New Right, 22, 24, 28, 106
Newcastle University, 148
Nicholls, Gill, 140
Nicholson, Tony, 203, 204, 205
non-mediated discussions, 166
North American universities, 43
northern history, 87
note-taking, 144
Nottingham University, 88, 100

Oberlin College, Ohio, 166
Ogilvie, Brian W., 205
Ohio State University, 47, 73–74, 90, 198, 201
Old and New History, 11–12, 15, 16, 17, 18, 67, 102
on-line learning, 165–167
on-line teaching, 154, 157, 158–162, 163, 165, 166–167
    advantages of , 159–162

drawbacks of, 162–164
Open University, xii
oral presentations, 42, 54, 123–124, 144, 164
    assessment of, 202–203
Organisation of American Historians, 22, 219
Oxford Brookes University, 204, 205

Parker, Jan, xii
patriarchy, 80
Pearl Harbor, 141
pedagogy, xii, 3, 88, 137, 138, 145, 149, 211
peer assessment, 184, 203–205
Pennell, Myra, L., 141
Pennington, Joanne de, 58
periodisaion, 75
Petrik, Paula, 165
placements, 127, 129
plagiarism, 196, 197, 208
political history, 79–80, 94, 211
political intervention, 24, 27
postcolonialism, 53
postmodernism, 18–21, 34–35, 88, 89
poststructuralism, 19, 53
presentations, 85, 190, 195
Preston, George, 150, 151, 152
primary evidence, 2, 52–53, 54–57, 58, 61–62, 64, 76, 94, 104, 111, 112, 126, 132, 142, 155, 162, 165, 184, 199, 201, 207
    see also sources
Privies, Privacy and Privation: the House and Home in Lancashire c.1600–1939, 143
problem-solving, 132
professional history, 12, 14
professional status, 32
programmes of study, 6, 40, 50, 58, 59, 61, 62, 63, 71, 79, 95
progression, 6, 62, 71, 77, 89–91, 92, 112, 117, 144, 213, 214

progression and differentiation,
    39–66, 151, 195, 197, 209, 216
  implementation, 40–42
progressive historians, 14
Prussian cultural revival, 13
psychohistory, 35
public duty, 85
public history, 10, 25–28, 126
purposeful learning, 61
pyramiding, 150

quality assurance, 211
Quality Assurance Agency, 3, 4, 31,
    33, 39, 41, 69, 187
Queen's University, Belfast, 112,
    180–181, 182, 183
questions, 141–142, 201–202

race and ethnic history, 83–84, 94
Race, Phil, 184
Randall, John, 69
Read, B., 200
Reconstructing History, 104
reflexive analysis, 9, 35, 131, 136, 137,
    155
reflexivity, 68, 72, 87, 89, 91, 95
Republic of Ireland, 110, 112
research, 137, 138
Research Assessment Exercise, 31
research methods, 11
research versus teaching debate,
    32–33, 137–138
resources, 161–162
Rethinking History, 90
Robson, J., 200
Rogers, Graham, 157
Rogers, Jennifer, 147
role-play, 149
Royal Holloway College, 46

Saint Joseph College, 85
Salem Witch Trials, 76, 151
Salmon, Patrick, 148

sampling approaches, 216–217
San Diego University, 149
school history, 22–5
  national curriculum, 36, 43
school leavers, 122
Schools Council History Project, 24
Scotland, 105
Scottish universities, 112
Second World War, 27
secondary material, 192
self-assessment, 127, 136,146,
    205–206
seminars, 60, 61, 62, 105, 132–133,
    134, 135, 146–152, 157, 315
  participation in, 148–153, 193
  size of, 148–149
Sheffield Hallam University, 54–55,
    120, 124, 125, 195, 204
Sheffield University, 51
Sicilia, David, 166
Simons, William, 76, 151
skills, 7, 29, 41, 42, 52–53, 55, 56,
    87–88, 107, 110–116, 121,
    123–126, 131, 211, 214, 216–217
  advanced, 116–117, 214
  and employability, 105–107
  generic, 98, 101, 119
  specific, 98, 101, 108–110
  teaching, 129
  transferable, 7, 107
  workplace, 119
skills versus content debate, 25,
    57–58
skills progression, 56–57
skills and qualities of mind of the
    historian, 96–131
Skip Knox, E.L,. 160, 163, 164
Smithsonian Institution, 26
social and cultural history, 6, 7,
    82–83
social and cultural upheavals, 14
social and economic history, 80
social history, 14,

social sciences, 15, 18, 70
sources, 13, 42, 45, 52–53, 72, 117, 118, 156
Spaeth, Donald, 153–154
Sport in American Society, 54
spreadsheets, 153
staff/student liaison meetings, 190
Stanford University, 83
state of the discipline, 9–38
State University of New York, 76, 151
State University of Virginia, 115
statements of attainment, 179–185, 208
Stearns, Peter, 75, 139, 141, 143, 144, 145, 152
Stoney Brook University, New York, 86
Subject Centre for History, Classics and Archaeology, 219
students, 2, 33, 39–40, 47–48, 50, 74, 75, 78, 84, 92, 111, 122, 127, 129–130, 136, 141, 142, 143, 144, 145, 146, 153, 155, 156, 161, 162, 167, 168, 173, 178, 190, 196, 200, 203, 208, 212, 213
asking questions, 141–142
and assessment, 172–177, 190–209, 215
contact with, 162–164
final year, 42, 47, 58, 60, 104, 114, 116, 120, 121, 195, 214
as learners, 134–139, 153–162, 166
level one, 51, 88, 89, 112, 113, 121
level two, 112, 114
profile of, 29–30
non-traditional, 29, 128, 187
part-time, 30
polling of, 142–143
as reflective thinkers, 146–152
second level, 54, 55
Student Assessment and Classification Working Group, 170, 174, 185–186, 191

survey on assessment criteria, 188–189
student-centred learning, 131
study logs, 124, 190
study skills, 120, 122
Studying History, 104
style, 173
surface learning, 76, 77
    see also, deep versus surface learning
survey programmes, 61
survey units, 45, 75, 82, 156
syndicates, 150

tautology, 182
Teaching History – A Journal of Methods, 220
teaching and learning, 5, 6, 7, 42, 60–61
    assessment, 57–58
    interactive approaches, 140–143
    and research, 137–138
Teaching and Learning Technology Project, 153
Teesside University, 203
television, 27
temporal coverage, 67, 68, 214
textual analysis, 20
Thatcher, Margaret, 24
thematic history, 94, 112
theoretical approaches, 36, 42, 50, 53
Thompson, E.P., 19
Three Sovereigns for Sarah, 151
time, 162, 168
time depth, 71, 72, 75, 77, 94
traditional teaching, 158–160, 167
transferable skills, 7, 106, 126, 203, 207
transparency, 184–185, 207
Trinity and All Saints College, Leeds, 93
tuition fees, 29

undergraduate history programmes,
2, 5, 6, 7, 11, 16–7, 36, 43–44, 50,
52, 54, 56, 62, 64, 87, 94, 102, 105,
109, 116, 157, 175, 179, 191, 196,
213
undergraduate history students, 8,
52, 77, 88, 92, 132, 133, 140, 164,
170, 207
see also students
understanding, 173
universities,
expansion of 28
Universities Defence Group, 137
University of Aberdeen, 65
University of Alabama, 84
University of Auckland, 103, 120
University of Berlin, 12
University of Birmingham, 54
University of Bristol, 51, 102
University of California, 22
University of California, Berkley, 86
University of California, Riverside,
106
University of Central Lancashire, vii,
viii, 55, 120, 121, 143, 150, 161,
176, 193, 204
University of Chicago, 84
University College, London, 124
University College, Northampton,
62, 113
University of Dundee, 120, 121
University of Durham, 201
University of Essex, 82, 90
University of Greenwich, 165
University of Hertfordshire, 93
University of Illinois at
Urbana-Champaign, 84
University of Liverpool, 58
University of Luton, 56
University of Mary Washington,
Virginia, 115
University of Massachusetts at
Amherst, 205

University of Melbourne, 53
University of New South Wales, 60,
73, 105
University of Newcastle Upon Tyne,
70, 109, 158, 159, 162, 163
University of North British
Columbia, 87, 103
University of Northumbria, 85
University of Nottingham, 94, 120,
121
University of Reading, 109
University of Sheffield, 90, 107
University of Southern Maine, 120,
125, 152
University of Staffordshire, 127
University of Sydney, 48, 49, 50,
171–172, 173, 174, 176, 180, 181,
182, 183
University of Tasmania, 52
University of Texas, 52
University of Utah, 120
University of Virginia, 82, 105
University of Wales, Bangor, 57, 62,
174
University of Warwick, 196
University of Washington, 73, 159
University of West of England, 83,
168
University of Western Australia, 114
University of Wisconsin-Marinette,
156
University of Wisconsin-Sheboygan,
156
University of York, 109, 114
United Kingdom, 36, 52, 60, 112, 116,
122, 125, 126, 130
US History, 13, 14, 23, 26, 36, 149,
155, 156, 159, 166, 201
US universities, 13, 32, 47, 49, 50, 52,
54, 60, 61, 76, 80–82, 102, 104,
105, 110, 115, 120, 125, 126, 130
views of, 36–37
Utah University, 54

Victorian Certificate in Education, 178

Victorian values, 25

Vietnam War, 198

virtual learning environments, 1, 8, 157, 163, 168

visual aids, 145, 156

Wabash College, Indiana, 102, 140, 199

web design, 190

web-based provision, 133, 159, 161, 162, 164–167

WebCT, 158

Western Civilisation, 23, 47

websites, ix, 2, 93, 156, 157, 158, 161, 164, 166–167, 196
  for learning and teaching, 218–220

widening participation, 187, 211

Winstanley, Michael, 154

Witchcraft, Magic and Science, 205

women's history, 15, 73, 79, 80–83, 87, 94

Woolf, Harvey, 182

Worcester University College, 117, 120

working-class housing, 143

workplace skills, 126–130
  see also skills

workshops, 60, 158

World Civilisation, 198

World History, 73, 155

World Wars, 27, 73

York University, 50